Foundations of
Library Services

LIBRARY SUPPORT STAFF HANDBOOKS

The Library Support Staff Handbook series is designed to meet the learning needs of both students in library support staff programs and library support staff working in libraries who want to increase their knowledge and skills.

The series was designed and is edited by Hali R. Keeler and Marie Shaw, both of whom teach in support staff programs and have managed libraries.

The content of each volume aligns to the competencies of the required and elective courses of the American Library Association–Allied Professional Association (ALA-APA) Library Support Staff Certification (LSSC) program. These books are both textbooks for library instructional programs and current resources for working library staff. Each book is available in both print and e-book versions.

Published books in the series include:

1. *Foundations of Library Services: An Introduction for Support Staff*
2. *Library Technology and Digital Resources: An Introduction for Support Staff*

Upcoming titles include:

3. *Cataloging and Classification: An Introduction for Support Staff*
4. *Collections: An Introduction for Support Staff*

Foundations of Library Services

An Introduction for Support Staff

Hali R. Keeler

Library Support Staff Handbooks, No. 1

ROWMAN & LITTLEFIELD
Lanham • Boulder • New York • London

Published by Rowman & Littlefield
A wholly owned subsidiary of The Rowman & Littlefield Publishing Group, Inc.
4501 Forbes Boulevard, Suite 200, Lanham, Maryland 20706
www.rowman.com

Unit A, Whitacre Mews, 26-34 Stannary Street, London SE11 4AB

British Library Cataloguing in Publication Information Available

Library of Congress Cataloging-in-Publication Data Available

ISBN 978-1-4422-5640-8 (cloth : alk. paper)
ISBN 978-1-4422-5641-5 (pbk. : alk. paper)
ISBN 978-1-4422-5642-2 (ebook)

Printed in the United States of America

To library support staff everywhere—
you are the backbone of our profession

Contents

PART III: ACCESS TO INFORMATION: A FUNDAMENTAL RIGHT

Figures

Tables and Textboxes

TABLES

TEXTBOXES

Preface

Foundations of Library Services: An Introduction for Support Staff is designed as an introduction to basic library services. It is aligned with the *Foundations of Library Service* competencies as determined by the Library Support Staff Certification (LSSC) Program of the American Library Association (ALA).

Each chapter begins with the LSSC competencies that are to be addressed, followed by a list of topics that will be covered, as well as a glossary of key terms. Chapters are then broken into easily readable sections that relate back to these key terms. Figures, tables, and photographs are included to highlight concepts that set them apart for emphasis. The language is uncomplicated but appropriate to the material being covered. Actual library experiences are included to illustrate how these concepts work in the real world. Each chapter concludes with a summary plus questions and opportunities for learning extensions. Readers of this text will come away with a basic knowledge of the workflow in a library as well as the skills to interact with patrons of all types.

Library support staff (LSS) are known by many names and have various levels of responsibilities. They may hold such titles as library assistants, library technical assistants, library associates, or library aides. This book can serve as a reference or refresher for them; it meets the needs of the student in a library certificate or degree program; and it can serve as a text for such a program. Both support staff and students in support staff programs are the audience for this book.

The book contains clear wording and ample definitions, and many figures, tables, and photos help illustrate the concepts that are presented. Additionally, end-of-chapter summaries, review questions, and activities, as well as a bibliography consisting of extensive "References, Suggested Readings, and Websites," provide access to supplementary resources that will provide further support for instructors or that will meet the individual interests of the student or the library worker.

Foundations of Library Service contains three parts, each devoted to one aspect of library service. Part I: "Materials," introduces the mission and roles of the library in general and how it relates to its community, as well as the ethics and values of the profession as explained by the Library Bill of Rights and the Library Code of Ethics.

The roles of the LSS in different kinds of libraries—public, school, academic, and special—are addressed, as is an overview of library services today, including the processes of acquisitions, collection development, and classification and related concepts such as bibliographic verification, selection policies, and various classification schemes. Part I goes on to cover special collections, including the wide range of what may constitute such a collection and its inherent challenges; nonbook materials in all formats, including the value of social media; and serials. This part also includes what are usually considered the "public services" of circulation, the advantages of current and future of Integrated Library Systems (ILS); reference services (both in the library and virtually) and the importance of the reference interview; the role of the reader's advisory and the tools to achieve it; the reserve process for both placing "holds" on materials for a patron and the reserve function in schools and colleges for classroom purposes; and interlibrary loan and other forms of resource sharing.

Part II: "Customer Service," covers the importance of customer service to all populations. Chapter 8: "Customer Service to Youth," presents the challenges inherent in working with children and includes valuable information on the best ways to serve this group. Service to the older adult takes into account what can be offered to the active older adult as well as to the homebound. Chapter 10: "Customer Service to Patrons with Special Needs," provides practical information, including tables and examples, about how library staff should conduct themselves to best serve this group. Customer service to those who present a challenge to the library and personnel is addressed, including how to defuse tense situations and tips on dealing with disruptive patrons. A chapter on the importance of programming and public relations for all service populations, including examples, resources, and checklists, is included as a factor in customer service.

Part III: "Access to Information: A Fundamental Right," consists of three chapters revolving around the principles of intellectual freedom and censorship. This section once again addresses the Library Bill of Rights as the right of everyone to have free and unfettered access to all materials. These chapters present the reasons people feel compelled to censor and how to counter those reasons; how to deal with book banning and media and Internet challenges; and the processes of relying on policies and procedures to respond to specific challenges.

This book breaks new ground as it is written expressly to align with the competencies required by the American Library Association Library Support Staff Certification Program. The author's experience teaching in a library technology program, as well as extensive research, has shown that there is a lack of appropriate instructional materials for the non-MLS student. Texts on the market are geared for the graduate level and, as such, are often too theoretical and technical for this level of study. Books in the Library Support Staff series are being created to meet this need, as well as to provide a resource and reference for those already working in the field.

There are many examples in which this book can be useful to LSS to build and improve their skills. The reference interview is a valuable exercise in finding out exactly what a patron is looking for, and the model reference behaviors contribute to getting a complete and correct result. The importance of customer service is emphasized and provides the LSS with the tools they need in order to work with a variety of populations and the problems that they can expect to encounter in these face-to-face interactions.

Additionally, the chapter questions and activities provide opportunities for the LSS to review what they have learned and practice these new skills in the workplace. The many tables are useful resources that the LSS can rely on as well to guide them or can be used as checklists as LSS experience these scenarios in the real world. This book is intended to be a guide to the actual day-to-day activities that LSS will encounter.

This book came about after years of teaching LSS courses using textbooks that were designed for graduate-level study. While full of good information, the students often found it difficult to wade through content that is overly technical, theoretical, and complex. Content for this book was then developed using the author's thirty-five years of experience as a children's librarian, a library director, and an adjunct professor in an LSSC certified program and was designed to align with the ALA-LSSC competencies. Instructional experience, the current literature, research, and hands-on practice contributed to the content. Courses taught by the author at Three Rivers Community College include Library Public Services, Library Technical Services, and Management Strategies.

Use of this text is intended to give the LSS the tools, skills, and basic knowledge that they would need to work at a variety of support-level positions in a library of any kind. Depending on the size and staff needs of the library, the LSS would be able to assist with anything from greeting the patrons as they come through the door to working at the circulation desk to performing limited reference service, interlibrary loan, cataloging, special collections, and programming and public relations. Their customer service training would be useful in all circumstances, and they would have the skills to assist patrons of all ages and abilities.

While designed as a textbook, this book is equally valuable for the student and for those who already work in a library. They will find it a handy reference and support in their work as it will give them supplemental information that they may lack or will serve to reinforce their existing skills.

Acknowledgments

There are several people I'd like to thank for their efforts on my behalf:

- My sincere thanks go to my colleague Marie Shaw for her support, advice, and friendship. Your help was invaluable and most appreciated.
- Thank you to my editor, Charles Harmon, for his encouragement, support, and patience. I am grateful that you saw the need for this project.
- I am indebted to the editorial advisory board for their professional appraisals, keen eyes, and suggestions—but mostly for taking the time out of their busy schedules to consult on this book.
- With love and thanks to my husband, Gerry, for his support, encouragement, and technical expertise. You have always been there for me.
- Finally, to all of the students and support staff I have worked with over the years—I continue to learn from you all.

Editorial Advisory Board

PART I

Materials

CHAPTER 1

Library Services Today

An Overview

Library support staff (LSS) will know the mission and roles of a library in its community and the mission of libraries in general. They will know the values of the profession, including an understanding of the Library Bill of Rights, the ALA Code of Ethics, freedom of information, confidentiality of library records, and privacy issues. The will also know the roles of LSS and other staff in libraries. (ALA-LSSC Competency #1, #2, #3)

Topics Covered in This Chapter:

- How Libraries Serve Society
- Ethics
- Library Users
- Different Types of Libraries
  - Public
  - School
  - Academic
  - Special
- Staffing
- Public and Technical Services

Key Terms:

Demographics: Demographics are the statistics of a given population by age, sex, race, and income. This is important for libraries so that they can know whom they are serving and so that they can provide the appropriate resources.

Library Bill of Rights: The Library Bill of Rights is a document created by the American Library Association (ALA, the national professional library association) affirming basic policies that guide library service.[1] It is based on the principles of the U.S. Constitution and guides librarians in providing equal service to all patrons.

Library Code of Ethics: The Library Code of Ethics is a document created by the ALA that recognizes the ethical responsibilities of library personnel toward the public and guides how the public is served.[2]

Public services: Public services are those tasks performed by LSS that involve direct contact with the customer. They include the circulation and reference functions, as well as helping the patron find materials of interest for research or pleasure reading and helping patrons with library computers and equipment. Public services also include the functions of interlibrary loan and reserves.

Technical services: Technical services are those tasks performed by library staff associated with selecting and preparing new materials for circulation, such as adding barcodes, spine labels, and plastic covers, so that the materials can be protected and ownership can be identified. They also include cataloging and classification of materials, acquisitions, and the mending, repair, and preservation of materials.

HOW LIBRARIES SERVE SOCIETY

Libraries serve society in the most fundamental way by providing free and equal access to all of their resources. They do this by acquiring, organizing, and storing information and by assisting patrons so that they can find what they need. Everyone needs information for daily work, for learning, and for recreation. Libraries are one way to provide large numbers of people with large quantities of information at a reasonable cost.

Providing free and equal access also applies to availability of technology. Contrary to what is shown in the media, not everyone has an iPhone, tablet, laptop, or even a home computer. The "digital divide" (the gap between those who have access to technology and those who do not) can be bridged by the availability of current technology at the library. Many libraries even loan laptops, tablets, and e-readers to their patrons for home use.

Those who fall into this "digital divide" may not just be economically disadvantaged. It is a social issue affecting

a. rural populations that may not have the availability of connectivity that an urban area would;
b. the disenfranchised (such as the mentally ill or the homeless), who may not have the ability to provide for themselves; and
c. the elderly, who may be so baffled as to avoid new technology completely.

The library has the ability, and the responsibility, to reach out and offer these services to those who have no other mode of access.

It has to be mentioned that there are those who feel that libraries not only do not serve society but that because of technology they are, or will be, irrelevant in the future. They believe that e-books will make paper books irrelevant; Google will

Figure 1.1. Electronic Devices. *Photograph courtesy of the Bill Memorial Library*

make librarians obsolete. However, libraries are likely to survive, particularly if they are vigilant about adapting to trends and expectations—and they are very good at that. "Two key elements for future library sustainability [are]: perception and adaptation to a new paradigm."[3] The Internet is a tremendous influence and source of information, but it is not necessarily the best source as it cannot interpret or evaluate information. For this, libraries are invaluable.

LIBRARY ETHICS

Regardless of the particular demographics of a library, all users must be treated equally. The rules that guide this principle come from the American Library Association (ALA) in the form of two documents: the **Library Bill of Rights**, and the **Library Code of Ethics**. These documents assert that all users deserve the same access to materials regardless of age, race, origin, or views. The ALA advocates in defense of the rights of library users to read, seek information, and speak freely as guaranteed by the First Amendment. This basic right is a core value of the library profession. These principles will be examined more fully in later chapters on intellectual freedom and censorship.

On a more practical level, library ethics are part of the regular routine in a library. Library users expect and are entitled to the utmost privacy about their transactions and personal information. Many years ago, before my library was automated, the

THE LIBRARY BILL OF RIGHTS

The American Library Association affirms that all libraries are forums for information and ideas, and that the following basic policies should guide their services.

I.   Books and other library resources should be provided for the interest, information, and enlightenment of all people of the community the library serves. Materials should not be excluded because of the origin, background, or views of those contributing to their creation.

II. Libraries should provide materials and information presenting all points of view on current and historical issues. Materials should not be proscribed or removed because of partisan or doctrinal disapproval.

III. Libraries should challenge censorship in the fulfillment of their responsibility to provide information and enlightenment.

IV. Libraries should cooperate with all persons and groups concerned with resisting abridgment of free expression and free access to ideas.

V.   A person's right to use a library should not be denied or abridged because of origin, age, background, or views.

VI. Libraries which make exhibit spaces and meeting rooms available to the public they serve should make such facilities available on an equitable basis, regardless of the beliefs or affiliations of individuals or groups requesting their use.

Adopted June 19, 1939, by the ALA Council. Amended October 14, 1944; June 18, 1948; February 2, 1961; June 27, 1967; January 23, 1980. Inclusion of "age" reaffirmed January 23, 1996.

Used with permission from the American Library Association

---

patrons were assigned numbers that would be written on the book card. One day a patron asked me who was #156. Of course, I could not tell her—but her motive was innocent. She apparently chose many of the same titles and thought it would be nice to meet and discuss their common interests.

A privacy policy, or confidentiality statement, is essential to protect the users' right to their own information and the library's right *not* to share personal information. This is often part of a library's policy handbook or is appended to the circulation policy. In the wake of the events of 9/11, privacy became even more important as it can be the first line of defense against law enforcement requests for a patron's reading records. There will be more discussion of this particular issue when we tackle the USA PATRIOT Act in a later chapter.

The Library Code of Ethics states:

As members of the American Library Association, we recognize the importance of codifying and making known to the profession and to the general public the ethical principles that guide the work of librarians, other professionals providing information services, library trustees and library staffs. Ethical dilemmas occur when values are in conflict. The American Library Association Code of Ethics states the values to which we are committed, and embodies the ethical responsibilities of the profession in this changing information environment. We significantly influence or control the selection, organization, preservation, and dissemination of information. In a political system grounded in an informed citizenry, we are members of a profession explicitly committed to intellectual freedom and the freedom of access to information. We have a special obligation to ensure the free flow of information and ideas to present and future generations. The principles of this Code are expressed in broad statements to guide ethical decision making. These statements provide a framework; they cannot and do not dictate conduct to cover particular situations:

THE LIBRARY CODE OF ETHICS

I. We provide the highest level of service to all library users through appropriate and usefully organized resources; equitable service policies; equitable access; and accurate, unbiased, and courteous responses to all requests.

II. We uphold the principles of intellectual freedom and resist all efforts to censor library resources.

III. We protect each library user's right to privacy and confidentiality with respect to information sought or received and resources consulted, borrowed, acquired or transmitted.

IV. We respect intellectual property rights and advocate balance between the interests of information users and rights holders.

V. We treat co-workers and other colleagues with respect, fairness, and good faith, and advocate conditions of employment that safeguard the rights and welfare of all employees of our institutions.

VI. We do not advance private interests at the expense of library users, colleagues, or our employing institutions.

VII. We distinguish between our personal convictions and professional duties and do not allow our personal beliefs to interfere with fair representation of the aims of our institutions or the provision of access to their information resources.

VIII. We strive for excellence in the profession by maintaining and enhancing our own knowledge and skills, by encouraging the professional development of co-workers, and by fostering the aspirations of potential members of the profession.

Used with permission from the American Library Association

LIBRARY USERS

What to call people who come into the library, either physically or virtually—users? patrons? customers? members?—is an oft-debated issue. In an article called "Just Whom Do We Serve?"[4] author Anthony Molaro argues that what we call these people influences how we interact with them. For example, he claims that "patron" connotes their superiority over library staff. "Customer" implies an exchange of money. "Members" implies fees and privileges, while "users" consume. What they are called will depend on the library; from my experience in public library service, "patron" seems to be the most widely used term among my colleagues. It is not the definitive answer, but it is the one we will use most often for this text.

Who uses a library depends on the kind of library and on the library's demographics. The *Merriam-Webster Online Dictionary* defines this as "the qualities (such as age, sex, and income) of a specific group of people."[5] According to a 2013 Pew Research study, 54 percent of Americans have used a public library in the past twelve months and 72 percent live in a "library household" (age sixteen and over).[6] Those aged thirty to sixty-four find that library services are very important, and in general, more women than men use library services.[7] These statistics will vary according to the library, specific services, and the particular community, but the results present an overall pattern. In a 2001 report of the Library Research Service, of all general library users, 74 percent read for pleasure; 56 percent learned about a skill, hobby, or other interest; and 46 percent found information needed for school, work, or a community group. Of all users who studied specific service responses, 59 percent said they use the library as a place—to think, read, write, or study. Fifty-three percent of those using local history or genealogical resources made progress in their research, and in the category of basic literacy, 36 percent read to a child or helped a child choose a book.[8]

Any given public library may have users who include children, teens, adults, seniors, patrons with special needs, and the homeless. Your demographic or service population determines what kinds of materials are offered and in what languages; what kind of programs are offered and for what ages. In later chapters, we will explore in detail the services offered to a range of populations. Figure 1.2 gives an idea of library use broken down between "library lovers" and the general population. Not surprisingly, there is not that much of a gap.

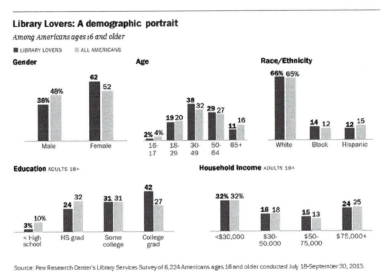

Figure 1.2. Demographic Portrait. *Used with permission from the Pew Research Center*

Table 1.1. Generation Chart

Generation Z	2000–today	Born with technology
Generation Y/Millennials	1980–2000	Technology is the norm
Generation X	1965–1979	Came of age technologically
Baby Boomer	1946–1964	Had to learn technology
The Greatest Generation	1930–1946	Technology didn't exist

Library users of all ages typically fall into two categories: digital natives and digital immigrants. Digital natives, those born between the early 1980s and the early 2000s, Millennials (or Generation Y), as they are known, have grown up with technology as the norm. Baby Boomers (post WWII, 1946–1964) and GenXers (mid-1960–early 1980s) have had to learn technology—some more enthusiastically than others. Many individuals from these groups are now as technologically fluent as their children. The Greatest Generation (1930–1946)—so called because they lived during the Depression and World War II—have had the greatest challenge. While some may be baffled by current trends, many in this demographic have adapted to all that technology has to offer.

DIFFERENT KINDS OF LIBRARIES

A library is a collection of information, formerly thought to be in book format (but which may be in a variety of formats and media), organized for use. All libraries acquire, organize, preserve, and disseminate books and/or other informational materials. Public, school, academic, and special libraries have features in common:

WHAT LIBRARIES HAVE IN COMMON

The particulars vary from type to type and even between libraries of the same type, but all libraries have

- books,
- other informational materials,
- a system for organizing the materials (a classification scheme),
- a catalog for finding the materials,
- a system for disseminating materials and/or information,
- personnel/staff,
- governing structure,
- a site/building/room/space, and
- mechanisms for telling clients about materials and services.

What distinguishes one type of library from another is the service population, not significant differences in service itself.

Public Libraries

Tax-supported public libraries are a relatively modern concept. The first one that the United States was created in Peterborough, New Hampshire, in 1833[9]; the

Boston Public Library, America's first large public library, was established in 1848.[10] By the end of the nineteenth century, the concept had flourished, and many cities and towns had public libraries. Not all public libraries are funded by their towns or municipalities. Many libraries, particularly in New England, were privately endowed and then given to their towns as a gift by philanthropists and run by a board of directors. Many of these "association" libraries exist today. Unfortunately, the philanthropists do not.

Public libraries have responded to changes in society by adjusting their role. They serve culturally diverse populations and ages and are thus the most heterogeneous of any type of library. Public service then is structured around these populations in order to best serve the library's particular demographic. The staff in public libraries must be generalists in order to meet the needs of this population, and foreign-language skills can be a requirement in some communities.

Today, public libraries provide more than books. They are places of cultural preservation of information in its various formats. They are often the hub of their community, providing a wide range of materials, Internet service, training and programs, meeting space, and in some cases, emergency shelter during natural disasters. Surprisingly, in the United States there are no national laws that govern public libraries, so each state must create its own. State libraries have been established in order to provide support and guidance to their towns. Some large states have county and municipal libraries, also considered to be public libraries, that do the same work on the local level.

While there may be no national laws, there are professional associations that provide guidance, professional development, and support to LSS at all levels. On the national level, there is the ALA and its divisions, such as the Public Library Association, Library Leadership and Management Association, or the Reference and Users Services Association. Further, each state has its own library association (e.g., CLA, the Connecticut Library Association; NJLA, the New Jersey Library Association; and WLA, the Washington Library Association) that can assist. Professional journals such as *American Libraries, Library Journal, Library Hotline, Library Quarterly, Publishers Weekly*, and *Library Trends* are also useful. The state or county libraries also offer workshops, webinars, and other opportunities for professional development.

School Libraries

As the United States does not have a national education system, it is once again up to each state to establish an agency to provide public education for K–12. This is done through each state's Department of Education. It is through these agencies that standards of accreditation are determined. While the states have responsibility for primary and secondary education, it's the local school districts that direct the curriculum and fund the libraries, usually via the local board of education.

The nature and function of school libraries has evolved since the nineteenth century, when school libraries became separate from public libraries.[11] They were typically a small collection of books but, paralleling the rise of media and technology in the public library, have become the resource centers that are found today.

The school librarian, or school media specialist (SMS), usually holds a master of library science (MLS) degree. Depending on which state they are in, they may also need to be a certified teacher. The SMS provides library instruction and works with teachers to coordinate lesson plans and materials for classroom support. They may also oversee budget and purchasing, offer reading programs, and provide reference, interlibrary loan, and digital instructional services. The school library or media center is occasionally the center of controversy and conflict over challenged materials (which will be studied in a later chapter on intellectual freedom and censorship). Professional organizations provide support, guidance, and professional development opportunities, such as the Association for Library Service to Children (ALSC, a division of ALA), and the Association of School Librarians (ASL), as well as journals such as *Library Media Connections, School Library Journal, Children and Libraries*, and *Kirkus Reviews*. Again, state or county libraries also offer workshops, webinars, and other opportunities for professional development.

Academic Libraries

Academic libraries serve society's need for education for those beyond high school, and there are several options from which to choose.

The community college is a public, two-year institution that is generally low cost and tax supported and has open enrollment and a comprehensive curriculum. Students are usually recent high school graduates, but some segment of the student body may consist of returning or continuing education students who are older. They may already have some college experience but choose to return to college for new skills. The libraries of such colleges, or learning resource centers, as they may be called, primarily support the students and their coursework, often offering tutoring services for the first-time and remedial college student. Community college students graduate with associate's degrees.

In the four-year college or university, the libraries partner in the educational mission of the institution to develop and support information-literate learners.[12] They may offer formal library instruction or information literacy, and the students are expected to be able to use the library independently. Depending on the size and funding of the institution (publicly funded or privately endowed), there may be more than one library that supports the curricula, such as an engineering library or an art library. These libraries serve the teaching needs of the institution as well as those of the students. They may also support faculty research. Support for these librarians comes from such organizations as the Association of College and Research Libraries (ACRL), the Reference and Users Service Association, and Library Leadership and Management Association (LLAMA), all divisions of ALA. College and university students graduate with bachelor's, master's, or PhD degrees. Journals of interest to this cohort include *College & Research Libraries News, CHOICE: Current Reviews for Academic Libraries*, as well as myriad digital publications such as *Keeping Up With . . .* (a service of ACRL).

Special Libraries

Special Libraries are those that don't fit into any other category. They include corporate, industrial, medical, law, museum, and military libraries. They may be referred to as information centers and are usually not open to the public, although

some, like museum libraries, may have special hours. Unlike the traditional libraries where we go to find what we need, special libraries perform information retrieval
and may alert constituents by e-mail, text, or other digital means. This service is
called selective dissemination of information, or SDI.

Special libraries are designed to support the organization for which they were
created and by whom they are funded and, as such, must prove their value to
the organization. They derive support from the Special Library Association, an
international association not affiliated with ALA; however, ALA's Association of
Specialized and Cooperative Library Agencies (ASCLA) can provide support and
guidance as well.

Another type of special library is the prison library, which also falls under
the auspices of the ASCLA. These tax-supported libraries serve to provide fiction
and nonfiction materials, with some restrictions. The ALA has developed service standards for the incarcerated and has adapted the Prisoner's Right to Read
in order to support library service to all populations.[13] There are two interest
groups that support prison libraries, ASCLA's Library Services for the Incarcerated
and Detained Interest Group and the ASCLA Library Services for Youth in Cus-
tody Interest Group. ASCLA has prepared standards of service for correctional
facilities.[14]

STAFFING

Staffing follows a general pattern in all types of libraries (see figure 1.3). The director of the institution is a professional librarian—someone who holds a master
of library science (MLS) or master of library and information science (MLIS). (Directors of academic or university libraries will generally hold doctorate degrees
as well.) There may be multiple professional librarians with an MLS on staff who
serve as department heads or in other professional capacities under the director;
some may, in fact, hold a bachelor's degree in library science. (While this degree
is not as common as the MLS, many colleges do offer it.) Library workers who
do not hold the MLS or BS are the support staff and can go by several titles:
paraprofessional, library technical assistant, library assistant, library associate, or
library aide. Although their backgrounds may range from a high school graduate
to a college degree, additional library education can lead to an associate's degree
or a library certificate. Those who pursue additional education through the ALA
Support Staff Certification Program become library support staff (LSS), a nationally accepted designation. LSS often take on the responsibilities that were once
the domain of professional librarians. Some libraries consider LSS for positions
formerly unavailable to them due to time, money, and technical expertise. The
current "graying" of professional librarians offers opportunities for LSS to take on
increasingly more responsibility.

According to the *Occupational Outlook Handbook*, "Library technicians and assistants help librarians with all aspects of running a library. They assist patrons,
organize library materials and information, and perform clerical and administrative
tasks."[15]

They also may

perform circulation activities, including patron registration;
shelve materials (and other related tasks, such as shifting and sorting);
do simple cataloging;
answer simple reference questions;
assist with programs; and
maintain the online computer records.

In a small library, there may be additional duties with increased responsibility; in a large library, LSS may be limited to a specific task, such as circulation or technical processing. With experience and additional training in the form of workshops, webinars, and coursework, the LSS can achieve increased responsibilities and opportunities for advancement.

The clerical staff performs the office-related tasks typical of any business and are usually not trained in library work but are essential to the running of the library. Some may serve as receptionists (answering phones), secretaries (record keeping, scheduling), bookkeepers (paying bills, processing payroll), or development staff (involved in fund-raising).

Volunteers round out the staffing picture. Volunteers can shelve, repair materials, create displays, assist with programs—their usefulness depends on the library and its needs. They can range from short-term workers (for a particular project) to long-term volunteers who commit to working a regular schedule and perform specific tasks.

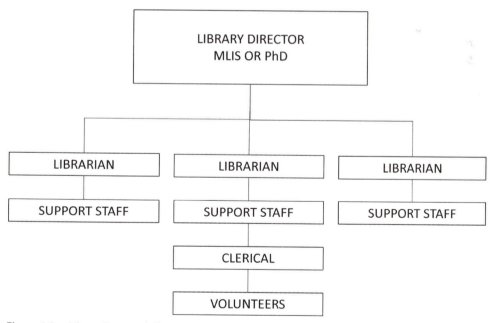

Figure 1.3. Library Personnel Chart

Another kind of volunteer is the community service worker, who is usually short term and needs to fulfill an obligation to their school, community, or the legal system.

LIBRARY PUBLIC AND TECHNICAL SERVICES

Although the lines between them are blurring in many libraries today, there is a fundamental difference between public services and technical services. Public service is exactly what it sounds like: *direct* contact with the patron on a daily basis.
   Public service functions include

   Reference—answering questions, assisting patrons
   Circulation—checking materials in and out, shelving, preservation

Technical service, on the other hand, involves *limited* contact with the public. Technical service functions include

   Acquisitions—bringing materials into the library
   Cataloging—organizing materials so that users can find them
   Preparation—making materials ready for circulation
   Storage—taking care of the physical collection, including conservation and preservation

As mentioned above, the line between public and technical service is blurring. The reality is that in many libraries, these tasks may be carried out by the same person.

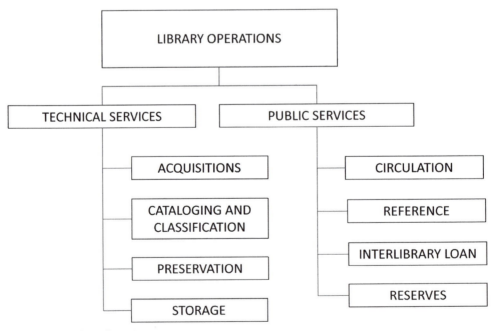

Figure 1.4.   Library Operations

In a small library, the same staff person who checks out your books may also be the one who processed them. In larger libraries, the staff may be cross-trained—technical service staff may take a shift at the reference desk and vice versa. The advantage is that all library personnel understand all of the facets of library service.

CHAPTER SUMMARY

In this chapter, we learned about the "nuts and bolts" of library service: who staffs the library and what their specific duties might be; who uses the library and the library's relationship to them; the timeliness of service that libraries provide; the various types of libraries and their relationship to their communities or funding structure; and the issues and ethics involved. LSS must know the values of the profession, including an understanding of the Library Bill of Rights, the ALA Code of Ethics, freedom of information, confidentiality of library records, and privacy issues. They must also know the roles of LSS and other staff in libraries.

DISCUSSION QUESTIONS AND ACTIVITIES

1. Explain the role of the LSS in a library, taking into consideration the overall library hierarchy.
   a. Do you feel there is opportunity for advancement?
   b. If so, how and why?
2. What role does *your* library—the one you work in or the one you regularly use— play in your community?
   a. If it is not a public library, what impact does it have on the community, if any?
3. What are some of the differences and commonalities among the different types of libraries?
   a. Visit one of each and comment on what you find.
4. What do you think will be the future of libraries?

NOTES

1. American Library Association. "Library Bill of Rights," American Library Association, http://www.ala.org/advocacy/intfreedom/librarybill.

2. American Library Association, "Library Code of Ethics," American Library Association, http://www.ala.org/advocacy/proethics/codeofethics/codeethics.

3. Lluís Anglada, "Are Libraries Sustainable in a World of Free, Networked, Digital Information?," *El Profesional de la Información* 23, no. 6 (November/December 2014): 603–11.

4. Anthony Molaro, "Just Whom Do We Serve?," *American Libraries*, last modified March 28, 2012, http://www.americanlibrariesmagazine.org/article/just-whom-do-we-serve.

5. "Demographic," in *Merriam-Webster Online Dictionary*, http://www.merriam-webster.com/dictionary/demographic.

6. Kathryn Zickuhr et al., "How Americans Value Public Libraries in Their Communities," Pew Internet and American Life Project, last modified December 11, 2013, http://libraries.pewinternet.org/2013/12/11/libraries-in-communities/.

7. Rachel Applegate, "Gender Differences in a Public Library," *Public Library Quarterly* 27, no. 1 (October 11, 2008): 19–31, doi:10.1080/01616840802122468.

8. Rochelle Logan et al., "Counting on Results: New Tools for Outcome Based Evaluations of Public Libraries," last modified November 2001, http://www.lrs.org/documents/cor/CoR_FullFinalReport.pdf.

9. Larry Nix, "Peterborough Town Library," The Library History Buff, last modified December 7, 2008, http://www.libraryhistorybuff.org/peterborough.htm.

10. Boston Public Library, "Boston Public Library: A Brief History and Description," Boston Public Library, http://www.bpl.org/general/history.htm.

11. Karen Muller, "First School Library?," American Library Association, http://www.ala.org/tools/first-school-library.

12. George M. Eberhart, ed., *The Whole Library Handbook*, 5th ed. (Chicago: American Library Association, 2013), 16.

13. American Library Association, "Prisoners' Right to Read," American Library Association, last modified July 1, 2014, http://www.ala.org/advocacy/prisoners-right-read.

14. Larry Nix, "Prison Libraries," American Library Association, http://www.ala.org/tools/prison-libraries.

15. U.S. Department of Labor, *Occupational Outlook Handbook*, Bureau of Labor Statistics, last modified January 8, 2014, http://www.bls.gov/ooh/education-training-and-library/library-technicians-and-assistants.htm#tab-2.

REFERENCES, SUGGESTED READINGS, AND WEBSITES

ALA Office for Intellectual Freedom Facebook page. https://www.facebook.com/ALAOIF.

ALA Office for Intellectual Freedom Twitter feed. https://twitter.com/OIF.

Anglada, Lluís. "Are Libraries Sustainable in a World of Free, Networked, Digital Information?" *El Profesional de la Información* 23, no. 6 (November/December 2014): 603–11.

American Library Association. "Library Bill of Rights." American Library Association. http://www.ala.org/advocacy/intfreedom/librarybill.

———. "Library Code of Ethics." American Library Association. http://www.ala.org/advocacy/proethics/codeofethics/codeethics.

———. "Prisoners' Right to Read." American Library Association. Last modified July 1, 2014. http://www.ala.org/advocacy/prisoners-right-read.

———. "The State of America's Libraries." American Library Association. Last modified 2014. http://www.ala.org/news/state-americas-libraries-report-2014.

Applegate, Rachel. "Gender Differences in a Public Library." *Public Library Quarterly* 27, no. 1 (October 11, 2008): 19–31. doi:10.1080/01616840802122468.

Boston Public Library. "Boston Public Library: A Brief History and Description." Boston Public Library. http://www.bpl.org/general/history.htm.

"Demographic." In *Merriam-Webster Online Dictionary*. http://www.merriam-webster.com/dictionary/demographic.

Eberhart, George M., ed. *The Whole Library Handbook*. 5th ed. Chicago: American Library Association, 2013.

Evans, G. Edward. *Introduction to Library Public Services*. Westport, CT: Libraries Unlimited, 2009.

Intellectual Freedom Manual. 8th ed. Chicago: American Library Association, 2010.

Library Standard for Adult Correctional Institutions. http://www.ala.org/ascla/asclaissues/librarystandards.

Library Support Staff Certification. http://ala-apa.org/lssc/lta-program-recognition-project/.

Logan, Rochelle, Keith Curry Lance, Nicolle O. Steffan, Marcia J. Rodney, and Suzanne Kaller. "Counting on Results: New Tools for Outcome Based Evaluations of Public Libraries." Last modified November 2001. http://www.lrs.org/documents/cor/CoR_FullFinalReport.pdf.

Molaro, Anthony. "Just Whom Do We Serve?" *American Libraries.* Last modified March 28, 2012. http://www.americanlibrariesmagazine.org/article/just-whom-do-we-serve.

Muller, Karen. "First School Library?" American Library Association. http://www.ala.org/tools/first-school-library.

Multigenerational Characteristics. http://www.brucemayhewconsulting.com/index.cfm?id=20209.

Nix, Larry. "Peterborough Town Library." The Library History Buff. Last modified December 7, 2008. http://www.libraryhistorybuff.org/peterborough.htm.

———. "Prison Libraries." American Library Association. http://www.ala.org/tools/prison libraries.

U.S. Department of Labor. *Occupational Outlook Handbook.* Bureau of Labor Statistics. Last modified January 8, 2014. http://www.bls.gov/ooh/education-training-and-library/library -technicians-and-assistants.htm#tab-2.

Wagner, Pat. "Everyday Ethics for Libraries Parts 1–6." Vimeo video, 15 minutes each. Kansas State Library. http://kslib.info/1069/Everyday-Ethics-for-Libraries-An-Overview.

Zickuhr, Kathryn, Lee Rainie, and Kristen Purcell. "From Distant Admirers to Library Lovers—and Beyond." Pew Research Center. Last modified March 12, 2014. http://www.pewinter net.org/2014/03/13/high-engagement/.

Zickuhr, Kathryn, Lee Rainie, Kristen Purcell, and Maeve Duggan. "How Americans Value Public Libraries in Their Communities." Pew Internet and American Life Project. Last modified December 11, 2013. http://libraries.pewinternet.org/2013/12/11/libraries -in-communities/.

CHAPTER 2

Acquisitions, Collection Development, and Classification

Library support staff (LSS) will know the basic principles of acquisitions, collection development, and current cataloging and classification systems. (ALA-LSSC Competency #5)

Topics Covered in This Chapter:

- Acquisitions
- Collection Development
- Classification

Key Terms:

Acquisitions: The acquisition of materials in a library means ordering and receiving print and nonprint materials. It does not refer to the selection of these materials, nor does it refer to the ordering of office supplies or library equipment. The former is done by collection development or selection staff, the latter by the business or technical services department. Some materials are not ordered at all but come to the library as gifts or through library exchange.

Bibliographic verification: Bibliographic verification is the process whereby items to be ordered are carefully checked to make sure that they exist, are in print, and can be acquired. This is done by checking the item against the library's catalog, a consortium or state catalog, the Library of Congress, or OCLC/WorldCat. It also includes making sure that the library doesn't already own the item or have it on order, in process, or in repair.

Classification systems: A classification system is the numerical or alphabetical system a library uses to organize materials by subject. The two most often used are the Dewey Decimal Classification System and the Library of Congress Classification System. These systems provide for the arrangement of materials on a shelf in a logical order, making it easy for patrons to find that for which they are searching.

Collection development: A library's objective is to serve the informational needs of its users. The purpose of collection development is to select materials that serve the needs
of the primary service population. This service population will vary by library type and
community and relies on the demographics of that community to determine what
choices the library makes.

Selection policies: A selection policy is necessary in order to provide guidance for the
librarian or LSS who do collection development. This policy follows a set of guidelines
to consider when choosing materials and includes such criteria as positive reviews,
reputation of the author, local interest, demand, and budget limitations.

ACQUISITIONS

The **acquisition** of materials in a library means ordering and receiving print and
nonprint materials. It does not refer to the selection of these materials, nor does
it refer to the ordering of office supplies or library equipment. The former is done
by collection development or selection staff, the latter by the business or technical
services department. Some materials are not ordered at all but come to the library
as gifts or through library exchange.

Books and printed materials represent the largest library purchases.[1] Books are
usually acquired through wholesale book vendors, or jobbers, who may special-
ize in specific subject areas, publishers, or materials for a type of library such as
public, school, or academic. Some titles from small or alternative presses may only
be available directly from the publisher. The advantages of ordering from vendors
include discount pricing and the opportunity to create a back order, cancellation,
and processing profile. Vendors can provide such vendor-added services (VAS) as
processing a book to be delivered shelf-ready, including MARC records, barcodes,
spine labels, and book covers. Each of these items incurs a small fee, but the added
cost can far outweigh the time it takes to do the processing in house. Free delivery is
often available, although it may require a minimum number of books in a specific
order. There are many wholesalers and vendors available; some of the more well
known include Baker and Taylor, Ingram, Follet, and BWI (Book Wholesalers, Inc.).

Nonbook formats include books on CD, musical CDs, DVDs, and Blue-ray and
can be acquired through such vendors as Recorded Books, Tantor Media, and the
Library Video Company, among others. Libraries that offer electronic books, or
e-books, have the options of purchasing as well as subscribing to lending services
such as Overdrive or Axis 360. Advantages to acquiring e-books, CDs, and streaming movies through these services include lower pricing based on library size or
membership in a consortium; the disadvantage is that titles can only be loaned for a
finite period of time, they may not allow renewals, and titles can be lost altogether if
the library discontinues the service. Purchasing e-books for the library makes them
a permanent part of the collection.

The first step in the acquisitions procedure is to receive the request (from library
staff, a patron in a public library, or a teacher or professor in a school or academic
library). Be sure to maintain the source of the request. The second step involves the
need for **bibliographic verification**, for two reasons:

1. To determine that the item actually exists. The way to accurately verify an item is to check the library's catalog, the state or local consortium, the Library of Congress, or OCLC/WorldCat (by author, title, or a combination of the two).
   a. Determine the format—print or nonprint?
   b. Determine the currency—if it is not a current title, is it still in print?
   c. Determine the language—is it a foreign title?
2. To determine that the library needs it.
   a. Make sure it is not already in the collection.
      i. If it is, is it a replacement for a worn or damaged book or a second copy?
   b. Make sure it is not on order but not yet in the catalog.
      ii. Check standing orders and automatic shipment plans.
      iii. Check with the processing department.

The third step is placing the order. There are various ways of placing an order with the vendor. Most libraries do this electronically through the vendor's website. Some libraries may want to create a paper copy to fax to the vendor (or to have on hand for the convenience of the patrons). Depending on the vendor, the order may include the complete and correct citation: author, title, publisher, date of publication, edition, and number of copies. The single most important piece of information in the citation, however, is the ISBN: the International Standard Book Number. This is a unique thirteen-digit number assigned to each edition of each publication—a unique and separate number is assigned for the hardbound, paperback, audio, or electronic versions of the same title. This number alone may be all that the vendor needs; the addition of the other information is helpful in case of mistyping the ISBN or to verify the correct format.

There are also various methods of acquisition:

- The firm order is a list of titles that the library knows it wants to order—this is considered a *micro selection*.
- The standing order is an open order for the library to receive everything on a particular topic or category (e.g., annual editions of certain reference materials).
  - A variation on this is when a library chooses to receive all titles of particular authors as they are published in fiction, nonfiction, or both.
- The approval plan is when the library is sent a selection of titles from which it may choose with the understanding that they can be returned.
  - The last two are referred to as *macro selection*, which adds large quantities of materials through mass buying plans, not by individual titles.[2]
- Another method of acquisition is known as gifts and exchange.
  - Gifts can be those materials actively sought by the library in order to fill needs in the collection.
  - Unsolicited materials given to the library also fall into this category. They may be useful to the collection or may be returned to the donor or used for other purposes, such as a book sale. The library needs a clearly worded policy on what gifts it accepts and their eventual disposition. No strings can be attached to a gift that would preclude the library from using the gift as it sees fit.
  - Exchange is the method some libraries, principally academic libraries, use to offer unused or no longer needed materials to another institution in exchange for something that fills a need in their collection.

Once the order is placed, the next step is to prepare for its receipt. In the meantime, there is a plethora of mail that may come to the library that the LSS must be able to handle. Know to whom it should be routed, including unsolicited material such as books, posters, and flyers. While unsolicited catalogs and flyers may be junk mail, they can be good sources for new information on products, services, and ideas.

When the shipment comes—which always felt like Christmas in my library—there is a procedure to follow:

1. Unpack the boxes.
2. Find the packing slip (the actual invoice is almost always sent separately).
3. Check the packing slip against the contents—item for item.
4. Check the shipment itself against the order form to make sure what was received was what was ordered and vice versa.

There could be problems with the shipment, including missing items, duplicate items, incorrect format, damage (missing pages, cover upside down, or incorrect spine label, for example), missing copies of volumes within a set, incorrect prices, discounts, or VAS indicated on the packing slip. If there are problems, then the vendor must be contacted immediately. Be prepared to give the order number, account number, or whatever other information the vendor requests. Most likely, they will issue a return authorization number (RTA) to allow the item to be returned; there may also be a return label in the enclosed paperwork. Once it all checks out, the materials can be processed (as needed) and the property marked. Be sure this is all done before paying the invoice, as materials may not be returnable unless a mistake was the vendor's error.

Besides using a vendor, there are other ways to acquire materials. Libraries may have an arrangement with a local bookstore for materials to supplement the collection or for new titles. Libraries may use or offer print-on-demand services and equipment. For some items, it may be necessary to order directly from the publisher; these prices and discounts will vary from vendor pricing. Outsourcing is another way that libraries acquire materials—they contract with a service that does the selection and processing without input from the staff. This takes the entire acquisition function out of the library altogether and may be an option for small libraries that lack trained staff to make these decisions or for large libraries that choose to put their energy into other functions. It can be argued that this is both a time and money saver for a given library.

COLLECTION DEVELOPMENT

The objective of any library is to serve the informational needs of their users. Who these users are will depend on the library's demographics. The U.S. Small Business Administration defines demographics thus: "Demographics are the characteristics of a human population. This information is often used by small business owners to conduct research into where opportunities exist within their market and in developing appropriate business and marketing strategies to target customers."[3] The Small Business Administration's website provides numerous links to utilities that can help a library determine their demographic. In library terms, we use these characteristics in order to tailor the information to our users' need. The purpose, then, of **collection development** is to select materials that serve the needs of the primary service population or demographic.

Like so many other facets of librarianship, a policy needs to be in place to guide collection development. A selection policy follows a set of guidelines to consider when choosing materials. The following textbox of a sample **selection policy** shows the criteria that must be considered.

There are many sources to choose from when selecting materials for a collection. The ALA offers much guidance in collection development and selection utilities for all formats and libraries.[4] Professional journals include *Publisher's Weekly*, *Booklist*, *Library Journal*, *School Library Journal*, *Kirkus Reviews*, and *Choice*. These journals are available both in print and electronic formats by subscription. Librarians or LSS responsible for selection would read the many reviews, grouped by genre in fiction and nonfiction alike, that these journals provide and choose those

---

SAMPLE SELECTION POLICY

1. Library Mission Statement or Statement of Purpose
2. Statement of Responsibility for Selection: Who does the selecting?
3. Purpose of Material Selection Policy: This would be a statement about the reasons materials are chosen and the inclusion of materials to appeal to a wide range of patrons. It would also include:
   a. Library Bill of Rights
   b. Freedom to Read Statement
4. Statement of Confidentiality
5. Types of Materials: print and nonprint, electronic, downloadable, media
6. Criteria of Selection: This would include such elements as
   a. Budget limitations
   b. Local interest
   c. Suitability of subject matter
   d. Reputation of author
   e. Positive reviews
   f. Demand
   g. Relevance to the community
7. Children's Materials Selection
   a. Specific criteria
8. Teen Materials Selection
   a. Specific criteria
9. Gift Acceptance
   a. Under what circumstances a library will accept materials
   b. What will be done with the items if they cannot be included in the collection
10. Weeding (or deselection)
    a. The criteria to follow to remove items from the collection
11. Disposal of Withdrawn Items
12. Request for Reconsideration of Materials

that fit the library's criteria according to their selection policy. Staff also have authorized booklists and web sources to consult, such as Read.gov from the Library of Congress, Fiction-L Booklists, NoveLists by EBSCO, and myriad lists produced by individual libraries. The H. W. Wilson Company produces a Core Collections series of bibliographies for public library nonfiction, fiction, children, middle and junior high, and senior high. This series is continually being updated, and while not technically a review source, they provide examples of the best choices for the above-named libraries. The professional judgment of the library staff is a valuable resource, as are user requests. User requests can run the gamut from the scholarly to those plucked from popular magazines and television shows. Oprah has become a one-woman review source—if she endorses a book, you can be sure that patrons will be asking for it.

CLASSIFICATION SYSTEMS

Classification systems arrange like items together. At a grocery store, all of the canned peaches are in the same area or shelf. This principle applies to libraries as well. The classification system is important because the classification number combined with the author designation form a unique notation that becomes the *location symbol* or *call number*. I like to think of this as the "address" or where the item "lives" on the shelf. This means that like or related materials are together or very close to each other.

Only two classification systems have been universally adopted—the Dewey Decimal System and the Library of Congress System.

Dewey Decimal System

The Dewey Decimal System (DDC) was created by Melvil Dewey, a librarian and the founder of the American Library Association, in 1876.[5] Primarily used in public libraries and schools (K–12), Dewey divided the world of knowledge into ten main classes:

DEWEY DECIMAL CLASSIFICATION MAIN CLASSES

000	Generalities
100	Philosophy
200	Religion
300	Social Sciences
400	Language
500	Pure Science
600	Technology
700	Arts
800	Literature
900	Geography and History

Source: Dewey Decimal Classification

These are then divided into the "hundreds divisions." An example of this in the 500 class, pure science, would look like this:

DEWEY DECIMAL CLASSIFICATION HUNDREDS CLASSES	
500	Science
510	Mathematics
520	Astronomy
530	Physics
540	Chemistry
550	Earth Sciences and Geology
560	Fossils and Prehistoric Life
570	Life Sciences; Biology
580	Plants (Botany)
590	Animals (Zoology)

Source: Dewey Decimal Classification

Taking it one step further, these divisions are broken down into what is called the "thousands." Chemistry, 540, would look like this:

DEWEY DECIMAL CLASSIFICATION THOUSANDS CLASSES	
540	Chemistry and Allied Sciences
541	Physical Chemistry
542	Techniques, Equipment, and Materials
543	Analytical Chemistry
544	[Unassigned]
545	[Unassigned]
546	Inorganic Chemistry
547	Organic Chemistry
548	Crystallography
549	Mineralogy

Source: Dewey Decimal Classification

As you can see, all classification numbers have three digits: the first digit is the *main class*, the second digit is the *division*, and the third digit is the *section*. A decimal point after the third digit may be used to further define the subject according to the tables in the DDC. This structure allows individual libraries to classify as broadly or as specifically as its collections demand. The Internet Public Library (http://www.ipl.org) has created a handy breakdown of all of the divisions.[6]

Library of Congress Classification

The Library of Congress Classification (LCC) is the second most widely used system in the United States, primarily by academic and special libraries. Created between 1897 and 1911,[7] LCC divides knowledge into twenty-one broad categories, using a letter to represent each subject field. (The letters I, O, W, X, and Y are not used.) Double or triple letters are used for subclasses. The letter notation plus a numerical value constitute the LC classification number. This combination of letters and numbers allows for greater specificity with fewer characters.

LIBRARY OF CONGRESS CLASSIFICATION

A	General Works
B	Philosophy, Psychology, Religion
C	Auxiliary Sciences of History
D	World History and History of Europe, Asia, Africa, Australia, New Zealand, etc.
E	History of the Americas
F	History of the Americas
G	Geography, Anthropology, Recreation
H	Social Sciences
J	Political Science
K	Law
L	Education
M	Music and Books on Music
N	Fine Arts
P	Language and Literature
Q	Science
R	Medicine
S	Agriculture
T	Technology
U	Military Science
V	Naval Science
Z	Bibliography, Library Science, Information Resources (general)

Source: Library of Congress

A classification number, then, is a number assigned to a book in order to distinguish it from others. A full call number will include a classification number and a letter or letters to represent the author's name.

These classification numbers help to identify the book on the shelf—an advantage for browsers. It also helps to identify what items the library holds by linking that item to the library's catalog. The information about the item must be translated into a language that the computer can read and understand. We currently use MARC records (*machine readable cataloging*). In a MARC record, each part of the bibliographic record, such as author, title, publisher, copyright date, ISBN, and local call number, is part of a string of identifiers. RDA, or Resource Description and Access, is a set of guidelines for how to enter data into MARC records; this allows the computer to "read" the information that these codes represent and create the record that can direct the user to the resource when displayed in a library catalog.[8] However, a new initiative called Bibliographic Framework, or BIBFRAME, is the "foundation for the future of bibliographic description that happens on the web and in the networked world. It is designed to integrate with and engage in the wider information community and still serve the very specific needs of libraries." It will eventually replace the MARC format in order to accommodate cataloging rules and new methods of data entry.[9]

Other Methods of Classification

Although DDC and LCC are the two most often used systems, there are other methods of classification. The U.S. government uses a system called SuDoc, after the superintendent of documents. This system is used for government documents and publications of the U.S. Government Publishing Office.[10] This system could be used in any library that houses government documents, particularly if it is a federal depository.[11] A federal depository library is so designated by Congress and is authorized to collect government documents in a variety of categories.

The National Library of Medicine has its own classification system as well—NLM. This provides for classification of medical and related scientific materials and is used internationally. It is a letter-based arrangement similar to LCC in that it uses letters for broad categories that are further defined by numbers.[12]

The Cutter method, also known as the Cutter Expansive Classification or Cutter-Sanborn, was created by Charles Cutter, librarian of the Boston Athenaeum (1868–1892),[13] and was later revised by Margaret Sanborn. While not technically a classification system, this alphanumeric method was devised to arrange works by author within a given class. Cutter tables are used to add short representations of names and words to call numbers for sorting and filing.[14] It can be used with both the DDC and LCC systems.

Some libraries may use a combination of both or all three (DDC, LCC, and Cutter). It is important for LSS to understand which system their library is using; even more important is that they understand how the system works. As mentioned previously, circulation staff is the frontline of the library. It is critical that they know their collection, be able to find material, and direct patrons on how to do so as well.

CHAPTER SUMMARY

In this chapter, LSS learned the basic principles of acquisitions, collection development, and classification. The library's objective to serve their users was examined, as was determining who the library's users are. The elements of a selection policy were presented as a guide to choosing materials appropriate for a given library. Additionally, this chapter presented an introduction to the major classification systems and how the LSS would use them to find materials in the library.

DISCUSSION QUESTIONS AND ACTIVITIES

1. Using the sample selection policy provided in this chapter as a guide, write a selection policy for a library of your choice: public, school, or academic.
   a. Take into consideration all of the elements of the policy relative to your chosen library, as well as the demographics of the community that you choose.

2. Visit a library of your choice and ask the librarians what review sources they prefer and why.
   a. Ask to see two hard copies (or ask for permission to log on to two online sources). Read reviews for several different items—books (adult, teen, or children; fiction and nonfiction), audio CDs, or other media that these sources offer.
   b. Is there is noticeable difference in style, format, or content?
3. Search online library catalogs (or visit two libraries) that use DDC and LCC classification and search for the same nonfiction book.
   a. Notice the differences in their call numbers. Using the DDC and LC tables, can you understand how those numbers were assigned?
   b. Do you find one system easier to use and why?

NOTES

1. G. Edward Evans, *Introduction to Technical Services*, 8th ed., Library and Information Science Text Series (Santa Barbara, CA: Libraries Unlimited, 2010), 85.

2. George M. Eberhart, ed., *The Whole Library Handbook*, 5th ed. (Chicago: American Library Association, 2013), 248.

3. U.S. Government, "Demographics," U.S. Small Business Administration, https://www.sba.gov/content/demographics.

4. American Library Association, "Resources for Library Collections," American Library Association, http://www.ala.org/alcts/resources/collect.

5. A&E Television Networks, LLC, "Melvil Dewey," Biography.com, http://www.biography.com/people/melvil-dewey-9273516.

6. Drexel University, "Dewey Decimal Classification System," Internet Public Library, http://www.ipl.org/div/aplus/dewey1.htm.

7. ITS.MARC, "Historical Note on the Library of Congress Classification," Cataloger's Reference Shelf. http://www.itsmarc.com/crs/mergedProjects/scmclass/scmclass/historical_note_on_the_library_of_congress_classification_scm.htm.

8. Library of Congress, "What Is a MARC Record and Why Is It Important?," Library of Congress, http://www.loc.gov/marc/umb/um01to06.html.

9. Library of Congress, "Bibliographic Framework Initiative," Library of Congress, http://www.loc.gov/bibframe/.

10. U.S. Government Publishing Office, "Superintendent of Documents (SuDocs) Classification Scheme Print Email Details," Federal Depository Library Program, http://www.fdlp.gov/catalogingandclassification/cataloging-articles/1791-superintendent-of-documents-sudocs-classification-scheme.

11. U.S. Government Publishing Office, "Federal Depository Library Program," U.S. Government Publishing Office, http://www.gpo.gov/libraries/?utm_source=rss&utm_medium=rss&utm_campaign=federal-depository-library-program.

12. National Institutes of Health, "NLM Classification 2014," U.S. National Library of Medicine, http://www.nlm.nih.gov/class/.

13. Boston Athanaeum, "Charles Ammi Cutter," Boston Athenaeum, http://www.bostonathenaeum.org/library/book-recommendations/athenaeum-authors/charles-ammi-cutter.

14. ITS.MARC, "G 63 Cutter Numbers," ITS.MARC, http://www.itsmarc.com/crs/mergedProjects/SCMshelf/scmshelf/g_63_cutter_numbers_shelf.htm.

REFERENCES, SUGGESTED READINGS, AND WEBSITES

A&E Television Networks, LLC. "Melvil Dewey." Biography.com. http://www.biography.com/people/melvil-dewey-9273516.

American Library Association. "Association for Library Collections and Technical Services." American Library Association. http://www.ala.org/alcts/.

———. "Resources for Library Collections." American Library Association. http://www.ala.org/alcts/resources/collect.

Boston Athenaeum. "Charles Ammi Cutter." Boston Athenaeum. http://www.bostonathenaeum.org/library/book-recommendations/athenaeum-authors/charles-ammi-cutter.

Drexel University. "Dewey Decimal Classification System." Internet Public Library. http://www.ipl.org/div/aplus/dewey1.htm.

Eberhart, George M., ed. *The Whole Library Handbook.* 5th ed. Chicago: American Library Association, 2013.

Evans, G. Edward. *Introduction to Technical Services.* 8th ed. Library and Information Science Text Series. Santa Barbara, CA: Libraries Unlimited, 2010.

Fister, Barbara. "The Dewey Dilemma." *Library Journal.* Last modified May 20, 2010. http://lj.libraryjournal.com/2010/05/public-services/the-dewey-dilemma.

ITS.MARC. "G 63 Cutter Numbers." ITS.MARC. http://www.itsmarc.com/crs/mergedProjects/SCMshelf/scmshelf/g_63_cutter_numbers_shelf.htm.

———. "Historical Note on the Library of Congress Classification." Cataloger's Reference Shelf. http://www.itsmarc.com/crs/mergedProjects/scmclass/scmclass/historical_note_on_the_library_of_congress_classification_scm.htm.

Library of Congress. "Bibliographic Framework Initiatives." Library of Congress. http://www.loc.gov/bibframe.

———. "The Center for the Book in the Library of Congress." Library of Congress. http://www.read.gov/cfb/.

———. "Read.gov Explore New Worlds: Read." Library of Congress. http://read.gov/.

———. "What Is a MARC Record and Why Is It Important?" Library of Congress. http://www.loc.gov/marc/umb/um01to06.html.

National Institutes of Health. "NLM Classification 2014." U.S. National Library of Medicine. http://www.nlm.nih.gov/class/.

Parrot, Kiera, and Karyn M. Peterson. "Ditching Dewey: Hot Topic in Hartford." *School Library Journal.* Last modified November 20, 2013. http://www.slj.com/2013/11/collection-development/ditching-dewey-hot-topic-in-hartford-aasl-2013/#_for.

University of Illinois at Urbana-Champaign. "Dewey Decimal System—a Guide to Call Numbers." University Library. http://www.library.illinois.edu/ugl/about/dewey.html.

USA.gov. "Library of Congress Classification Outline." Library of Congress. http://www.loc.gov/catdir/cpso/lcco/.

U.S. Government. "Demographics." U.S. Small Business Administration. https://www.sba.gov/content/demographics.

U.S. Government Publishing Office. "Federal Depository Library Program." U.S. Government Publishing Office. http://gpo.gov/libraries/?utm_source/rss&utm_medium/rss&utm_campaign/federal-depository-library-program.

———. "Superintendent of Documents (SuDocs) Classification Scheme Print Email Details." Federal Depository Library Program. http://www.fdlp.gov/catalogingandclassification/cataloging-articles/1791-superintendent-of-documents-sudocs-classification-scheme.

CHAPTER 3

Special Collections and Nonbook Materials

Library support staff (LSS) will know the roles of a library in its community, the basic principles of information services, and will be able to recognize and respond to diversity in user needs for resources and services. (ALA-LSSC Competencies #1, #5, #11)

Topics Covered in This Chapter:

- Special Collections
- Serials
- Media

Key Terms:

Access: Access is a way of getting to something. In the context of libraries, it means facilitating the means of getting information to the user.

Archives: Archives are a collection of documents or records that are not available to the general public because they may be valuable or fragile. It also can refer to the place where these items are stored, such as a special room in the library. LSS can provide access to archives or archived materials for their patrons.

Media: While *media* refers to any means of communication, including books, newspapers, magazines, CDs, DVDs, television, and radio, for example, in libraries, *media* is often the term used for formats other than print.

Preservation: *Preservation* is a term in general use to define activities that will prolong the life of materials. It includes concerns about the environment, handling, and storage. Preservation can be done by LSS trained in a few basic concepts.

Serials: *Serials* is an all-inclusive term covering a variety of publications in various forms, content, and purpose, like magazines and newspapers. They are issued in successive parts, at regular intervals, and are intended to continue indefinitely.[1]

SPECIAL COLLECTIONS

As we discussed in chapter 1, libraries serve society in the most fundamental way by providing free and equal access to all of their resources. They do this by acquiring, organizing, and storing information and by assisting people in finding that information. When we think of libraries, we often think of people borrowing books and other materials to use at their convenience. There are, however, materials that many libraries contain that are not available for circulation; they might not even be available to the general public. These are archives and **special collections**.

Archives are usually thought of as a place where old documents are stored, but that is only partially true. An archive is a collection of materials that are, for various reasons, unsuitable for general use but are nonetheless a valuable resource. They consist of materials collected because of the value of the materials or of the information that they contain. Their major purpose is the preservation of original and/or primary materials that make up a society's history. Many items are unique and irreplaceable, although reproductions of rare materials can also be part of such a collection. A library's special collection can range from one small shelf of local history material to a dedicated room to an entire library, such as the Folger Shakespeare Library in Washington, DC.[2]

The main functions of special collections are the *preservation of material* that is important to a particular constituency and *controlled access* to these materials. The two basic criteria for an item to be included in a special collection are the item's *suitability for the scope* or subjects of the collection and its *need for special handling* to ensure long-term preservation. The public service philosophy is that library material is for *use*. For special collections, the objective is to *preserve* the work, both its physical being and its information, by limiting access to essential rather than casual use. For the librarian, special collections present a conundrum because you want the material to be used, but you also don't want it to be destroyed. You must strike a balance between conservation and legitimate use. That's not easy, but it is important if you want the collection to continue to have value.

What a library chooses to collect depends on its demographic. So, too, the inclusion of a special collection supports an interest that the library wants to foster. For example, many public libraries will have a local history collection. These collections document the history of the local community and its people. At the library where I formerly worked, the special collection consisted of local history and biographical information of the founding families. Since this library was also located near a historic battlefield site, the collection included extensive information on the events that took place there. The information sought was not always about the events but also about the people. Genealogy is a popular pastime, and our archives held much of the kind of information that people seek for their family research.

Other special collections in libraries may consist of materials on a particular subject or the works of an individual author. (This brings to mind a neighboring library that received the entire body of work of a famous author after his death.) Besides books, these collections may contain photographs, manuscripts, theses, government documents, music, artwork, plays, maps, and audiovisual and digital materials, for example.

Figure 3.1. Special Collection of Historic Materials in a Small Public Library. *Photograph courtesy of the Bill Memorial Library*

Figure 3.2. Special Collections of Historic Materials Housed in Separate Room. *Photograph courtesy of the Groton Public Library*

Many special collections take on the characteristics of a museum and include artifacts, not just paper-based materials, especially in small communities lacking a museum. This was actually quite common for libraries in New England in the late 1800s and early 1900s; many of these libraries still retain some of their museum artifacts.

It is generally not the mission of school or community college libraries to house such collections; and while special collections are often found in public libraries, they can more often be found in college and university libraries. At Yale University, for example, the Beinecke Rare Book and Manuscript Library contains only rare books and manuscripts and serves as Yale's principal repository for literary archives.[3]

Access to a special collection is limited. Since most researchers need access to the content, the format may be irrelevant. Digitizing material is one way to meet both the need for access and the need to preserve the material, and increasingly libraries are digitizing their collections. Using these surrogates makes access easier and preserves the originals.

Access to a special collection must be controlled and patrons must be monitored in order to prevent the theft or mutilation of materials. There are various ways to do this, including requiring the patron to sign in, show identification, and give the reason for their research so that the staff know what area of the collection is being accessed. Identification such a driver's license may be held until the patron is done. Patrons may be required to "check" bags, briefcases, or purses or to put them in a secure locker. They may also have to wear gloves in order to handle fragile primary sources.

A library that is designated as an archive will have staff members specially trained in acquisition, processing, and communication with donors or other departments. They will understand the basic principles, objectives, and techniques for the preservation and conservation of original objects in various formats.[4] More information about conservation and preservation can be accessed through such sites as the Northeast Document Conservation Center, which is listed in the suggested websites at the end of this chapter.

There are differences as well in how material is processed. Special collections items are cataloged but often are not stamped, glued, or marked up as we do for circulating items. Issues of preservation involve decisions on climate control and environmental and security concerns, as well as the care of the documents themselves.

Special collections require promotion, publicity, and good public relations if they are to grow and thrive. They are expensive in terms of the actual material (in some cases, priceless), as well as in labor and maintenance. Good publicity reminds the public about the existence of a special collection and helps to procure funds to maintain and expand it. It can be a fascinating and challenging area in which to work.

Sometimes the gift of materials to a special collection will come with restrictions placed on them by their donors. According to a joint statement put out by the Association of College and Research Libraries (ACRL) and the Society of American Archivists (SAA), gift policies, and all of the policy decisions that go into restricted use, need to be clearly articulated by the library in accordance with published institutional polices.[5]

SAMPLE GIFT POLICY
1. The library accepts gifts of materials without restrictions and without commitment to their final disposition.
2. The library will not appraise materials for income tax purposes but will acknowledge the receipt of such gifts.
3. Acceptance of gifts materials into the collection will be subject to the same criteria as selection of purchased materials.
4. The library welcomes funds to be used for the purchase of memorials. A thank-you note is sent to the donor, and the family of the person honored is notified.

SERIALS

Serials is an all-inclusive term covering many publication variations in form, content, and purpose. Like its homophone, *cereals*, they come in a variety of forms to suit everyone's interests. Serials are defined as *publications issued in successive parts, at regular intervals, usually bearing numbers, and intended to continue indefinitely.*[6] They include periodicals, annual reports, and yearbooks, for example. *Periodicals* are publications with a *distinctive title intended to appear in successive numbered parts at regular intervals.* Each part generally contains articles by several contributors.

To further clarify:

- Magazines are often what we think of when we refer to serials
  - Monthly or weekly mass-market titles such as *Time* or *People* magazine.
  - Popular subject-oriented serials like *Sports Illustrated.*
  - Those that popularize science like *National Geographic* or *Smithsonian.*
  - Those that focus on opinion (social, political, literary, artistic, or religious) like the *National Review* or *Common Cause.*
- Journals
  - Journals are targeted to a narrower segment: the well-informed layperson or for professional specialties, such as *Library Journal* or the *Journal of the American Medical Association.*
- Newspapers
  - Newspapers fit into the definition of serials. In print they pose storage and access problems but may be stored on microfiche. As many newspapers are now digitally accessible, this can eliminate the storage issue altogether.
- Superseding serials
  - Superseding serials are those where the new issues replaces the previous one. Examples of these are phonebooks and product catalogs.
- Nonsuperseding serials
  - Nonsuperseding serials, however, are those that provide loose-leaf updates that *add* to the publication, such as local zoning regulations.

- Newsletters
  - Newsletters are generally short term and not lengthy. While corporate or special libraries may actively seek those in support of marketing, lobbying, and public relations, public libraries would accept them from local organizations and institutions. They are generally available for free by signing up to a distribution list.
- Yearbooks
  - Yearbooks are annuals, biennials, and occasional publications that include almanacs, proceedings, and directories of a society or association. These are usually collected by academic and special libraries.
- Institutional reports
  - Institutional reports can be annual, semiannual, quarterly, or occasional reports of corporations. These would mostly be of interest to corporate libraries.[7]

The advantage to using serials is that they are the source for the *most current information* as the update interval is very short compared to a book. Books on subjects such as finance may be out of date by the time they are published. This is important for LSS to understand when helping patrons find needed information.

Serials are available both in print and digitally:

- Print
  - The advantages of print serials include ease of use and ownership of the hard copy.

Figure 3.3.   Library Print Magazine Display. *Photograph courtesy of the Groton Public Library*

- ○ A disadvantage is storage, although libraries can choose to have serials bound into annual volumes to minimize storage space. How long serials are kept depends on the size and storage capacity of the library.
  - ○ Challenges to serials may include the public's objection to the library owning certain titles or to the content of a particular issue (such as the *Sports Illustrated* swimsuit edition). This will be explored in later chapters on censorship and intellectual freedom.
  - ○ Another challenge relevant to this discussion is that of copyright as it pertains to the copying or duplication of print articles.
  - ○ Print serials are costly, with academic subscriptions costing hundreds of dollars per year. Theft and loss can add to the overall cost.
- • Digital
  - ○ The advantage of digital serials is that only the desired article is downloaded.
  - ○ There is no advertising to clutter the content.
- However
  - ○ Content is not owned, only licensed, and may expire after the current issue.
  - ○ Content may only be available in abstract form, not in full text.
  - ○ There is no access to back files.
  - ○ Content may not be current if the serial is digitized after the publication of the hard copy, not simultaneously.
  - ○ There may be problems with download times and search delays.
  - ○ There may not be enough workstations available for the users.
  - ○ Fees can be high, no matter how many or how few people use the service.
    - ■ The cost of electronic serials may be based on the number of users (per service population or the number enrolled in a college, for example).
    - ■ The cost may be based per search or transaction (whether it was completed or not).
    - ■ There may be a flat license fee.
    - ■ The fee may be based on being part of a bundle (including titles that you don't want).
    - ■ The technology used to access a digital serial today may not be available in the future, making saved files unreadable.

While this may sound like there are few advantages to digital serials, they are in fact a smart choice for large public libraries, academic libraries, and special libraries.

The LSS must understand how serials are managed in their library. With print serials, individual issues are shelved in one of three ways:

- • Alphabetically by title
- • Alphabetically by title within a broad grouping (health, science, sports, etc.)
- • Classification by subject using call numbers

There are problems associated with print serials in the library. We already mentioned the high cost, but we also have to deal with occasional title changes. A magazine can change its title in the middle of a run due to changes in editor, philosophy, or ownership. An example of this is *McCall's* magazine, a long-running women's service magazine that in May 2001 was updated and renamed *Rosie* after its purchase by Rosie O'Donnell.[8] The popular teen magazine *Young Miss* changed its format and became *Young and Modern* in the 1980s; it was renamed yet again in 2000 as *YM*.[9] Both of these magazines have since ceased publication. The *Ladies' Home Journal*, another long-running title, transitioned to a quarterly publication in July 2014; it also maintains an online presence.[10] Some magazines will abruptly cease publication, and the user's subscription is then fulfilled with another title until the expiration date of the original title. These changes must be carefully tracked and accounted for in order to maintain accurate records.

The LSS need to know how print serials are managed in the library, including how they are shelved; how, or even if, they circulate; and how they are indexed. Indexing allows for the search and retrieval of a particular article. For many years, the Reader's Guide to Periodical Literature, a series of books, was the standard choice in libraries, and while it can still be helpful for articles that are not available online, most articles can be found in a variety of databases. Indexing services charge fees, but libraries usually absorb that cost and provide access to a database at no cost to the patron.

The key component in serials control is the *serial file*: a way to keep track of each title. This can be done by using a serial card, an index card, or the serial component

Title _____ Frequency _____

Ordered _____ Source _____ Cost _____

Vols. Begin _____ Vols. Per year _____ Tp. And Ind. _____

Year	Vol.	Jan.	Feb.	Mar.	April	May	June	July	Aug.	Sept.	Oct.	Nov.	Dec.

Daily

	1	2	3	4	5	6	7	8	9	10	11	12	13	14	15	16	17	18	19	20	21	22	23	24	25	26	27	28	29	30	31
January																															
February																															
March																															
April																															
May																															
June																															
July																															
August																															
September																															
October																															
November																															
December																															

Figure 3.4. Sample Serials Record Cards

of the integrated library system (ILS). The serials are usually alphabetical by title, and the records contain the following information:

Title
Price
Frequency
When subscription began
Renewal periods
Binding information
Bibliographic data

MEDIA

Information comes in all kinds of packages these days. At their inception, nonbook formats were treated as marginal additions to the library's collection. First appearing in school and college libraries and based mainly on the instructional needs of the teachers, examples of equipment consisted of overhead projectors, 16 mm films, and filmstrips. Public libraries added record albums, circulating art prints, audiovisual adaptations of children's books, toys, and puzzles. At the time, these were costly additions to the collection and posed challenges to library staff. If these items were circulated at all, they may have had differing loan periods, and shelving and storing these materials in the library also posed logistical problems. As time has passed, all manner of nonprint devices have been accepted and incorporated into collections and are taken very much for granted. Currently, technology has moved media to the forefront of most libraries. Examples to be found now include

- DVDs, Blue-ray, streaming video:
  - Associated issues include movie ratings and the age at which a library determines movies can be borrowed and copyright infringement (showing movies publicly without buying a public performance license).[11]
- Audio recordings
  - Books on CD
  - Play-aways (preloaded one title per device)
  - Downloadable from a site or service to a device (iPod, MP3, Kindle, Computer, etc.)
  - Music CDs (current, classical, children's, opera, etc.)
  - Audio choices fill a need for vision-impaired patrons. (More information on materials from the Library for the Blind and Physically Handicapped will appear in a later chapter.)

Other nonprint formats include electronic resources, microforms, gaming software (Guitar Hero, Wii), cameras, LCD projectors, nature backpacks, science kits, models—whatever the latest technology is, it will likely be available to borrow from the library at some point. Map collections may still exist for reference or historical purposes, but Internet mapping sources may eliminate the need for anything other than local street and road maps in libraries.

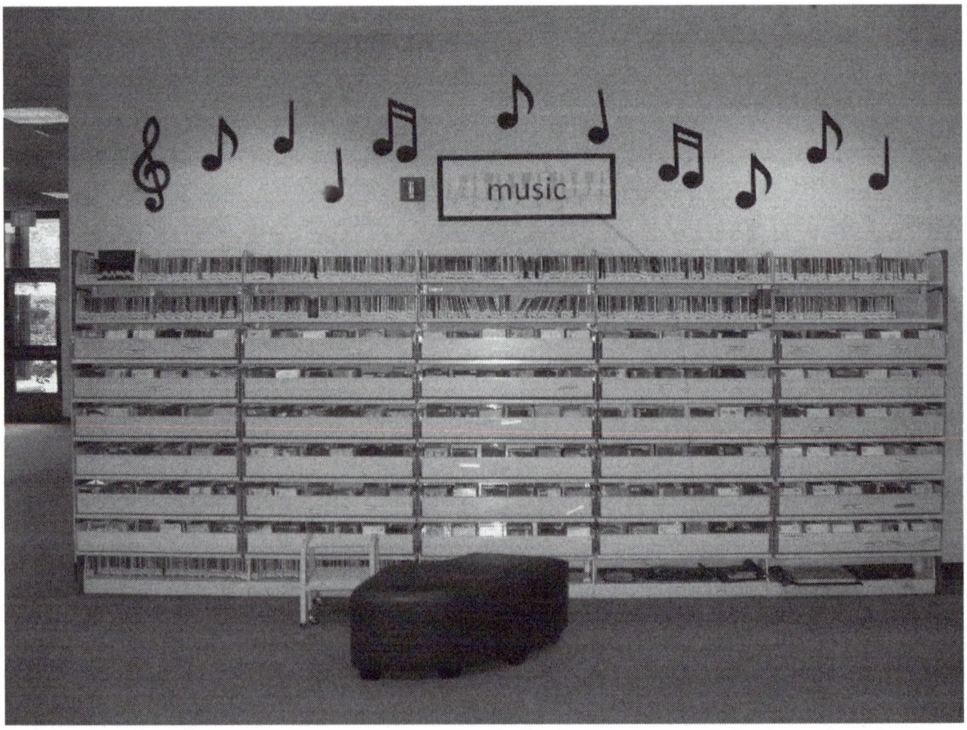

Figure 3.5. Shelving for Nonprint Materials. *Photograph courtesy of the Groton Public Library*

There are repercussions for the LSS as storage and shelving can potentially pose problems for nontraditional formats. So, too, does the processing of these nonstandard materials pose problems. There may be a separate set of rules or even policies governing the use and circulation of media, and LSS need to understand what these policies are. The LSS may also have to explain or demonstrate the use of some of the items and equipment to their patrons.

Social Media

Social media is the online or virtual interaction among people using established sites in order to communicate. Examples of social media that may be used in libraries can include Facebook, Twitter, Tumblr, Foursquare, and Pinterest, among others.[12] These sites are used to promote library programs and services, as well as a means of communication between patron and staff, and the management of these sites can be the responsibility of the LSS. In these increasingly technological times, it is important to be familiar with and understand the concepts and use of social media. This topic will be addressed again in later chapters.

CHAPTER SUMMARY

This chapter helped LSS understand the importance of special collections and archives and their purpose, use, and role in a community with diverse needs. It addressed access to these collections as an information resource and the basic principles of information services. The LSS should be able to recognize and respond to user needs for resources and services. This chapter also explored the inclusion of media and serials in the collection.

DISCUSSION QUESTIONS AND ACTIVITIES

1. Visit a library that has a special collection.
   a. How is it managed in terms of access, security, and preservation?
   b. How do you think it can be improved or made more accessible?
2. If you had to manage a special collection, what are some things you would do to promote the collection, and how would that add to its value?
3. What is a serial file, and what use does it serve?
4. Media in all its formats has become mainstream in many libraries.
   a. Do you feel that there is an impact on traditional library books and services, either positive or negative?
   b. Do you feel that this will affect the future of libraries?

NOTES

1. Library Corporation, "What Is a Serial?," Cataloger's Reference Shelf, http://www.its marc.com/crs/mergedProjects/conser/conser/module_2_1__ccm.htm.

2. Folger Shakespeare Library, "Folger Shakespeare Library," Folger Shakespeare Library, http://www.folger.edu/.

3. Yale University, "Beinecke Rare Book & Manuscript Library," Yale University Library, http://beinecke.library.yale.edu/.

4. American Library Association, "ACRL/SAA Joint Statement on Access to Research Materials in Archives and Special Collections Libraries," Association of College and Research Libraries, last modified July 2009, http://www.ala.org/acrl/standards/jointstatement.

5. American Library Association, "ACRL/SAA Joint Statement on Access."

6. Library Corporation, "What Is a Serial?"

7. G. Edward Evans, Sheila S. Intner, and Jean Riddle Weihs, *Introduction to Technical Services*, 8th ed., Library and Information Science Text Series (Santa Barbara, CA: Libraries Unlimited, 2011), 161–63.

8. Heather Holliday, "How '*McCall's*' Lost Its Way," *Advertising Age* 72, no. 11 (March 12, 2001): 24.

9. Writers Write, Inc. "Conde Nast Purchases Assets of *YM* Magazine," The Write News, last modified October 22, 2004, http://www.writenews.com/conde-nast-purchases-assets-of -ym-magazine-102220041.

10. Noam Cohen, "*Ladies' Home Journal* to Become a Quarterly," *New York Times*, last modified October 24, 2014, http://www.nytimes.com/2014/04/25/business/media/ladies-home -journal-to-become-a-quarterly.html?_r=1.

11. Motion Picture Licensing Corporation, "Welcome to the MPLC," Motion Picture Licensing Corporation, http://www.mplc.org/.

12. Linda Hofschire and Meghan Wanucha, "Public Library Websites and Social Media," *Computers in Libraries* 34, no. 8 (October 2014): 4–9.

REFERENCES, SUGGESTED READINGS, AND WEBSITES

American Library Association. "ACRL/SAA Joint Statement on Access to Research Materials in Archives and Special Collections Libraries." Association of College and Research Libraries. Last modified July 2009. http://www.ala.org/acrl/standards/jointstatement.

———. "Guidelines: Competencies for Special Collections Professionals." Association of College and Research Libraries. Last modified July 1, 2008. http://www.ala.org/acrl/standards/comp4specollect.

Association for Library Collections and Technical Services. "Low Cost Ways to Preserve Family Archives." YouTube. Video file posted by Karen E. K. Brown, April 29, 2014. https://www.youtube.com/watch?v=5v2hAEAAeg8&feature=youtu.be.

Cohen, Noam. "*Ladies' Home Journal* to Become a Quarterly." *New York Times*. Last modified October 24, 2014. http://www.nytimes.com/2014/04/25/business/media/ladies-home-journal-to-become-a-quarterly.html?_r=1.

Eberhart, George M., ed. *The Whole Library Handbook*. 5th ed. Chicago: American Library Association, 2013.

Evans, G. Edward, Sheila S. Intner, and Jean Riddle Weihs. *Introduction to Technical Services*. 8th ed. Library and Information Science Text Series. Santa Barbara, CA: Libraries Unlimited, 2011.

Folger Shakespeare Library. "Folger Shakespeare Library." Folger Shakespeare Library. http://www.folger.edu/.

Hofschire, Linda, and Meghan Wanucha. "Public Library Websites and Social Media." *Computers in Libraries* 34, no. 8 (October 2014): 4–9.

Holliday, Heather. "How 'McCall's' Lost Its Way." *Advertising Age* 72, no. 11 (March 12, 2001): 24.

Library Corporation. "What Is a Serial?" Cataloger's Reference Shelf. http://www.itsmarc.com/crs/mergedProjects/conser/conser/module_2_1__ccm.htm.

Motion Picture Licensing Corporation. "Welcome to the MPLC." Motion Picture Licensing Corporation. http://www.mplc.org/.

Northeast Document Conservation Center. https://www.nedcc.org/.

Perry, Margaret. "A Reference Librarian in Special Collections Making the Most of a Learning Opportunity." *Reference & User Services Quarterly* 50, no. 4 (Summer 2011): 319–21. http://blog.rusq.org/wp-content/uploads/2011/06/For-Your-Enrichment.pdf.

Ulrich's Web Global Serials Directory. http://www.ulrichsweb.com/ulrichsweb/faqs.asp#About_Ulrichs.

United States Copyright Office. "Copyright in General." United States Copyright Office. http://copyright.gov/help/faq/faq-general.html#automatic.

———. "Fees." United States Copyright Office. http://copyright.gov/docs/fees.html.

———. "What Does Copyright Protect?" United States Copyright Office. http://copyright.gov/help/faq/faq-protect.html#website.

United States Patent and Trademark Office. "Trademark, Patent, or Copyright?" United States Patent and Trademark Office. Last modified January 18, 2013. http://www.uspto.gov/trademarks-getting-started/trademark-basics/trademark-patent-or-copyright.

Writers Write, Inc. "Conde Nast Purchases Assets of *YM* Magazine." The Write News. Last modified October 22, 2004. http://www.writenews.com/conde-nast-purchases-assets-of-ym-magazine-102220041.

Yale University. "Beinecke Rare Book & Manuscript Library." Yale University Library. http://beinecke.library.yale.edu/.

CHAPTER 4

Circulation Services

Library support staff (LSS) will know the basic principles of circulation, including classification systems and stack maintenance. (ALA-LSSC Competency #5)

Topics Covered in This Chapter:

- Circulation Services
  - Borrower Registration
  - Overdue Materials
  - Shelving and Stack Maintenance
  - Reader-Interest Shelving
- Nonprint Materials
- Security and Theft Detection

Key Terms:

Circulation: Circulation is the process of checking materials out to a patron and back in to the library. The book is stamped or the borrower is provided with a receipt with the date that the material is due back. There are several other associated circulation tasks, including placing holds, tracking overdues, and interlibrary loan.

ILS: An integrated library system, or ILS, is the system that a library uses to perform the many functions of circulation, such as checking materials in and out. An ILS also tracks overdue materials, assesses fines, and provides for statistics and reports relevant to the library, as well as keeping a database of patrons and materials. Other modules provide for cataloging, acquisitions, and serials.

Nonprint materials: Nonprint materials refers to those items not in the traditional form of a book, such as audiobooks on CD, DVDs, and electronic books. Some libraries also maintain maps, microforms, games, and toys. Virtually all libraries have most of these materials in their collections.

Shelving and stack maintenance: Shelving and stack maintenance refers to returning materials to the shelves and the maintenance of materials on those shelves in proper order so that they can be easily found in the library. Stack maintenance also includes shifting and weeding.

CIRCULATION SERVICES

Circulation means the process of checking out a library's materials to patrons and checking them back in when they are returned, but it is actually much more complex. Who borrows materials? What materials are borrowed? What happens to materials when they are returned—or when they are not?

The circulation department fills two important roles:

- *Circulation control* or keeping track of library materials
- *Public relations*

Since circulation personnel are often the first people encountered, their behavior can determine whether users come back or not. We will talk more about this public relations interface and its potential problems when we discuss customer service in detail later in the book.

Most libraries use an integrated library system (**ILS**). All ILS consist of modules—circulation, acquisition, cataloging, serials, and public catalog—that are integrated so that they can be accessed from a single point. There are two graphical interfaces—that is, two ways to access: staff access and patron access. Patrons can only see what's in the catalog; they cannot modify it. But by logging in to their own account, a patron may change their passwords and request and renew materials. Staff access allows librarians to use some or all of the modules in order to catalog, order materials, set permissions, or change circulation parameters, among other things.

There is a multitude of ILS on the market. Circulation systems may be integrated (one that has modules for circulation, online catalog, and acquisitions, for example) or stand-alone (a single module or several modules that do not share data or one that is not connected to a network of libraries).[1] The annual "Library Systems Report" by Marshall Breeding, an independent library consultant, includes the vendor profiles of several dozen companies that produce automated library systems.[2] These company-owned products are proprietary, and changes can only be made by the vendor. The annual costs of these systems can reach many thousands of dollars for support, maintenance, and upgrades.

Most libraries keep their systems for ten to twelve years, although some keep them for up to twenty-five years without changing. Libraries need to keep up to date on ILS for the newest technology and best value for their library. However, we need to ask ourselves if we are providing the services that are appropriate for patrons and staff before changing systems—in other words, make sure you know what works best for your staff and your patrons. Don't embrace customization as much as learning what is there and how to use it. If everything is working well, there may be no need to change.[3]

If the need to change systems does occur, there are some new trends to consider. In another article by Breeding, "Open Source Library Automation," he describes the open source model as "free to use, free to modify, and free to share."[4] With open source software (OSS), libraries get licensed use of the source code and can modify or manipulate their ILS to suit their individual library needs. OSS is usually created by a collaborative group of individuals that can then distribute the source code to programmers, who can alter it as needed. OSS allows for faster improvements to the software than a vendor-owned system.[5] Systems using OSS function the same way as any ILS; the difference is barely detectable by the user.

Other trends that may be possible in future iterations of the ILS include simply scanning a patron's driver's license to automatically create his library account or providing real-time integrated downloads of ordered materials from vendors. Additionally, cloud developments may allow libraries to collaborate across different systems within and across states.[6] Imagine how these changes could improve the ILS and, ultimately, circulation services!

Which system a library uses depends on the size of the collection, the volume of activity, and the cost both to buy into and to maintain annually. When my library first automated, we chose a stand-alone system designed for small libraries, and pricing was based on the size of the collection. It did everything we needed it to do, but it was a closed system—that is, it only operated in-house, not on the web. We were not able to connect remotely or see the catalogs of any other libraries. We subsequently joined a consortium of several libraries, and while it is a bit more cumbersome, the ability to share catalogs more than makes up for it. While individual ILS may vary from library to library, they *all* share several characteristics. They should all

1. be relatively easy to use,
2. be reliable,
3. allow staff to identify materials borrowed and their due date,
4. provide a record of overdue materials,
5. provide for holds or reserves of requested materials,
6. automatically delete the link between user and item,
7. allow for the creation of statistics,
8. be cost effective, and
9. integrate with other modules in the ILS.

Circulation operations have four functions:

1. Charge or check out.
2. Charge or check in.
3. Shelve returned materials.
4. Housekeeping—that is, keeping materials accessible by "reading" the shelves (monitoring the shelves to make sure that materials are in order), checking for overdue materials, troubleshooting "lost" books, and so on.

There is a process for the patron to follow in order to check out an item. In this scenario, the patron approaches the desk with an item and his or her library card. The person at the circulation desk scans the barcode on the user's card and may see any of the following messages: the card has expired, the patron has a fine or overdue materials, or something is on hold for the patron. If there are no messages, then the library staff member can go on to scan the item. Again, the screen will tell the staff member if there is an issue, such as if the barcode is not found or the item is on hold for another patron. If there are no issues, it will automatically charge out the item. At this point, the item is stamped or a receipt is given, and any theft detection devices are deactivated. The same process is followed if the library uses a self-checkout system—one that is used without staff help. The screen will give the patron instructions (see figure 4.2).

This is a good time to mention patron confidentiality. At no time do we share the reading habits of others; in fact, it is no longer even possible in most systems today to go into a patron's record to see what she or he may have read in the past. Most systems wipe this information when the transaction is complete. This is to protect the library from unauthorized requests for confidential patron information. It is worth noting that while state statute protects the confidentiality of patron records,

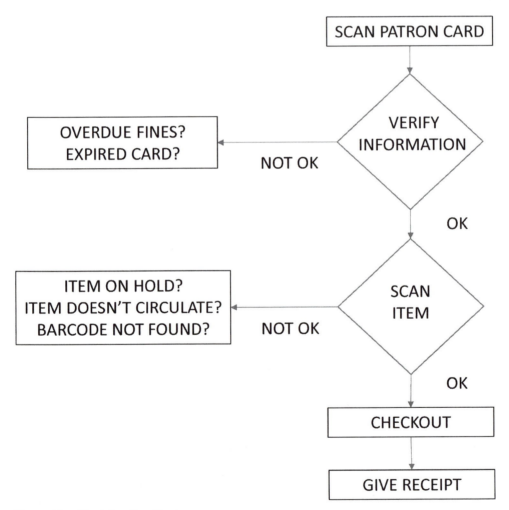

Figure 4.1. Circulation Flow Chart

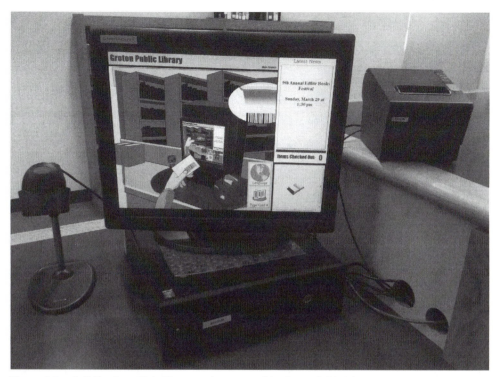

Figure 4.2. Self-Checkout Unit. *Photograph courtesy of the Groton Public Library*

the Supremacy Clause of the Constitution (Article 6, Paragraph 2) establishes that federal law generally takes precedence over state law[7] and, thus, can override it. (This concept will be revisited when the topics of intellectual freedom, censorship, and the USA PATRIOT Act are studied.[8])

To check an item back into the system, the same process is followed in reverse, and the theft detection device is reactivated.

Borrower Registration

Borrower registration is usually required in order to get a library card. There are several important reasons to do so:

- To identify who has the right to borrow materials
- To give the patron a means to check materials out
- To obtain communication information
- To obtain information on demographics for statistical purposes
- To inform patrons of their responsibilities
- To provide for expiration dates (which allows staff to verify all of the above at regular intervals)

To identify who has the right to borrow, public libraries usually require a photo ID and proof of residency. Academic libraries require a school ID, special libraries would use a corporate ID, and school libraries usually do not require any identification.

The ILS will also allow for the reporting of other statistics, including circulation of materials by item type and by patron group, interlibrary loan statistics, missing items, and overdue item reports, among others. Most systems allow for the creation of numerous custom reports.

Overdue Materials

Libraries spend a lot of money on materials. If they are not returned, then they are not available for others to borrow; thus, libraries often charge fines as an incentive to bring materials back—not as a punishment.[9] There is much debate about whether this is effective, but no one can argue the financial loss of unreturned items. If you are going to charge fines, it is important that a procedure is established, follow-up is timely, and enforcement is consistent. Fines do generate income, which, for many libraries, is essential.

There is a procedure to follow for overdue materials. First, check the shelves. Many times an item may not have been charged back in and ends up on the shelf. This happens more often than not. Then, keep an accurate record of what has been done to retrieve the materials—phone calls, e-mails, texts, or letters. Have a billing procedure in place and use it. Some libraries will even engage collection agencies to help get their items back. Alternatives to fines may include grace days, amnesty days, a voluntary collection jar, or food donations in lieu of fines. Above all, remember to be flexible, especially with those truly unable to pay.

Shelving and Stack Maintenance

Shelving materials **and stack maintenance** is an important part of circulation. Among those items needing to be shelved are new acquisitions, circulated materials, and materials used in-house. Items are usually shelved by format: books on standard shelving, media such as DVDs and CDs may be kept on standard shelving, bins, or racks. Some libraries interfile all titles so that those in multiple formats can be found in the same place. In fact, many libraries interfile their reference materials as well, giving up the traditional reference room.

Books (and other formats) are shelved alphabetically by author for fiction and numerically by call number for nonfiction. It may seem simple, but one misshelved item may as well be lost. A good way to shelve is to check the three books on either side of the one being shelved, as well as those on the shelves above and below to be sure that they are in order. Even when not shelving returned items, *shelf reading* is an important and ongoing activity, particularly in problem areas where there may be several authors with the same last name or several nonfiction books with the same call numbers. Shelf reading is exactly what it sounds like—looking at each book on a shelf to make sure that they are in order.

Finally, *collection shifting*, a necessary task, is ongoing. Inevitably, as more items are added to the collection the shelves become crowded, requiring shifting of the materials in order to make more room. This simply means moving books from one shelf to another in order to create more space. If not kept up, it can turn into a large project where entire shelves worth of books need to be shifted until room is made for everything.

Ultimately the collection will need to be *weeded*—selectively withdrawing items from the collection due to age, condition, or lack of circulation. This is not done arbitrarily; there are guidelines for withdrawing materials from a collection. The gold standard for weeding is a manual called *CREW* (Continuous Review Evaluation and Weeding). Along with the library's collection development policy, using the CREW method allows for the withdrawal of books following MUSTIE guidelines: M=misleading (factually inaccurate), U=ugly (worn binding), S=superseded (newer books on the subject), T=trivial (of no literary or scientific merit), I=irrelevant (to the library community's needs), and E=available elsewhere.[10]

Other Circulation Issues

Circulation statistics are needed for collection management and tell us what materials are being used: the number of adult books or children's books being circulated and in which subjects; when the library is the busiest; collection strengths; money collected; questions answered. This helps determine what to buy and when and how to staff the library.

Reader-Interest Shelving

Many libraries choose to house the fiction collection by broad subjects such as mystery, romance, science fiction, or Westerns. This is done so patrons can more easily find the specific genre they prefer; these books usually have a special sticker on the spine that designates the category. This is called reader-interest shelving. Some libraries also choose to interfile reference materials with the circulating collection in order to keep all material on a subject in the same location.

When we think of libraries, the picture that comes to mind is of long rows of shelved books. This model is changing, however, as libraries choose the "bookstore" model of shelving: books are shelved face out.[11] Some libraries have also rejected traditional shelving by arranging their books by *subject* rather than by call number.[12] This also makes use of the bookstore model by using the Book Industry Standards and Communication (BISAC) subject headings, a subject-driven system used by bookstores. The principle behind this change is that it makes libraries more inviting, it makes browsing easier, and it makes more sense to have like subjects together in a less formal way. To go a step further, many libraries are mimicking bookstores by adding comfortable reading areas and coffee bars.

After attending a particularly compelling presentation at a Public Library Association conference on using the bookstore model as a marketing tool, I gave this a try at my library. We were able to rearrange the existing shelving to display new books face out (see figure 4.3). Although we considered rearranging the shelving by subject, we opted to go with small changes. We were also able to acquire a coffee machine, and within weeks, we had a new look. It was an instant success, and the new books just flew off the shelves. Patrons were delighted to "see" the books they were looking for and to sit down with a cup of coffee.

As you can see by the following photos (figures 4.3–4.5), coffee service in libraries can range from the modest (a tabletop) to the quite elaborate—the in-house café run by a vendor.

Figure 4.3. New Books Display. *Photograph courtesy of the Bill Memorial Library*

Figure 4.4. "Catalog Café" Coffee Bar. *Photograph courtesy of the Bill Memorial Library*

Figure 4.5.   Vendor-Run Café. *Used with permission from Chocolati, Inc. @ Seattle Public Library*

NONBOOK MATERIALS

Most ILS systems can handle all types of materials. **Nonbook materials** include such items as periodicals, books on CD, DVDs, e-readers, laptops, and other equipment. These nontraditional formats are treated the same way as books as far as cataloging and processing into the collection, although their formats demand variations in their catalog records in order to differentiate them.

Another category is electronic books, or e-books. Libraries can make these available in a couple of ways. They can purchase electronic copies of books and add them to their catalog. Borrowers then download the e-books to their devices or borrow a device from the library with the titles already loaded. The cost of e-books is quite high, and price and availability to libraries has been the subject of much debate and even litigation over the past few years.[13] However, once an e-book is purchased, it is a permanent addition. On the other hand, many libraries choose to use a third-party system that can be joined for a fee, such as Overdrive or Axis 360. Based on the terms of the agreement, the library can then choose titles to add to their collection. Some of these titles may have metered use—after a certain number of circulations, the title disappears and would have to be repurchased. They also can only circulate for a defined period and cannot be renewed. The disadvantage to using such a service is that the library does not own the titles. If they leave the vendor, the titles go with the vendor even if the library paid for a copy for their patrons.

SECURITY AND THEFT DETECTION

Libraries lose materials not just because patrons don't bring them back but because of theft. The circulation staff is still the frontline for item control, but to avoid items simply "walking away," many libraries will use theft detection systems. This consists of security strips and tags, radio frequency detection tags (RFID),[14] or security gates. Some magnetic media cannot be used with certain anti-theft systems as it can damage the item and make it unplayable.

RFID tags are equipped with a microchip and an antenna. When attached to an item, that item can be tracked through radio frequencies. The use of RFID can be an asset to libraries because one can always know where the items are. However, this does pose privacy issues—understandably, patrons look down on being tracked.

Materials with anti-theft devices must be deactivated during check out to avoid alarms or other signals that material is leaving the building without being checked out. (Think of the plastic tags put on clothing in a department store—they must be manually removed by store staff using a special device or it will trigger an alert. If this item is taken without being paid for, and the anti-theft device is removed at home, it can release ink that will damage the clothing.) When the library item is returned, the security sensor is reactivated until it circulates again.

CHAPTER SUMMARY

In this chapter, we learned about the basic principles of library circulation that an LSS member would be expected to know and practice, as well as the attributes and functions of ILS. Topics covered included nonprint library materials and e-books, the basic principles of circulation, stack and collection maintenance, the problems of theft protection, and security of library materials.

DISCUSSION QUESTIONS AND ACTIVITIES

1. What is an ILS?
   a. Describe its components.
   b. Describe what an ILS is supposed to do for a library.
2. Describe the difference between open source and proprietary software as it applies to ILS.
   a. Find examples of both in your area or online.
   b. Can you determine any difference?
3. Libraries require patrons to register for a card.
   a. Please describe some of the reasons why this is important.
   b. Do you feel it is an invasion of privacy?
4. Many libraries provide patron access to electronic collections of books and audiobooks.
   a. Examine one in your local library and comment on its ease of use and the availability of materials compared to a print collection.
   b. Do you favor one over the other and why?
5. Should libraries charge fines for overdue materials?
   a. What might be an alternative, if any?

NOTES

1. John J. Burke, *Library Technology Companion*, 2nd ed. (New York: Neal-Schuman, 2006), 75.

2. Marshall Breeding, "Library Systems Report 2014: Competition and Strategic Cooperation," *American Libraries*, last modified April 15, 2014, http://www.americanlibrariesmaga zine.org/article/library-systems-report-2014.

3. *American Libraries*, "Integrated Library Systems," YouTube, video file, 60 mm, posted by Dan Freeman, May 14, 2015, https://www.youtube.com/watch?t=23&v=F8XgyROqOm0.

4. Marshall Breeding, "Open Source Library Automation: Overview and Perspective," *Library Technology Reports*, no. 8 (November/December 2008), https://www.webjunction.org/content/dam/WebJunction/Documents/webJunction/LTR_44n8_nov08_chap1.pdf.

5. Burke, *Library Technology Companion*, 85.

6. *American Libraries*, "Integrated Library Systems."

7. Cornell University Law School, "Supremacy Clause," Legal Information Institute, http://www.law.cornell.edu/wex/supremacy_clause.

8. American Library Association, "The USA PATRIOT Act," American Library Association, http://www.ala.org/advocacy/advleg/federallegislation/theusapatriotact.

9. Alison Flood, "For and Against Library Fines," Guardian.com, last modified August 18, 2008, http://www.theguardian.com/books/booksblog/2008/aug/18/forandagainstlibraryfines.

10. Jeannette Larson, *CREW: A Weeding Manual for Modern Libraries*, rev. ed. (Texas State Library and Archives Commission, 2012).

11. Corrado Di Tilllio, "The Retail Revolution @ Your Library," Public Libraries Online, last modified June 18, 2013, http://publiclibrariesonline.org/2013/06/the-retail-revolution -your-library.

12. Barbara Fister, "The Dewey Dilemma," *Library Journal*, last modified May 20, 2010, http://lj.libraryjournal.com/2010/05/public-services/the-dewey-dilemma.

13. Digital Book World, "Libraries Annual Report: Relations between Libraries and Publishers over Ebooks Improving," Digital Book World, last modified April 14, 2014, http://www.digitalbookworld.com/2014/libraries-annual-report-relations-between-libraries-and -publishers-over-ebooks-improving/.

14. Digital Book World, "Libraries Annual Report."

REFERENCES, SUGGESTED READINGS, AND WEBSITES

A&E Television Networks, LLC. "Melvil Dewey." Biography.com. http://www.biography .com/people/melvil-dewey-9273516.

American Libraries. "Integrated Library Systems." YouTube. Video file, 60 mm, posted by Dan Freeman, May 14, 2015. https://www.youtube.com/watch?t=23&v=F8XgyROqOm0.

American Library Association. "The USA PATRIOT Act." American Library Association. http://www.ala.org/advocacy/advleg/federallegislation/theusapatriotact.

Bonsor, Kevin, and Wesley Fenlon. "How RFID Works." How Stuff Works. http://electronics .howstuffworks.com/gadgets/high-tech-gadgets/rfid.htm.

Boston Athenaeum. "Charles Ammi Cutter." Boston Athenaeum. http://www.bostonath-enaeum.org/library/book-recommendations/athenaeum-authors/charles-ammi-cutter.

Breeding, Marshall. "Library Systems Report 2014: Competition and Strategic Cooperation." *American Libraries*. Last modified April 15, 2014. http://www.americanlibrariesmagazine .org/article/library-systems-report-2014.

————. "'Open Source Library Automation: Overview and Perspective." *Library Technology Reports*, no. 8 (November/December 2008). https://www.webjunction.org/content/dam/WebJunction/Documents/webJunction/LTR_44n8_nov08_chap1.pdf.

Burke, John J. *Library Technology Companion*. 2nd ed. New York: Neal-Schuman, 2006.

Cornell University Law School. "Supremacy Clause." Legal Information Institute. http://www.law.cornell.edu/wex/supremacy_clause.

Digital Book World. "Libraries Annual Report: Relations between Libraries and Publishers over Ebooks Improving." Digital Book World. Last modified April 14, 2014. http://www.digitalbookworld.com/2014/libraries-annual-report-relations-between-libraries-and-publishers-over-ebooks-improving/.

Drexel University. "Dewey Decimal Classification System." Internet Public Library. http://www.ipl.org/div/aplus/dewey1.htm.

Enis, Matt. "Can You Read Me Now?" LibraryJournal.com. Last modified June 23, 2014. http://lj.libraryjournal.com/2014/06/lj-in-print/can-you-read-me-now-product-spotlight/#.

Evans, G. Edward. *Introduction to Technical Services*. 8th ed. Library and Information Science Text. Santa Barbara, CA: Libraries Unlimited, 2010.

Fister, Barbara. "The Dewey Dilemma." *Library Journal*. Last modified May 20, 2010. http://lj.libraryjournal.com/2010/05/public-services/the-dewey-dilemma.

Flood, Alison. "For and Against Library Fines." Guardian.com. Last modified August 18, 2008. http://www.theguardian.com/books/booksblog/2008/aug/18/forandagainstlibraryfines.

ITS.MARC. "G 63 Cutter Numbers." ITS.MARC. http://www.itsmarc.com/crs/mergedProjects/SCMshelf/scmshelf/g_63_cutter_numbersshelf.htm.

————. "Historical Note on the Library of Congress Classification." Cataloger's Reference Shelf. http://www.itsmarc.com/crs/mergedProjects/scmclass/scmclass/historical_noteon_the_library_of_congress_classification_scm.htm.

Ketchum, D. H. "The Future: E-books and Interlibrary Loan." Slideshare.net. Last modified September 23, 2013. http://www.slideshare.net/davidhketchum/the-future-ebooks-and-interlibrary-loan.

Larson, Jeannette. *CREW: A Weeding Manual for Modern Libraries*. Rev. ed. Texas State Library and Archives Commission, 2012.

Library of Congress. "What Is a MARC Record and Why Is It Important?" Library of Congress. http://www.loc.gov/marc/umb/um01to06.html.

Middle Tennessee State University. "Let's Do Dewey." James E. Walker Library. http://library.mtsu.edu/dewey/.

Mosley, Shelley, and Anna Caggiano. "The 'Self-Weeding' Collection: The Ongoing Problem of Library Theft, and How to Fight Back." *Library Journal* 121, no. 17 (October 15, 1996): 38.

National Institutes of Health. "NLM Classification 2014." U.S. National Library of Medicine. http://www.nlm.nih.gov/class/.

Opensource.com. "What Is Open Source?" Opensource.com. http://opensource.com/resources/what-open-source.

Parrot, Kiera, and Karyn M. Peterson. "Ditching Dewey: Hot Topic in Hartford." *School Library Journal*. Last modified November 20, 2013. http://www.slj.com/2013/11/collection-development/ditching-dewey-hot-topic-in-hartford-aasl-2013/#_.

Tilllio, Corrado Di. "The Retail Revolution @ Your Library." Public Libraries Online. Last modified June 18, 2013. http://publiclibrariesonline.org/2013/06/the-retail-revolution-your-library/.

University of Illinois at Urbana-Champaign. "Dewey Decimal System—a Guide to Call Numbers." University Library. http://www.library.illinois.edu/ugl/about/dewey.html.

USA.gov. "Library of Congress Classification Outline." Library of Congress. http://www.loc.gov/catdir/cpso/lcco/.

U.S. Government Publishing Office. "Federal Depository Library Program." U.S. Government Publishing Office. http://www.gpo.gov/libraries/?utm_source=rss&utm_medium=rss&utm_campaign=federal-depository-library-program.

——. "Superintendent of Documents (SuDocs) Classification Scheme Print Email Details." Federal Depository Library Program. http://www.fdlp.gov/catalogingandclassification/cataloging-articles/1791-superintendent-of-documents-sudocs-classification-scheme.

"Using the LC Cutter Table." https://pantherfile.uwm.edu/kipp/public/courses/511/511 exercise-cutterhowto.pdf.

CHAPTER 5

Reference Services, Reader's Advisory, and Reserves

Library support staff (LSS) will know the basic principles of reference and information services. They will also be familiar with the services of reader's advisory and reserves, and the relationship among library departments or functional areas. (ALA-LSSC Competency #4, #5)

Topics Covered in This Chapter:

- Resources
- Reference Services
- Service to Off-Site Users
- The Reference Interview
- Reader's Advisory
- The Reserve Function

Key Terms:

Behaviors: Behaviors are the ways in which one acts toward another. This is important for LSS to understand when dealing with the public, as people have a variety of ways in which they respond to various situations.

Copyright: Copyright is a form of protection grounded in the U.S. Constitution and granted by law for original works of authorship fixed in a tangible medium of expression. Copyright covers both published and unpublished works[1] and protects them from unauthorized use.

OPAC: The **o**nline **p**ublic **a**ccess **c**atalog in a library is the online bibliography or database of a library's holdings. This is searchable from a computer in the library, and often from home, and contains a record of all print and nonprint materials held by that library.

Open-ended questions: An open-ended question is one that cannot be answered by "yes" or "no." This is useful when conducting a reference interview and encourages the patron to tell the LSS what, specifically, he or she is looking for.

Reference: Reference transactions are information consultations in which LSS recommend, interpret, evaluate, and/or use information resources to help others meet particular information needs.[2]

RESOURCES

Before providing even the most basic information services, all personnel need to know the library's **resources** or collection—the library's contents, the location of various elements of the collection, and outside sources. The staff at the circulation, information, and/or reference desks should be familiar with

1. the policies and procedures of the library and all of its departments;
2. the library's collection: print, nonprint, electronic resources, special shelving of genres and formats, and the library's special collections;
3. the organization of the reference area: where it is in the building or if it even exists, as many libraries interfile reference materials in the regular stacks;
4. where the reserves and other materials held for patrons are located; and
5. the library's calendar and program information.

It is the responsibility of all personnel to give the most accurate information possible and to be able to tell the patron what the source of your information is. You must also give the best service possible to all, regardless of age, ethnicity, or political, sexual, or religious affiliation. The Library Bill of Rights guarantees this.

Service should be positive, efficient, open, and amiable. It is also important to know what information you can and cannot give: While you can direct a patron to medical resources, you cannot give medical advice; nor can you give legal or tax advice. You may be viewed as an authority by virtue of your position, so these questions will be asked. Even if you happen to know the answer, do not share it, but instead refer the patron to the appropriate source. Be familiar with where these resources can be found in your library. In all cases, confidentiality must be protected.

Let's take a look at the various resources available to you. Not only must LSS be familiar with their library, they must be aware of their community. LSS should read the paper—know who the local and state officials are, what elections are being held and when, and the issues and places of interest to the community. It is helpful for a library to maintain a file related to local history, places, and people, as well as local organizations and events. Know, also, where the neighboring libraries are and how to get in touch with them, as well as what special collections and services they may offer.

Be aware of the technology in the library, such as the availability of a public fax machine, public copy machines, Internet-access computers, electronic resources and databases, and downloadable materials. Know what the policies and fees for use of this technology may be. Be familiar with what is on the library's webpage—the catalog, library calendar, and links to databases and test preparation sites, for example. It will differ from library to library, so be sure to know what your library offers.

We previously read about classification systems and catalogs, so be sure to know which system your library uses and how it works. Become familiar with the features of your online public access catalog (OPAC) and how it is organized. Does it offer access from home (reserve or renew materials) (see figure 5.1) or links to other online systems, and if so, which ones (local, state, regional, national)? Things you can learn from your OPAC include all of the materials in all formats by a particular author; an author's personal names, pseudonyms, and birth and death dates; other subjects an author may have written about; and the collation of an item: format, size, number of pages, maps, illustrations, and the like.

Other sources LSS should become familiar with will vary by library but may include dictionaries, encyclopedias, atlases, biographical sources, pamphlet collections, and periodical indexes. Not all libraries will hold a variety of print-based sources, so be aware of what databases the library may subscribe to, links to government resources, search engines, and other recommended Internet sites. This is the kind of information that you may be called upon to provide at any given time. If you are not familiar with it, then you cannot give your patrons the information that they may need.

REFERENCE SERVICES

The reference or information desk is one of the two most frequently visited public service points in the library (the other being circulation). The *purpose* of **reference service** is to facilitate access to information. The *role* of reference service is to make information available to the library user. Many libraries do not use the traditional reference desk anymore but rather group it all into one category: information.

Making information available to the user is done in three ways:

1. Finding the information for the user
2. Helping the user to find the information
3. Teaching the user to use library resources in order to find the information for him- or herself

Not all reference transactions take place at a reference or information desk. In fact, some libraries, such as a school library or a small public library, may not have a reference desk (or a reference collection, for that matter) at all. In a library that combines all activities at the circulation desk, you may very well be expected to answer a number of questions:

1. Directional questions, such as, "Where are the bathrooms?"
2. Technical and mechanical questions, such as how to use the copier or fax machines.
3. Ready reference or questions that can be answered by using a standard source, such as an almanac or fact book, government census, or Bureau of Labor statistic

websites. These questions could include population statistics, a list of U.S. presidents; notable sports figures for the year, and so on. (While it's easy to find these answers using a search engine such as Google, good library practice dictates using authoritative and documentable print and electronic sources, as mentioned previously.)

It is important that LSS know what they are expected to be able to answer. Complicated reference questions or those beyond the scope of the LSS's knowledge should be referred to a specially trained librarian.

SERVICE TO OFF-SITE USERS

Technology has enabled us to extend our **services to off-site users**. Web-based library catalogs allow users to reserve and renew books from home.

E-mail, chat, instant messaging (IM), and text are now routinely being used by libraries to provide information and reference service to those who are not in the library building. This information can range from the library's hours to reserving materials to complicated reference questions. One of the best sources for online information is the Library of Congress's Ask a Librarian Virtual Reference Shelf, [3] which provides a wide range of information on a variety of subjects.

Off-site questions can be as simple as an answer needed to settle a bet ("Who won the World Series in 1938?") or homework help. The difference between providing homework help and doing someone's homework for them can be difficult to determine, and a properly conducted reference interview will help you figure out just what the patron is asking. Regardless of the question, it is imperative that you document your answer with the correct and complete source information.

THE REFERENCE INTERVIEW

When a patron approaches with a question, I have often observed that the first reaction is for the staff member to turn to the computer to look up an answer. This

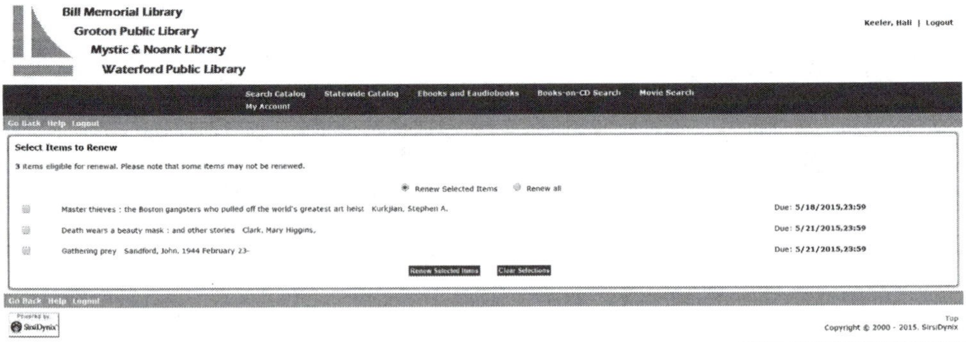

Figure 5.1. Item Renewal Screenshot. *Sirsi*

is frequently done because the staff member "panics" and turns to the "authority" rather than taking a moment and thinking it through. The second thing I have observed is that the staff member assumes that they know what the patron wants and goes off searching without determining the exact nature of the request. Patrons can be intimidated by libraries and librarians and may fail to speak up or do not know how to articulate their needs. They may assume that the librarian knows what they want, and the end result is that they take what is offered to them or they leave without anything. Both scenarios are disappointing—but not infrequent. What the staff member should do first is to conduct a **reference interview**.

The reference interview is the process whereby staff members communicate and interact with the patron in order to determine how to best answer an informational need and to determine the true nature of the question. This is critical because too much or too little information from the patron can lead to a wrong answer. A good rule of thumb is to use *open-ended questions*—those that cannot be answered by yes or no, such as "What is the assignment?" or "What specifically are you looking for?" Yes or no questions can shut off the interview or lead it in the wrong direction.

There are also a variety of model behaviors that contribute toward a successful reference interview. "Approachability, making people comfortable, and asking the questions used in successful reference interviews are all reference behaviors. Research and studies have been done showing that these behaviors and actions improve reference service success."[4] Many years ago I participated in a series of workshops that emphasized the elements of a successful reference interview. When approached by someone looking for information, these are some *model reference behaviors* that I was taught to follow:

I like to use sample scenarios of reference interviews where one person role plays the patron and another, the librarian. These exercises show how easy it is to misunderstand and how important it is to elicit complete information before beginning

---

MODEL REFERENCE BEHAVIORS

1. Welcoming: Smile, make eye contact, and give a friendly greeting.
2. Attending: Give your full attention, maintain eye contact, and make attentive comments such as "I see" and "Uh-huh."
3. Listening: Do not interrupt; paraphrase or repeat the patron's question to demonstrate understanding and clarify if the question is unclear.
4. Eliciting: Use open probes to elicit the specific question (not yes or no questions).
5. Searching: Find the answer in the first source searched; search other sources if the answer cannot be found in the first source and report on the progress of your search. If you are truly unable to answer the question, then offer a referral to another staff member or library that can help.
6. Informing: Speak clearly, confirm that your answer is understood, and cite your source.
7. Follow up: Ask "Does this completely answer your question?" Ask other follow-up questions as necessary.

your search. I have included two sample reference interview scenarios at the end of this chapter.

Additionally, keep the patron informed of your progress. Many a patron can feel abandoned if the librarian rushes off to find an answer and leaves the patron waiting, unsure of where the librarian has gone and when he will return. It is helpful to leave the patron with something to look at while you are off searching. I often like to find a primary resource and tell the patron to look through this book or article while I am searching for more information. Avoid using jargon: speaking simply and clearly will be more effective.

The procedure for providing *off-site* or *virtual reference services* is not much different in that you will still use many of the above-mentioned behaviors. Remote, online, virtual, or digital reference is "the provision of reference services, involving collaboration between library user and librarian, in a computer-based medium. These services can utilize various media, including e-mail, Web forms, chat, video, Web customer call center software, Voice over Internet Protocol (VoIP), etc."[5] Except in the case of video, the main difference is that since you cannot see the patron, you may be missing vital visual clues. The patron cannot see that you are off searching for information, so it is critical that you continue to communicate what you are doing and how long you may be out of touch. Use simple conversational language, not jargon, and cite your sources. For a more personal touch, use the patron's name in all communications.

READER'S ADVISORY

While not specifically a reference interview, **reader's advisory** (RA) involves engaging library users in finding information of another kind: what to read. It's a conversation about books. Not very many years ago, the concept of reader's advisory fell out of favor. It was seen as frivolous and not a good use of professional time and resources. Happily, this has turned around, and librarians and LSS engage daily with patrons who are eager for recommendations.

There are a couple of ways to do this. Passive RA involves creative displays of materials: book displays, "shelf talkers" (signage such as "Staff Picks" or "Hot off the Press"), book lists on the library's webpage, or printed lists to take home. There are a number of books available that offer reading suggestions, such as the Book Lust series by Nancy Pearl or *Read This!* edited by Hans Weyant. The Genreflecting Advisory series is a staple in most libraries, offering guidance for a variety of genres. Individual publishers offer book discussion guides for specific titles, and websites and blogs are also prolific. Examples of these can be found at the end of this chapter. Social media sites—Facebook and Pinterest, for example—are also a good source for suggested readings. There are valuable databases such as NoveList and What Should I Read Next, which are excellent resources, although some require a paid subscription. The good news is that many libraries have such a subscription, making these databases available to a larger audience. Many of these sites allow searching by subject, genre, time period, country, and so on. The choices can be limitless. I put this to use once when a young woman came in looking for a book. When asked about subjects, she was very specific. It had to be a book about a nurse who goes skiing in the Alps, breaks her leg, and meets a handsome doctor. Needless to say, the only title we could find was the one she had just read. That was a little too specific!

Another more proactive way to provide reader's advisory services is through the use of book talks given in the library or off-site to various groups. If possible, produce book talk podcasts for broadcast through the library's webpage, through social media, or even through local or municipal television.

Not every library offers a formal RA program or specialized staff, but every library that has personnel can offer personal RA service. The key is to make sure that personnel are approachable and willing to give their time. No one has to be an expert, and as stated previously, there are a plethora of great tools available to help every staff member succeed. A good first rule to follow is to put yourself on the same level as the patron—because you really don't know what he or she is looking for. Help the patron define his or her needs and interests. Ask the patron about a book they recently read that he or she especially liked. Don't make judgments about the patrons based on their age, dress, or sex. In that same vein, never refer to a book as "clean" unless the patron specifically asks—and don't make it sound "cleaner" than it really is. Some years ago we had an elderly patron at the library who returned a book and loudly proclaimed to all within earshot that the book was filthy dirty. She then proceeded to ask where this author's other books could be found! Avoid, also, telling a patron that they will "love" a book—he or she may not share your tastes and could be disappointed. In fact, the patron might even avoid asking you for further suggestions.

Learn about "now" books—recent best sellers by authors who churn out half a dozen books a year on current or contemporary issues—as opposed to "forever" books, dealing with relationships, philosophy, history, or the human condition, that stand the test of time.[6] Serving different purposes, all of these books are important.

You do not have to read every book in the library, nor do you need to read a book cover to cover to still be able to offer valuable suggestions. You do need to be aware of what's in the collection, what's on the most recent best-seller lists, and what may have recently won awards. Become familiar with review sources such as *Publishers Weekly* and the *New York Times Book Review*; skim popular magazines for their recommendations. Read the newspaper; browse in bookstores. Get a feel for what's going on in publishing. Consider this as a jumping-off point to thinking or starting a conversation about books.

Keep track of what you read, and, as everyone on staff has different interests, ask your coworkers about their recent favorites or what they didn't like about a particular book. I used to start off the monthly staff meeting by asking everyone what they were reading and to give a mini review. Take notes so that you will remember; it can be helpful to keep a record for your files. Whatever you do, when a patron approaches for help, do not turn immediately to the computer to stall for time! You may not always have an appropriate title to recommend right off the bat, but remember, you can start the conversation.

THE RESERVE FUNCTION

There are two things that come to mind when we talk about "**reserves**" in libraries. The first is the service whereby the library will reserve, or "hold," an item that a patron has requested for personal use. The second is the function of academic and school libraries whereby materials needed for a class are held aside at the request of the instructor for the exclusive use of the students of that class.

In the first case, a patron will make a request for an item that may be unavailable. The patron places a hold, or a reserve, on the item so that he or she can check it out when it comes back. Some circulation systems allow a patron to do so from home by logging into her account and accessing the reserve function. In some cases, the patron may request that a staff member do it for him. Either way, the patron's name is placed in the queue and she is notified when the item becomes available. When done from home, other patrons on the reserve list are not visible on the screen, thus ensuring confidentiality.

There are a few ways to inform the patron of the reserve. Depending on the size of the library, it may be as simple as a phone call. Some integrated library systems (ILS) automatically send an e-mail or text. Because of confidentiality, the information goes only to the patron. If a phone message is left, it has to be generic, such as "a book is being held for you at your request." The LSS will then place the reserved item on a separate shelf until the patron can get it, allowing him or her a few days or up to a week or more.

Many libraries use a self-service model where the item is shelved in a semipublic area with a slip of paper in the book with the patron's identification—the first few letters of their last name, for example. Some libraries put a wrapper around the book so that it cannot be identified. Access is limited to those patrons who have a legitimate reason to be in those stacks, although I visited a small branch library in the Pacific Northwest that held the reserves in plain view, albeit near the circulation desk. This

Figure 5.2.   Reserve Book Holds Area. *Photograph courtesy of the Seattle Public Library*

challenges the traditional concept of confidentiality as, I have observed, people do like to snoop. I like to think of this as interest or curiosity in what someone else may be reading, however. (Because people are so interested in what others are reading, we have often put low circulation books on the return cart. It is amazing how many people will pick from this cart if they believe someone else just returned the book.)

In the second case, an instructor asks the library to put aside a particular title or article to be used by the students in that class. The item is shelved in a special area (often behind the circulation or information desk) and must be requested. The student has to show identification in order to gain access to the item, and he or she is typically only able to use the item in the library and for a limited amount of time. This ensures that all of the students in the class will get a chance to use it. By removing this item from general circulation, however, it denies access to anyone else who would like to use it while it is reserved.

Reserves of this sort can pose a challenge to staff in an academic or school library, as the administration of the reserve—from the instructor's request, through the process of identifying it for a course, to monitoring students' use—can be time consuming, particularly at the beginning or end of a semester. Once again, confidentiality is an issue, as no one can ask who has used the material—neither the instructor nor the other students.

Copyright also has to be considered. In the case of an article, it is acceptable to make one copy for the reserve shelf as *fair use* applies:

> Section 107 [of the copyright law] contains a list of the various purposes for which the reproduction of a particular work may be considered fair, such as criticism, comment, news reporting, teaching, scholarship, and research. Section 107 also sets out four factors to be considered in determining whether or not a particular use is fair.

> 1. The purpose and character of the use, including whether such use is of commercial nature or is for nonprofit educational purposes
> 2. The nature of the copyrighted work
> 3. The amount and substantiality of the portion used in relation to the copyrighted work as a whole
> 4. The effect of the use upon the potential market for, or value of, the copyrighted work[7]

While no longer required by law, the reserved material should have a copyright notice attached to the work to protect it from unlawful reproduction, or such notices should be posted by the photocopier:

Both meanings of the reserve function, then, illustrate that an item is requested to be held aside for the use of one person at a time. The circumstances dictate the methods used.

CHAPTER SUMMARY

This chapter focused on the basic principles of reference and information services, including model behaviors, the reference interview, the function of reserves in the library, and the related issue of copyright. It also introduced the concept of reader's advisory and encouraged the LSS's familiarity with collections, resources, and the relationship among functional areas in the library and in the community.

DISCUSSION QUESTIONS AND ACTIVITIES

1. Describe the elements of the reference interview.
   a. What can the LSS do to ensure that it is successful?
2. There are several ways that the LSS can provide service to off-site or virtual users.
   a. Please describe what they are.
   b. How can they be achieved?
3. Considering the model behaviors described in this chapter, observe how they are carried out in your library or one that you frequent.
   a. Are they being done?
   b. If so, are they effective?
4. Describe how the concepts of privacy and confidentiality impact the reserve function in the library.
5. Copyright is multifaceted and potentially confusing.
   a. Using the federal copyright website (http://www.copyright.gov/), read up on the nuances of copyright.
   b. What is your understanding of what can and cannot be copyrighted?

SAMPLE SCENARIOS

SAMPLE REFERENCE INTERVIEW SCENARIO 1

In this case, the patron is a student.

Patron: I need to do a report on custard.

Librarian: May I see your assignment sheet?

Patron: I didn't bring it with me.

Librarian: What class is this for?

Patron: History.

Librarian: OK, is this American History or World History?

Patron: I don't know. All I remember is that it has something to do with custard.

Librarian: Custard is a type of pudding.

Patron: No, it's not about food; it's about a guy.

Librarian: Do you mean Custer—General George Custer?

Patron: Yes, that's it.

Librarian: All right then, that would be the American Civil War. What specifically do you need to know about General Custer?

Patron: I think I'm supposed to find out about a battle he was in and when he died.

Librarian: So your question is: You need to find out which Civil War battle General Custer fought and died in?

Patron: Yes, that's it.

Librarian: OK, we'll start by looking for biographies of General Custer. We can also look up the call number for the American Civil War to locate this information. [Search ensues.] Let's see . . . it seems that General George Armstrong Custer fought and died in the Battle of the Little Big Horn on June 25, 1876. This was referred to as "Custer's Last Stand." Does that completely answer your question?

Patron: Yes, thank you! May I take that book out? My teacher will be proud of me.

SAMPLE REFERENCE INTERVIEW SCENARIO 2

Patron: My friend recommended a book she recently returned, but I don't remember the name.

Librarian: Do you remember what it's about?

Patron: It has something to do with dreams.

Librarian: What about dreams?

Patron: It's a scary book.

Librarian: Is it fiction or nonfiction?

Patron: It's like Stephen King, but it's not by him.

Librarian: So let me make sure I understand. You are looking for a scary novel about dreams?

Patron: No, but I think it has dream in the title.

Librarian: All right. You are looking for a novel with the word *dream* in the title that is a scary story.

Patron: Yes.

Librarian: OK, let's take a look at the OPAC and do a search for titles with the word dream in it. There are several titles that have come up. Do any of these look familiar?

Patron: Yes—that one! *Disturb Not the Dream*.

Librarian: So the book that you are looking for is called *Disturb Not the Dream*? That is by Paula Trachtman. Is that the correct title? It looks like it is on the shelf.

Patron: Yes. I'd like to take that out please. My friend thought I'd really like it, and I can't wait to read it.

NOTES

1. U.S. Copyright Office, "Copyright in General," U.S. Copyright Office, http://copyright .gov/help/faq/faq-general.html#what.

2. American Library Association, "Guidelines for Behavioral Performance of Reference and Information Service Providers," Reference and User Services Association, last modified May 28, 2013, http://www.ala.org/rusa/resources/guidelines/guidelinesbehavioral.

3. Library of Congress, "Virtual Reference Shelf," Library of Congress, http://www.loc.gov/rr/askalib/virtualref.html.

4. Ohio Library Council, "Model Behaviors," Ohio Reference Excellence on the Web, last modified June 2014, http://www.olc.org/ore/3model.htm.

5. Ohio Library Council, "Virtual or Remote Services, Chat," Ohio Reference Excellence on the Web, http://www.olc.org/ore/2remote.htm.

6. Mary K. Chelton, "Tips on Self-Training for Readers Advisory Work with Adults," Readers Advisory: The Complete Spectrum, last modified 1998, http://www.sjrlc.org/RAhandouts/selftraining.htm.

7. U.S. Copyright Office, "Copyright: Fair Use," U.S. Copyright Office, http://www.copyright.gov/fls/fl102.html.

REFERENCES, SUGGESTED READINGS, AND WEBSITES

American Library Association. "Guidelines for Behavioral Performance of Reference and Information Service Providers." Reference and User Services Association. Last modified May 28, 2013. http://www.ala.org/rusa/resources/guidelines/guidelinesbehavioral.

Chelton, Mary K. "Tips on Self-Training for Readers Advisory Work with Adults." Readers Advisory: The Complete Spectrum. Last modified 1998. http://www.sjrlc.org/RAhandouts/selftraining.htm.

Gers, Ralph. Effective Reference Performance: Participant Workbook. Rev. ed. Columbia, MD: Transform, Inc., 1990.

Goodreads. http://www.goodreads.com.

Library of Congress. "Copyright in General." U.S. Copyright Office. http://copyright.gov/help/faq/faq-general.html#what.

——. "Virtual Reference Shelf." Library of Congress. http://www.loc.gov/rr/askalib/virtualref.html.

Library Thing. http://www.librarything.com.

Modern Library. http://www.modernlibrary.com.

Ohio Library Council. "Model Behaviors." Ohio Reference Excellence on the Web. Last modified June 2014. http://www.olc.org/ore/3model.htm.

——. "Model Reference Behaviors Checklist: Face-to-Face." Ohio Reference Excellence on the Web. Last modified 2014. http://www.olc.org/ore/3checklist.htm.

——. "Virtual or Remote Services, Chat." Ohio Reference Excellence on the Web. http://www.olc.org/ore/2remote.htm.

Orr, Cynthia, and Diana Trixier Herald. Genreflecting: A Guide to Popular Reading Interests. Genreflecting Advisory Series. Santa Barbara, CA: Libraries Unlimited, 2013.

Pearl, Nancy. Book Lust. Seattle, WA: Sasquatch Books, 2003.

Reading Group Choices. http://www.readinggroupchoices.com.

Schwartz, Meredith, and Henrietta Thornton-Verma. "The State of Readers' Advisory." Library Journal 139, no. 2 (February 1, 2014): 30.

U.S. Copyright Office. "Copyright: Fair Use." U.S. Copyright Office. http://www.copyright.gov/fls/fl102.html.

——. "Copyright in General." U.S. Copyright Office. http:copyright.gov/help/faq/faq=general.html#what.

Weyant, Hans, ed. Read This! Handpicked Favorites from America's Indie Bookstores. Books in Action. Minneapolis, MN: Coffee House Press, 2012.

CHAPTER 6

Resource Sharing

Library support staff (LSS) will know the basic principles of interlibrary loan, resource sharing, and the value of cooperating with other libraries to enhance services. (ALA-LSSC Competencies # 5 and # 7).

Topics Covered in This Chapter:

- Interlibrary Loan
- Ethical Considerations
- Preservation Concerns
- Sharing of Other Resources
- Trends in Interlibrary Loan

Key Terms:

Copyright: Copyright is a form of protection granted by law to protect original works of authorship, such as a book, poem, music, and so on.[1] Only the copyright holder has the right to allow his or her material to be reproduced.

Document delivery: Document delivery is the means to provide electronic or digital copies of materials to a patron, instead of a book or physical journal. This is most commonly done in academic and special libraries.

Interlibrary loan (ILL): Interlibrary loan is the process by which one library will provide books and other materials to another library. This is usually done by obtaining or delivering materials not owned by one library to another library or sharing multiple copies for a book discussion.

> *Resource sharing:* Resource sharing is not limited to interlibrary loan and document delivery but also applies to cooperative purchasing of library materials and supplies. It can also refer to physical collections when libraries agree to collect materials in different subject areas.

INTERLIBRARY LOAN

No library can own everything. Interlibrary loan (ILL) is the process by which a library borrows an item from another library for one of its users. It is another method of providing access to information. The Interlibrary Loan Code for the United States, which guides this practice, was prepared by the Reference and User Services Association of the American Library Association (ALA). Most state and regional systems will have their own codes that mirror that of ALA, and all LSS should be familiar with it.[2]

INTERLIBRARY LOAN CODE FOR THE UNITED STATES

Introduction

The Reference and User Services Association, acting for the American Library Association in its adoption of this code recognizes that the sharing of material between libraries is an integral element in the provision of library service and believes it to be in the public interest to encourage such an exchange.

In the interest of providing quality service, libraries have an obligation to obtain material to meet the informational needs of users when local resources do not meet those needs. Interlibrary loan (ILL), a mechanism for obtaining material is essential to the vitality of all libraries.

The effectiveness of the national interlibrary loan system depends upon participation of libraries of all types and sizes.

This code establishes principles that facilitate the requesting of material by a library and the provision of loans or copies in response to those requests. In this code, "material" includes books, audiovisual materials, and other returnable items as well as copies of journal articles, book chapters, excerpts, and other non-returnable items.

1.0 Definition

1.1 Interlibrary loan is the process by which a library requests material from, or supplies material to, another library.

2.0 Purpose

2.1 The purpose of interlibrary loan as defined by this code is to obtain, upon request of a library user, material not available in the user's local library.

3.0 Scope

3.1 This code is intended to regulate the exchange of material between libraries in the United States.

3.2 Interlibrary loan transactions with libraries outside of the United States are governed by the International Federation of Library Associations and Institutions' International Lending: Principles and Guidelines for Procedure.

4.0 Responsibilities of the Requesting Library

4.1 The requesting library should establish, maintain, and make available to its users an interlibrary borrowing policy.

4.2 It is the responsibility of the requesting library to ensure the confidentiality of the user.

4.3 Some requesting libraries permit users to initiate online ILL requests that are sent directly to potential supplying libraries. The requesting library assumes full responsibility for these user-initiated transactions.

4.4 Requested material should be described completely and accurately following accepted bibliographic practice.

4.5 The requesting library should identify libraries that own the requested material. The requesting library should check and adhere to the policies of potential supplying libraries.

4.6 When no libraries can be identified as owning the needed material, requests may be sent to libraries believed likely to own the material, accompanied by an indication that ownership is not confirmed.

4.7 The requesting library should transmit interlibrary loan requests electronically.

4.8 For copy requests, the requesting library must comply with the U.S. copyright law (Title 17, U.S. Code) and its accompanying guidelines.

4.9 The requesting library is responsible for borrowed material from the time it leaves the supplying library until it has been returned to and received by the supplying library. This includes all material shipped directly to and/or returned by the user. If damage or loss occurs, the requesting library is responsible for compensation or replacement, in accordance with the preference of the supplying library.

4.10 The requesting library is responsible for honoring the due date and enforcing any use restrictions specified by the supplying library. The due date is defined as the date the material is due to be checked-in at the supplying library.

4.11 The requesting library should normally request a renewal before the item is due. If the supplying library does not respond, the requesting library may assume that a renewal has been granted extending the due date by the same length of time as the original loan.

4.12 All borrowed material is subject to recall. The requesting library should respond immediately if the supplying library recalls an item.

4.13 The requesting library should package material to prevent damage in shipping and should comply with any special instructions stated by the supplying library.

4.14 The requesting library is responsible for following the provisions of this code. Disregard for any provision may be reason for suspension of service by a supplying library.

5.0 Responsibilities of the Supplying Library

5.1 The supplying library should establish, maintain, and make available an interlibrary lending policy.

5.2 The supplying library should consider filling all requests for material regardless of format, but has the right to determine what material will be supplied on a request by request basis.

5.3 It is the responsibility of the supplying library to ensure the confidentiality of the user.

5.4 The supplying library should process requests in a timely manner that recognizes the needs of the requesting library and/or the requirements of the electronic network or transmission system being used. If unable to fill a request, the supplying library should respond promptly and should state the reason the request cannot be filled.

5.5 When filling requests, the supplying library should send sufficient information with each item to identify the request.

5.6 The supplying library should indicate the due date and any restrictions on the use of the material and any special return packaging or shipping requirements. The due date is defined as the date the material is due to be checked-in at the supplying library.

5.7 The supplying library should ship material in a timely and efficient manner to the location specified by the requesting library. Loaned material should be packaged to prevent loss or damage in shipping. Copies should be delivered by electronic means whenever possible.

> 5.8 The supplying library should respond promptly to requests for renewals. If the supplying library does not respond, the requesting library may assume that a renewal has been granted extending the due date by the same length of time as the original loan.
>
> 5.9 The supplying library may recall material at any time.
>
> *Used with permission from the American Library Association*

There are two philosophies at work in library materials collection: One is that the collection should consist of books that someone might need at some point in the future—"just in case." The other is that the library should provide what the patrons want right now—"just in time." ILL provides the solution to this dilemma. As mentioned earlier, it is impossible for any library to own every book that is in print. Even with that in mind, however, it is often difficult for library staff to dispose of any books that are not being used and are taking up valuable shelf space. The knowledge that a system is in place to put that book in the hands of the patron without taking up space on your very crowded shelf makes it easier to make these decisions and still satisfy the user.

However, ILL is not a substitute for purchasing needed titles. If the LSS gets more than two or three requests for a particular title, the library should consider purchasing it. Many libraries will not lend materials that are newer than, say, six months, which is something to be considered when new and popular titles are released. There was a situation at my library where a book was requested by a fairly small library. The book was very overdue, and sending automated overdue notices was having no effect. Finally, the other library was called, and the person who answered said that the book was out, as it was very popular with their patrons—they had been using an ILL as if it was their own book, and lending it to a long list of patrons. Clearly, this is not the intention of ILL.

There are two components to ILL. The first is that of the borrower—the library that requests and receives the materials from another library. The second is that of the lender—the items that one library loans to another. There are multiple steps involved. To borrow materials from another library, the LSS must follow these steps:

- Take the request from the patron—and be sure to get as much information as possible.
- Verify that the library does not already own the item or that it is not on order.
- Verify the existence of the item (bibliographic verification). This can be done by checking local, regional, and national databases.
- Once the item has been verified (the network will determine which libraries own the item), then make the request. This is done electronically using the ALA-approved Interlibrary Loan form or a form established by OCLC or another network—such as your integrated library system (ILS). It may also be done by e-mail, phone, or fax.
- While there may be no paperwork involved, it is important to check the system regularly for updates on the status of the item and to keep the records updated.

- Once the item has been received, it has to be prepared for lending to the patron who requested it. This involves entering the bibliographic information into the receiving library's circulation system and marking the item so that it can be returned to the *requesting library*. This is very important, since the item has to be accounted for before being returned to the library of origin.
- Notify the patron who made the request that the item is now available for pickup.

Instructions for Completing Delivery Form

1. Clearly Print Delivery Address and Shipping Date

2. Put Town or City of Destination Before the Date

3. Use the Remarks Section to Identify the Branch Library or the Person to whom this item is being sent

4. Fold This Part of Form inside the Material Being Sent

ILL Number: _____

Title: _____

Author: _____

Fold On Dotted Line   This Portion Remains in Item

Fold Shipping Information Over Front Cover and Secure With Rubber Band

---

To:

Date: _____

Address: _____

Town: _____

Library Name: _____

From:

Town: _____

Library Name: _____

__ILL Request __ILL Return __Other Return __Fines Paid

Remarks: _____

_____

Figure 6.1.   Sample Interlibrary Loan Delivery Slip

Figure 6.2. Sample Bin of Items with Labels Ready for Delivery. *Photograph courtesy of the Bill Memorial Library*

To loan materials to another library, the LSS must follow these steps:

- Receive the request, usually by checking the library's ILL network.
- Find the item on the shelf. It is not enough just to verify that it is on the shelf by checking the catalog.
- Approve the request and check out the item to the requesting library.
- Prepare the item for shipping.

Some problems that may come up include a book not being on the shelf as indicated, or it may not be lendable if it's very new, rare, reference, or in poor condition. Other issues to consider include the loan period. A library typically may allow books to circulate for two or three weeks. For ILL, it is necessary to factor in delivery and patron notification times, so the library may have a special loan period for ILL materials of six weeks, for example.

For ILL to work, there needs to be a cooperative network of library databases either regionally, statewide, nationally, or worldwide.

- Regional networks can be as simple as a consortium of ILS such as Sirsi/Dynix, Follett, or Innovative Interfaces—only a few examples of the many ILS available for libraries of all sizes.[3] Searching often starts here.

- Larger networks include, for example, individual state libraries, which provide a database of the holdings of all of the participating individual libraries in the state, including public, school, special, and academic. This allows for the searching of materials anywhere in the state for the purpose of ILL.
- An example of an even larger network is Lyrasis, a membership cooperative of libraries combining the former NELINET (New England), SOLINET (the Atlanta area), and PALINET (the mid-Atlantic region).[4]
- Nationally and globally, one of the major providers of library management systems is OCLC:

In 1967, a small group of library leaders founded OCLC with an ambitious public purpose, to:

- ○ improve access to the information held in libraries around the globe, and
- ○ find ways to reduce costs for libraries through collaboration.

This vision launched an effort to share the world's information via library collaboration—first in Ohio, then across North America and today in 113 countries. The first step was to combine technology with library cooperation through shared, computerized cataloging. Today, the OCLC cooperative helps libraries define their place in the digital world with new cloud-based services that amplify and extend library collections and resources.[5]

Libraries can subscribe to their software packages, such as OCLC/WorldCat Resource Sharing or OCLC ILLiad, in order to facilitate resource sharing nationally or internationally.[6] WorldCat is a union catalog—that is, a combined library catalog of many libraries, available through OCLC. It is a web-based platform for searching, viewing, and selecting potential lenders. ILLiad is a software product that allows a library to manage all of its borrowing and lending through a Windows interface. Both are managed by OCLC and are subscription products. The size and cost make these systems more appropriate for academic and large public library systems. Because interlibrary loan is labor intensive, it is a relatively expensive service for libraries to provide. Fees to join systems range from several hundred dollars for a regional consortium to many thousands of dollars for systems such as OCLC. These fees may seem high, but the per unit cost of a transaction is lowered because of volume.

An integral part of ILL is delivery—how materials get from one library to another. In the case of local, regional, or consortium libraries, delivery may be contracted to a commercial vendor that provides vans, buses, or trucks for this purpose. ILL materials are placed in bins or bags that are then picked up, brought to a central processing area for sorting, and then delivered to the appropriate libraries (see figure 6.2). Interestingly, a number of years ago, the Ames Public Library and Iowa State University, only two miles apart, implemented ILL delivery by bicycle![7] Interstate and international delivery is by mail or parcel post. Guidelines for international delivery can be found through the International Federation of Library Associations and Institutions website.[8]

When articles or documents are requested through ILL, it is called document delivery. Traditionally, libraries mailed or faxed photocopies of articles. Today it is usual to scan and/or send articles electronically, although public libraries will occasionally send an entire journal or magazine. Document delivery is more common in the academic and special library environment. It is not uncommon for relevant articles in the selected fields to be automatically routed to a professor or scientist without prior request. In academic and special libraries, this would be a regular and expected library service.

While libraries in general prefer not to charge for services, the cost for the delivery of materials and documents can be considerable. In the region to which my library belonged many years ago, out-of-state ILL services were available on a fee basis through a centralized system. A designated library with an OCLC subscription had the responsibility for arranging out-of-state loans for those libraries that did not have a subscription, and each library paid a yearly fee to be debited when such loans were requested. (This cost was not passed on to the patron.) When the amount on account was spent, we had the option of paying more or suspending out-of-state loans until the next fiscal year. As it turned out, we usually had just enough in our account to cover the cost of these loans.

While charging fees is anathema to the library philosophy of free and equal access, the reality is that ILL is expensive. For this reason, many libraries will limit ILL requests to three or four requests at a time, for example. The public doesn't understand how much time and effort goes into the process, and it can quickly add up. A 2010 study in Connecticut determined the cost of an ILL transaction relative to the salary and benefits of the staff person, the number of hours they spent on the task, and the number of transactions conducted. The more requests that were filled, the lower the cost per unit—an incentive in itself to encourage ILL.

In general, the volume of ILL in academic libraries is greater than that for public libraries. There are patrons who think nothing of requesting a dozen books at a time. Other patrons will request books that they don't really want or need and, after considerable effort to obtain them, will decide that they don't want them after all. ILL is a valuable but costly service.

Once again considering the hidden cost of an ILL item, some libraries, particularly academic libraries, may charge fees for ILLs. Most libraries will only provide ILL service to its registered cardholders. A library must be able to identify and track its users, so it makes sense not to extend this service to those who might not return the item. There are libraries that will provide a number of services to noncardholders, such as temporary residents or those from out of state who work in the community, but the library usually requires some kind of deposit against loss.

Table 6.1. Total Unit Cost for ILL

Findings: Total Unit Cost	
Range	$1.92 to $27.63
Median	$9.58
Average	$11.25

Source: Mary E. Jackson, "So Really, How Much Does ILL Cost in CT?" (lecture, Connecticut Library Association Conference, Hilton Stamford, CT, May 2, 2011)

The request for renewals of ILL materials is another issue. The LSS cannot auto-matically renew the item in the library's circulation system. The request has to go back to the library that originated the loan. Depending on how quickly that library responds, there can be a gap of several days; meanwhile, the items become overdue. (In reality, some libraries will go ahead and renew the item in their system with the caveat that if the lending library won't renew it, the patron will return it right away. This is determined by individual libraries.)

ETHICAL CONSIDERATIONS

Once again we are faced with **copyright** concerns, particularly as it relates to docu-ment delivery, since the requested materials are reproduced from books, journals, microforms, software, and other materials. The copying, scanning, or otherwise providing access to these materials comes under the protection of copyright law. We are reminded of fair use in the reproduction of articles: One can make photocopies of some pages but cannot copy an entire work, cannot profit from it, and cannot use copies instead of buying the work.

In interlibrary loan and document delivery, we must remember also to respect the confidentiality of user records. If at all possible, the user's identity should not be part of the ILL request, and, as in circulation, the transaction should be deleted once it is complete. As we saw in chapter 1, it is essential to protect the users' right to their own information and the library's right *not* to share personal information without a legally obtained court order or subpoena.

PRESERVATION

It was mentioned in an earlier chapter that LSS are the frontline for item control and preservation. Those who prepare materials for ILL, if not the circulation staff, are re-sponsible for noting the condition of the items that are loaned and that in which they are returned. The condition of some requested books can be appalling, for example, broken spines, loose pages, or markings (see figure 6.4). LSS should be instructed to send the items back with a note that the book was received in that condition, lest the lending library think it was damaged by the patron of the borrowing library (see fig-ure 6.3). It is important that staff at both ends take responsibility for the condition of the items as they are loaned and as they are checked back in. We have received ILL re-turns that were wet, ripped, and stained, with no notation as to the cause. Being aware of the condition of items before lending can prevent further damage by first repairing the item or by denying the loan due to its condition. ILL policy should clearly address this preservation issue so as to prevent damage to valuable materials.

SHARING OF OTHER RESOURCES

The concept of resource sharing is not limited to interlibrary loan and document delivery, although that is what we think of first. There are other ways in which

Anytown Library
123 Main Street
Anytown, USA
555-123-4567
www.anytownlib.org

Date: _____
To: Interlibrary Loan Department
Re: Condition of Item Received

This Item Was Received From You
With Condition Problems:

_____

_____

Our Patron Was Notified of the Condition Before Receiving It
Thank you
ILL Department, Anytown Library

Figure 6.3.   Sample Item Condition Slip

libraries can effectively share resources. Purchasing cooperatives are common. It is well known that volume purchasing brings down individual costs. You don't have to look further than Costco, Sam's Club, and other warehouse stores to see this principle at work. The Connecticut Library Consortium, a member-driven organization, in partnership with the Capital Region Education Council (CREC) negotiates discounts for books, supplies, furniture, equipment, technology, e-resources, and training. The Massachusetts Library System partners with the Massachusetts Higher Education Consortium; Texas, Wisconsin, and so on, provide similar cooperative

Figure 6.4.   Example of Damaged Book. *Photograph courtesy of the Bill Memorial Library*

arrangements for member schools and libraries. Libraries must always prove their worth to their funding bodies, and cooperative buying is one way to demonstrate that responsibility.

Another example of resource sharing is cooperative collection development, in which libraries collect materials on a specific subject. For example, one library in a region can build a collection of business materials, the neighboring town can collect in the area of law resources, and another can concentrate on health. This provides for a better allocation of resources, as no one library has to collect in all three areas, yet the materials are available to the patrons of all of the libraries. This model can include physical collections, electronic resources and databases, and serials—virtually any area of library collection is a potential source for resource sharing for public, school, and academic libraries.

TRENDS IN INTERLIBRARY LOAN

It is now common for libraries to allow patron-initiated requests from their home computers. While this may bypass the patron-librarian transaction, the request should still be subject to approval by library staff. This access does not allow a patron to renew an ILL item, however. As previously stated, the renewal of an ILL must be determined by the lending library.

Gaylord Product #	Demco Product #	Member #	Demco Product Description	Old Demco Price	New Contract Price	List Price
PT1125	1227970	3800	Demco Premium Book Tape 1 ½" x 15 Yards	$1.89	$1.89	$5.09
PT1125	20260770	3800	Gaylord Crystal Clear Book Repair Tape 1"x15" Yards	----	$2.25	$4.59
344L	14942262	4020	Demco White Paper 1"x1 1/2" 5000 Labels	$9.79	$9.79	$40.99
147 R	12817080	4060	Circulation Labels 500/ Roll Day Loan	$2.39	$2.39	$9.54
367R	12814970	4050	Demco Circulation Label ¾" x 1" 500 Roll	$1.98	$1.98	$8.19
G978	12281420	3020	Vistafoil Laminate 4-mil Gloss Finish 12"W x 400'L	$12.09	$12.09	$28.19
1141	16740600	3650	Scotch 845 Book Tape 2"x15" Yards	$4.89	$4.66	$7.79
6115	16285950	9010	Avery Permanent Glue Stick .26 ounces	----	$1.00	$1.49
GBCPDVD 1	12142870	5298	Checkpoint DiscMate Single DVD Case 5-3/8"x 7 ½ x1/2"	-----	$2.49	3.69
----	12217060	5350	Amaray DVD Album Insert Tray 2-capacity Charcoal	$0.39	$0.39	$0.69
----	12985610	9060	Patron Card/Key Tag Combo with Signature Panel	$0.79	$0.79	$1.69

Figure 6.5. Consortium Discounts

Another innovation in ILL is offering an electronic copy to the user. Libraries can purchase devices such as Kindles; if the library does not own the requested title, it can quickly be purchased and downloaded to an e-reader. The electronic titles are added into the online public access catalog (OPAC), and the device is then loaned to the patron instead of the physical book. It is faster than the traditional ILL model and immediately puts the title in the hands of the patron. This involves creating a policy for the lending of devices, including locking the devices so that the patron cannot buy additional titles on the library's account.[9] However, the lending of such devices has become common in many libraries.

Yet another innovation in electronic-book ILL is the use of Occam's Reader, a software program that allows the interlibrary loan of electronic books directly between libraries using ILLiad software. This collaboration between Texas Tech University, the University of Hawaii at Manoa, and the Greater Western Library Alliance[10] has been well received, and there are plans for further improvements to this exciting technology. Clearly, the nature of ILL is expanding.

CHAPTER SUMMARY

LSS must be familiar with the many ways in which libraries share resources, from cooperative collection development and cooperative purchasing to the interlibrary loan of physical and electronic resources and the value of cooperating with other libraries in order to enhance services. All resource sharing represents a way to save space and money while ultimately benefiting the patron and taxpayer. Important considerations include the preservation of loaned materials and the ethical responsibility of LSS in relation to copyright.

DISCUSSION QUESTIONS AND ACTIVITIES

1. Interlibrary loan is a valuable tool that has an impact on collection development. Please explain this.
2. Besides the interlibrary loan of books, identify several other resources that libraries can share. Please be specific.
3. How is preservation an important part of the circulation process?
   a. What impact does interlibrary loan have on this, and how can it be managed?
4. There are many potential new trends in interlibrary loan.
   a. Do you think these new trends will make traditional interlibrary loan obsolete?
   b. If so, why and how?

NOTES

1. United States Copyright Office, "Copyright in General," United States Copyright Office, accessed February 22, 2015, http://copyright.gov/help/faq/faq-general.html#what.

2. American Library Association, "Interlibrary Loan Code for the United States," Reference and Users Services Association, accessed February 22, 2015, http://www.ala.org/rusa/resources/guidelines/interlibrary.

3. Marshall Breeding, "Library Systems Report 2014: Competition and Strategic Cooperation," *American Libraries* 45, no. 5 (May 15, 2014): 21–33.

4. Marshall Breeding, "SOLINET, PALINET and NELINET Merge to Form Lyrasis," *Smart Libraries Newsletter* 29, no. 7 (March 1, 2010): 2–3, http://www.librarytechnology.org/ltg-displaytext.pl?RC=14582.

5. "What Is OCLC?," OCLC.org, last modified 2013, http://www.oclc.org/content/dam/oclc/services/brochures/211510ukb_what_is_oclc.pdf.

6. George Eberhart, ed., *The Whole Library Handbook*, 5th ed. (Chicago: American Library Association, 2013), 309–11.

7. Superpatron, "Bicycle Powered Inter-library Loan in Iowa," Superpatron, last modified June 25, 2008, http://vielmetti.typepad.com/superpatron/2008/06/bicycle-power-1.html.

8. International Federation of Library Associations and Institutions, "Guidelines for Best Practice in Interlibrary Loan and Document Delivery," International Federation of Library Associations and Institutions, http://www.ifla.org/files/assets/docdel/documents/guidelines-best-practice-ill-dd-en.pdf.

9. Joyce Neujahr, "Lightning Fast Interlibrary Loan," *College and Research Library News* 72, no. 9 (2011): 531–41.

10. David H. Ketchum, "The Future: E-books and Interlibrary Loan," last modified September 23, 2013, http://www.slideshare.net/davidhketchum/the-future-ebooks-and-interlibrary -loan?next_slideshow=1.

REFERENCES, SUGGESTED READINGS, AND WEBSITES

American Library Association. ALA Library Fact Sheet 8: Interlibrary Loan Form. American Library Association: Interlibrary Loans. http://www.ala.org/tools/libfactsheets/alalibraryfact sheet08.

———. "Interlibrary Loan Code for the United States." Reference and Users Services Association. Accessed February 22, 2015. http://www.ala.org/rusa/resources/guidelines/inter library.

———. "RUSA STARS' 5 Things Every New Resource Sharing Librarian Should Know." Reference and User Services Association. http://www.ala.org/rusa/sections/stars/5-things-every -new-resource-sharing-librarian-should-know.

Baich, Tina, and Erin Silva Fisher. Interlibrary Loan Systems. In *The Whole Library Handbook*, edited by George M. Eberhart, 309–11. Chicago: American Library Association, 2013.

Breeding, Marshall. "Library Systems Report 2014: Competition and Strategic Cooperation." *American Libraries* 45, no. 5 (May 15, 2014): 21–33.

———. "SOLINET, PALINET and NELINET Merge to Form Lyrasis." *Smart Libraries Newsletter* 29, no. 7 (March 1, 2010): 2–3. http://www.librarytechnology.org/ltg-displaytext.pl? RC=14582.

Eberhart, George, ed. *The Whole Library Handbook*. 5th ed. Chicago: American Library Association, 2013.

Evans, G. Edward. *Introduction to Library Public Services*. 7th ed. Westport, CT: Libraries Unlimited, 2009.

International Federation of Library Associations and Institutions. "Guidelines for Best Practice in Interlibrary Loan and Document Delivery." International Federation of Library Associations and Institutions. http://www.ifla.org/files/assets/docdel/documents/guidelines -best-practice-ill-dd-en.pdf.

Jackson, Mary E. "So Really, How Much Does ILL Cost in CT?" Lecture, Connecticut Library Association Conference, Hilton, Stamford, CT, May 2, 2011.

Ketchum, David H. "The Future: E-books and Interlibrary Loan." Last modified September 23, 2013. http://www.slideshare.net/davidhketchum/the-future-ebooks-and-inter library-loan?next_slideshow=1.

Lyrasis. http://www.lyrasis.org/Pages/Main.aspx.

Neujahr, Joyce. "Lightning Fast Interlibrary Loan." *College and Research Library News* 72, no. 9 (2011): 531–41.

Northeast Document Conservation Center. Storage and Handling Practices. https://www
    .nedcc.org/free-resources/preservation-leaflets/4.-storage-and-handling/4.1-storage
    -methods-and-handling-practices.

OCLC. http://www.oclc.org/en-US/home.html.

Superpatron. "Bicycle Powered Inter-library Loan in Iowa." Superpatron. Last modified June
    25, 2008. http://vielmetti.typepad.com/superpatron/2008/06/bicycle-power-1.html.

United States Copyright Office. "Copyright in General." United States Copyright Office.
    http://copyright.gov/help/faq/faq-general.html#what.

"What Is OCLC?" OCLC.org. Last modified 2013. http://www.oclc.org/content/dam/oclc/
    services/brochures/211510ukb_what_is_oclc.pdf.

PART II

Customer Service

CHAPTER 7

Twenty-First-Century Library Customer Service

An Overview

Library support staff (LSS) will know the basic concepts, skills, and practices of customer service. They will be able to communicate and promote the library's values and services to the staff, volunteers, users, and the community and recognize and respond to user needs and services. (ALA-LSSC Competencies #9, #10)

Topics Covered in This Chapter:

- Customer Service—Overview
- Customer Service Skills
- Body Language
- Telephone and Remote Protocol

Key Terms:

Attending skills: Attending skills are those that show that the LSS is giving full attention to the patron. They show active interest in what patrons say and do and show respect for their needs.

Body language: Body language is a constant, nonverbal flow of communication, including eye contact, posture, hand gestures, touch, and the use of space. The LSS must be aware of this in his or her interactions with patrons.

Customer service: Customer service means assisting patrons (users, customers) with their needs in person, by phone, or electronically by providing high-quality service. The LSS does this in order to achieve a goal or complete a transaction while showing respect, courtesy, and interest in the patron.

> *Internal customer service:* Internal customer service means assisting coworkers, subordi-
> nates, or managers in the workplace by providing the same high-quality service in order
> to achieve a goal or complete a transaction, showing respect, courtesy, and interest, as
> the LSS would to a patron. Treating coworkers with this same level of customer service
> ensures excellent relations throughout the library.

CUSTOMER SERVICE—OVERVIEW

We have all heard the expression, *you only get one chance to make a first impression.* How many times have we all wished for a "do-over" when meeting someone for the first time? The impression that we give the first time a patron walks through the library door could set the tone for that person's impression of and relationship with the library. It's a simple concept borrowed from the business world—customers will remain loyal if they are satisfied with the quality of the service that they receive. As libraries are essentially a customer-focused profession, it is a good model to follow, and a customer service plan should be part of the library's mission. A good plan can improve customer relations by focusing on customer needs. That plan begins with the library's mission statement—it should include what the library believes to be its service mission. Statements such as "to serve our community," to "provide resources for our patrons," and so on specifically set a service goal. Determining the library's demographic helps to focus services on *patrons'* needs. Patrons should be made to understand what the library can and cannot provide, such as how long interlibrary loan (ILL) service may take or if individualized computer training is available. Patrons should be made to feel that they will be heard, whether they have a question or a complaint. Service quality includes the physical appearance of the library and the willingness of staff to help, to be courteous and competent, and to provide a safe atmosphere.

The governing body of the library establishes the policies, procedures, and rules that make clear the expectations of both staff and patrons. They determine the policies that define the principles of operation, the procedures that define and interpret the policies, and the rules—what is actually done. This gives the staff the flexibility that they need to make decisions that, while based in policy, can satisfy the patron. For example, the library may establish a policy stating that fines will be collected for overdue materials. The procedure is that fines are $0.05 a day per item. The rule, however, may be that fines will be forgiven for seniors. This empowers the LSS to make decisions on the spot, as warranted by the situation.

Customer service is the interaction between the user and the service provider; good customer service adds value and goodwill. Most people who choose to work in libraries genuinely like what they do, and for them, providing good customer service is second nature. Customer service can be *transaction* based or *relationship* based. Transaction-based service is *point of service*: checking out a book. Relationship-based service *implies a relationship* between the LSS and the patron. This can be done by remembering the patron's name or knowing the patron's reading preferences, for example, so as to recommend titles when he or she comes into the library.[1] This creates value to the patron and encourages loyalty. Think about the stores that you shop in. If the employee is chatting with another, checking his phone, or otherwise ignoring you, you are not likely to return to that store. Negative interactions with a business are spread to twice as many people as positive ones.[2] When the store personnel greet you by name and go out of their way to be helpful, it makes you want to return to that particular store. So it is with libraries. The customer is the most important part of your job. Remind yourself that the patrons are *not* an interruption but the reason that you are there every day.

CUSTOMER SERVICE SKILLS

The reference skills that we learned in chapter 5 apply here as well. These behaviors—welcoming, **attending**, listening, eliciting, searching, informing, and follow up—should become routine to the LSS in all patron interactions and contribute to excellent customer service.

Additionally, there are six basic customer service needs[3]:

BASIC CUSTOMER SERVICE NEEDS

1. **Friendliness**

   Friendliness is the most basic of all customer needs, usually associated with being greeted graciously and with warmth. We all want to be acknowledged and welcomed by someone who sincerely is glad to see us. A customer shouldn't feel they are an intrusion on the service provider's work day!

2. **Understanding and empathy**

   Customers need to feel that the service person understands and appreciates their circumstances and feelings without criticism or judgment. Customers have simple expectations that we who serve them can put ourselves in their shoes, understanding what it is they came to us for in the first place.

3. **Fairness**

   Everyone needs to feel they are being treated fairly. Customers get annoyed and defensive when they feel that someone is getting better service or treatment than they are.

4. **Control**

   Control represents the customers' need to feel they have an impact on the way things turn out. Our ability to meet this need for them comes from our own willingness to say "yes" much more than we say "no."

5. **Options and alternatives**

   Customers need to feel that other avenues are available to getting what they want accomplished. They depend on us to have all the answers, and if one way doesn't work, they expect us to provide another means to that end.

6. **Information**

   Patrons need to be educated and informed about our products and services, and they don't want us leaving anything out. They look to us to be the source of all information.

Source: Lifehack.org

One of the most effective customer service skills the LSS can use is to *listen*. There are fourteen keys to good listening.[4]

FOURTEEN KEYS TO GOOD LISTENING

1. Limit Your Own Talking: You can't talk and listen at the same time.
2. Think Like the Speaker: His problems and needs are important and you'll understand and retain them better if you keep his point of view in mind.
3. Ask Questions: If you don't understand something or feel you may have missed a point, clear it up now before it may embarrass you later.
4. Don't Interrupt: A pause . . . even a long pause . . . doesn't always mean he finished saying everything he wanted to.
5. Concentrate: Focus your mind on what she is saying. Practice shutting out distractions.
6. Take Notes: This will help you remember important points; and be selective—trying to jot down everything she says can result in being left far behind or in retaining irrelevant details.
7. Listen for Ideas, Not Just Words: You want to get the whole picture, not just isolated bits and pieces.
8. Interjections: An occasional "Yes" or "I see" shows the speaker you're still with him, but don't overdo it or use it as a meaningless comment.
9. Turn Off Your Own Words: This isn't always easy: your personal fears, worries, and problems not connected with this conversation form a kind of static that can block out the speaker's message.
10. Prepare in Advance: Remarks and questions prepared in advance, when possible, free your mind for listening.
11. React to Ideas . . . Not the Person: Don't allow irritation at things he may say, or his manner to distract you.
12. Don't Jump to Conclusions: Avoid making unwarranted assumptions about what the speaker is going to say, or mentally try to complete his sentences for him.
13. Listen for the Overtones: You can learn a great deal from the speaker from the way she says things.
14. Practice Listening: Make your conversations with your colleagues a learning tool for improving your listening skills.

Source: Learning Tree International Blog

In 2014, a program was given by the Customer Service Section of the Connecticut Library Association. Called "Knock Their Socks Off: Easy Ways to Deliver Exceptional Customer Service," it reinforces and goes beyond the concepts mentioned above.[5]

As in all areas of library service, we must continually reassess what we do in order to be sure that we are meeting our patron's needs. There are several ways to do this. Many libraries will periodically conduct surveys. The staff may compile a

KNOCK THEIR SOCKS OFF!

First Impression
Friendly facial expression
Resting smile
Alert and relaxed posture
Calm movements
Sociable demeanor
Comfortable and work-appropriate outfit
Tidy desk area

Initial Contact
Acknowledge patron
Soft eye contact
Genial greeting: "How may I help you?"
Listen attentively
Let them finish
Confirm or redirect

Closing the Interaction
Confirm that the need was met
Ask if you can do anything else
Pleasant send-off

Verbal Communication
Soothing and firm tone of voice
Speak slowly, clearly, and deliberately
Use layperson vocabulary; avoid jargon

Build Rapport
Show recognition
Say their name
Offer suggestions

Business at Hand
Complete transaction quickly and correctly
Talk through the process

Prevent Burnout
Breathe deeply and regularly
Remember your purpose
Focus on positives
Find joy in your day
Take your breaks
Commiserate sparingly
Leave work at work

Used with permission from Brandie Doyle, MLS @ CLASS Conference, 2013

list of questions that reflect various areas of service. The resulting survey can then be printed out and given to patrons; the questions can go on the library's website, or they can be structured within a free data-gathering tool such as Survey Monkey, Zoomerang, or Google Forms, for example. These sites can correlate and interpret data, and for a fee or subscription, they can be more finely tuned and detailed. Interviews can be conducted by library staff using a selected list of questions randomly asked of patrons. For a more structured approach, focus groups can be formed and subsequently interviewed using the same set of predetermined topics. A less formal evaluation can be made by observation: what resources are being used, when, and by whom? Patron requests are also indicative, such as if they are consistently asking for materials that are not being collected. Of course, so are patron complaints—anything that is brought to the staff's attention must be taken into consideration for evaluation purposes.

BODY LANGUAGE

It should go without saying that the first thing to do when someone walks through the door is to smile and acknowledge him or her. Beyond that, we need to recognize the messages that we are sending with our **body language**—the constant nonverbal flow of communication. Professor Albert Mehrabian, who pioneered the work in nonverbal communication beginning in the 1960s, gives us a communication model that shows that 55 percent of what we learn comes from body language, while 38 percent comes from the tone of voice and only 7 percent from words.[6]

While some may disagree with Mehrabian's research, it is worth paying attention to the concept. Since body language is not conscious, here are some examples of what to aim for:

- Face: use a relaxed and pleasant expression.
  - Make eye contact: this is an attending skill, as it lets the patron know that you are interested.
  - Smile.
  - Try for an open, relaxed expression. Be careful not to let personal worries or stress show.
- Body posture: this shows your energy level and interest.
  - Nod: one of the best ways to show attention. Be careful though—overdoing it can signal impatience.

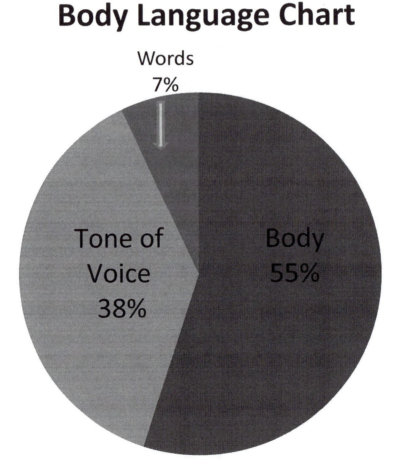

Figure 7.1. Body Language Chart

- ○ Face the patron.
- ○ Lean slightly forward: leaning back or stepping away gives negative signals.
- Hand gestures: this is a natural way of expression.
  - ○ Use an open handed gesture, flat hand, palm up or out.
  - ○ Avoid a closed hand or pointing fingers.
  - ○ Avoid tapping fingers, clicking pens, jingling coins. This conveys annoyance or impatience.
- Touch: the most acceptable form of public touch is handshaking.
  - ○ Touch can convey caring and concern.
  - ○ Nonthreatening touch is in the area between the elbow and the wrist.
  - ○ Avoid the more intimate gestures, such as hugging, putting an arm around someone, or slapping his or her back.

Be aware also of *personal space*: the distance between you and another person. Those who stand too close invade your personal space. The guidelines are:

- Zone 1: intimate, zero to two feet, for family members, friends, romantic partners
- Zone 2: personal or casual, two to four feet, for customers and patrons—it's a safe and comfortable distance
- Zone 3: social, four feet or more, for teachers, instructors, librarians
- Zone 4: public, beyond twelve feet

There may also be cultural differences in your library. People in some cultures, such as Asian cultures, tend not to touch when greeting; other cultures, such as Italian or Latin American, tend to be more physical. Some Middle Eastern cultures prohibit any touch between men and women at all. It helps to take your cues from the patron and act accordingly.[7]

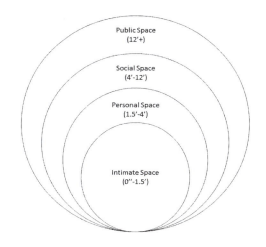

Figure 7.2.   Personal Zone Chart

TELEPHONE AND REMOTE CUSTOMER SERVICE

Not everyone gets their information by physically coming into the library. Current technology makes it easy to access virtually all aspects of library service from the comforts of home. Computers, tablets, and mobile devices allow new ways for libraries to provide service to their patrons. Chapter 5 addresses service to off-site users, so we already know about e-mail, chat, IM, and text as a communication tool. While this kind of communication is by nature impersonal, the principles of the Fourteen Keys to Effective Listening can still apply, such as asking questions, not jumping to conclusions, and being prepared in advance. We have to remember that we are dealing with our patrons on the other end, and that their needs are as legitimate as the patron standing in front of us.

Another method of remote communication is the telephone. Even though we cannot see the patron, we owe him or her the same level of service that he or she would receive in person. Although you may not be having your best day, for all intents and purposes this patron is the first person you have spoken to all day—and he doesn't care what your problems are. Turn off your own worries and concerns. When taking a phone call, body language disappears and your voice becomes 86 percent of the story. A monotone suggests that you are bored, slow speech might imply that you are depressed, and a very loud tone can be interpreted as anger. Developing telephone skills is critical. Beware of your inflection—the highs and lows in your pitch. It also reflects how interested you are in the conversation. If you don't have an interesting voice, then practice your inflection. The best advice is to smile and to breathe—it can be heard in your voice.[8]

Be friendly yet businesslike, and speak distinctly. How many times have you called a business only to have to ask the person on the other end to repeat themselves

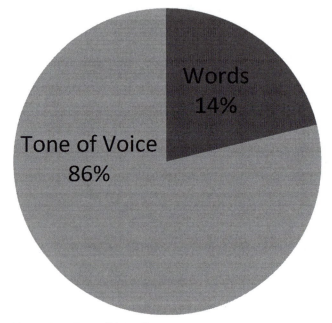

Figure 7.3.   Tone of Voice Chart

because you couldn't understand them and weren't sure that you called the right number. Speak slowly and avoid mumbling or speaking too quietly. Learn to take messages and to get them to the right person promptly; it is a good idea to note the date, time, and your initials so that the recipient can get back to you with questions. Don't be afraid to ask the caller to spell his or her name, and make sure you repeat back the phone number as well. I have gotten many message slips over the years with the names misspelled or the numbers mixed up; it makes it very difficult to return such a call—not to mention the lack of professionalism that it shows.

If you must put a patron on hold, be sure to ask his or her permission first. You can briefly explain that the library is very busy or that you are on another line and will return to the patron's call shortly. If the caller agrees, thank them and let them know that you'll be with them in a moment. Do not simply lay the phone down or tell them to "hold on." If the patron must be placed on hold while you find an answer to her question, tell her that's what you will be doing. Try not to leave anyone on hold longer than two or three minutes. With or without a sound track, that's a long time to wait. If you cannot satisfy her question in that amount of time, then offer to call her back when you have located the information. When you do return to the call, make sure to thank the caller for her patience.[9]

Be sure that you learn to use the hold button on the phone. I have observed staff people cover the mouthpiece with a hand or hold it to their body while they ask another staff member a question—or to ask if they want to take the call! Know the difference, too, between the hold button and the flash button, which allows you to switch between calls. Unless you're careful, you can disconnect the call. Sometimes a caller will not want to be placed on hold. In a case like this, see if the question can be answered quickly; if not, take the caller's name and number and tell him that his call will be returned soon. And make sure that it is! Use all of your customer service skills to ensure that the caller is treated courteously.

Internal Customer Service

Just as the LSS uses customer service and listening skill behaviors with all patrons, so too must they practice **internal customer service**—that is, with coworkers. Treat the staff and board members as customers. They should be treated with the same respect and skills that are used with the patrons. Make sure that you are on time, particularly if it means that someone else can't leave until you show up. In fact, it is usually appreciated if you can be a few minutes early for your shift. This allows time to hang up your coat, review the day's issues, and be ready to greet your patrons.

Internal customer service also applies to your volunteers. They may not be paid staff, but they are performing an invaluable service. They, too, deserve to be treated well and with respect. Volunteers can make the job of the LSS much easier, and your attitude should reflect that.

CHAPTER SUMMARY

Customer service, or the way that we interact with library patrons and each other, is important to understand and to practice. The many behaviors and skills we use—attending skills, listening skills, and body language—help to communicate the values and services of the library to the staff, board, volunteers, and the community.

Knowing and using these skills is the difference between having an empty building full of materials and equipment and providing essential services to an enthusiastic public—and ensuring that they return.

DISCUSSION QUESTIONS AND ACTIVITIES

1. There are two ways to approach customer services: transaction based and relationship based.
   a. What is the difference between the two?
   b. Why does it matter?
2. Think of an interaction that you have had at a library or a business.
   a. What customer service behaviors were used, if any?
   b. How could the transaction have been improved?
3. What is body language, and how does it affect the relationship of the LSS to the patron?
   a. Give five examples.
4. How does service to remote users differ from that of a face-to-face user—or does it?

NOTES

1. G. Edward Evans, *Introduction to Library Public Services* (Westport, CT: Libraries Unlimited, 2009), 43.
2. Hulya Aksu, "Customer Service: The New Proactive Marketing," *Huff Post*, last modified March 26, 2013, http://www.huffingtonpost.com/hulya-aksu/customer-service-the-new-_b_2827889.html.
3. Rosa Say, "The Six Basic Needs of Customers," *Lifehack: Tips for Life* (blog), http://www.lifehack.org/articles/work/the-six-basic-needs-of-customers.html.
4. Carl Sawatzky, "Project Leaders: Learn to Listen . . . 14 Keys to Effective Listening," *Learning Tree International Blog*, last modified April 29, 2010, http://blog.learningtree.com/project-leaders-learn-to-listen-14-keys-to-effective-listening/.
5. Brandi Boyle, "Knock Their Socks Off: Easy Ways to Deliver Exceptional Customer Service" (address, CLASS Conference, University of Hartford, West Hartford, CT, November 1, 2013).
6. Albert Mehrabian, *Silent Messages* (Belmont, CA: Wadsworth, 1972).
7. Keith Bailey and Karen Leland, *Customer Service for Dummies* (Foster City, CA: IDG, 1999), 56–57.
8. Bailey and Leland, *Customer Service for Dummies*, 60–63.
9. Bailey and Leland, *Customer Service for Dummies*, 75–78.

REFERENCES, SUGGESTED READINGS, AND WEBSITES

Aksu, Hulya. "Customer Service: The New Proactive Marketing." *HuffPost*. Last modified March 26, 2013. http://www.huffingtonpost.com/hulya-aksu/customer-service-the-new-_b_2827889.html.
Antell, Karen. "Should Libraries Be Run Like Businesses?" *Reference and User Services Quarterly*, Spring 2013, 182–85.

Bailey, Keith, and Karen Leland. *Customer Service for Dummies*. Foster City, CA: IDG, 1999.

Boyle, Brandi. "Knock Their Socks Off: Easy Ways to Deliver Exceptional Customer Service." Address, Class Conference, University of Hartford, West Hartford, CT, November 1, 2013.

Cuddy, Amy. "Your Body Language Shapes Who You Are." TED Talk, October 2012. https://www.ted.com/talks/amy_cuddy_your_body_language_shapes_who_you_are/transcript?language=en.

Dunselman, Marijke. "7 Ways to Achieve Great Internal Customer Service and Happy Staff!" MarketingWhizz. http://www.marketingwhizz.com/weekly-marketing-tip/7-ways-to-achieve-greatinternal-customer-service-and-happy-staff.

Evans, G. Edward. *Introduction to Library Public Services*. Westport, CT: Libraries Unlimited, 2009.

Mehrabian, Albert. *Silent Messages*. Belmont, CA: Wadsworth, 1972.

"Patron Service 101: Training for Staff." YouTube. https://www.youtube.com/watch?v=gzbDdgWiaS0&list=PLE8BD99D71383C4D8.

Pellack, Loraine J. "Now Serving Customer 7,528,413." *Reference and User Services Quarterly*, Summer 2012, 316–18.

Say, Rosa. "The Six Basic Needs of Customers." *Lifehack: Tips for Life* (blog). www.lifehack.org/articles/work/the-six-basic-needs-of-customers.html.

Sawatzky, Carl. "Project Leaders: Learn to Listen . . . 14 Keys to Effective Listening." *Learning Tree International Blog*. Last modified April 29, 2010. http://blog.learningtree.com/project-leaders-learn-to-listen-14-keys-to-effective-listening/.

Schmidt, Aaron. "Developing a Service Philosophy." *Library Journal*, November 1, 2014, 21.

"Telephone Etiquette: Making Lasting First Impressions." YouTube. https://www.youtube.com/watch?v=leabFC3ec6w.

CHAPTER 8

Customer Service to Youth

Library support staff (LSS) will know the basic concepts and skills of customer service. They will be able to recognize and respond to diversity in user needs and preference for resources and services. (ALA-LSSC Competencies #9, #11)

Topics Covered in This Chapter:

- Service to Children
- Service to Teens
- Social Media for Children and Teens

Key Terms:

Child development: Child development is the physical, intellectual, language, and social stages that occur in children from birth to young adulthood. This is especially important when planning library services for that age group.

Common Core Standards: The Common Core is a set of high-quality academic standards in mathematics and English language arts/literacy (ELA). These learning goals outline what a student should know and be able to do at the end of each grade.[1] Libraries are aligning material selection to this concept.

Microcosm: A microcosm is a smaller version of something else or having the characteristics of a larger version. The children's room is a microcosm of library service to adults as it provides all of the same services, such as reference and reader's advisory, to children as it does to adults.

Social media: Social media is the interactive, web-based electronic communication through which users create online communities in order to share information, ideas, and personal messages. This is a popular use for library computers for patrons and can be used by staff to share library news.

SERVICE TO CHILDREN

When the word library is mentioned, the first thing that comes to many people's minds is "children." Children are the best public-relations tool that a library can have, and bringing children in for story time or programs is also the reason many adults come to the library. By introducing children to the pleasure of reading and books, we are teaching them how to use the library and ways of gathering information, as well as satisfying their curiosity. Visiting the library can teach children that the library is part of the community. According to a Pew Internet Study called "Parents, Children, Libraries, and Reading":

- 94% of parents say libraries are important for their children and 79% describe libraries as "very important." That is especially true of parents of young children (those under 6), some 84% of whom describe libraries as very important.
- 84% of these parents who say libraries are important say a major reason they want their children to have access to libraries is that libraries help inculcate their children's love of reading and books.
- 81% say a major reason libraries are important is that libraries provide their children with information and resources not available at home.
- 71% also say a major reason libraries are important is that libraries are a safe place for children.

Almost every parent (97%) says it is important for libraries to offer programs and classes for children and teens.[2]

Browse through the program listings in your local paper and you'll see many of them are for children's activities at the public library. However, as we saw in chapter 1, library service for children in both schools and the public library didn't arise until the mid-nineteenth century, and the first professionally trained school librarian wasn't appointed until 1900.[3] Until library education became standard, these librarians would have been self-taught. Because women were the traditional caregivers, it stands to reason that they were the first "children's librarians." However, the first qualification for someone to serve children in a library, then as now, is a genuine fondness for children. They must like, respect, and enjoy them. Then they must have training in **child development**: to understand the mind of a child, how a child thinks at different stages of her life, and how a child processes vocabulary as she grows.[4] A professional children's librarian will hold the MLS degree; a school media specialist will also have teacher training. Many school districts require school library media specialists to be certified teachers.

Additionally, the children's librarian must know and enjoy children's literature. There is a wide variety of writing and art styles, and the librarian must become familiar with them in order to be able to evaluate books and nonprint materials. While of course it is not possible to read everything in the collection, a certain familiarity is expected—to be gained through reading. The inclusion of **Common Core** Standards in the curriculums of many state education systems provides consistent, strong, clear benchmarks for learning.[5] This is impacting libraries, changing the way that traditional library skills are being taught and encouraging a close collaboration between school and public librarians. Figure 8.1 illustrates the effect that Common Core has on the public library[6]:

Common Core Shift   Public Library Response

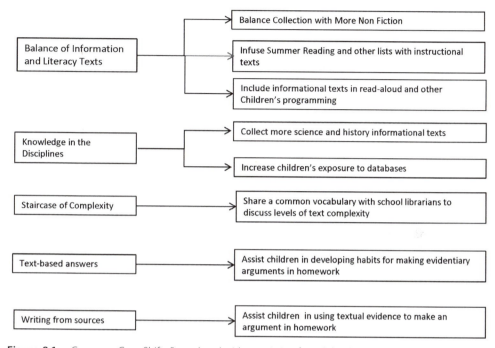

Figure 8.1. Common Core Shift. *Reproduced with permission from School Library Journal @ Copyright Library Journals, LLC. A Wholly Owned Subsidiary of Media Source, Inc.*

This is applicable to even the youngest patrons. Story programs for children from babies to toddlers may have once simply been an activity in and of itself: children sit and listen to a story. These same programs now incorporate elements of core standards in that librarians are meant to encourage language skills and concepts (shapes, colors), as well as the development of fine and gross motor skills into these programs. Commercial programs such as Mother Goose on the Loose, a popular and successful early literacy program for children ages birth to three, are on the market and provide manuals, instructions, and ready-to-use materials that complement the concepts of Common Core Standards.[7] Librarians also rely on standard and authoritative sources such as H. W. Wilson's *Children's Core Collection*, the *Middle & Junior High School Core Collection*, and the *Senior High Core Collection* to assist in selecting appropriate materials for each of these age groups.

Back in the 1980s, the American Library Association (ALA) produced an instructional video tape titled *Kids Are Patrons, Too!* In it, a young boy dressed as a newspaper reporter went through the library with his microphone interviewing the other children about their library needs. Although it is no longer available, the concepts it taught were invaluable—that all people should be treated with respect, friendliness, and personalization. Children's librarians have an obligation to their young users, who have legitimate needs. They must guide their young patrons to find the resources that they need and to learn the value of literature.[8]

However, children do have different needs than adults and should be treated as such. For them, even approaching the librarian or the help desk can be scary. They often have a harder time expressing themselves than adult patrons do, so the reference interview is even more critical. It must be geared to their level. The librarian must be open and friendly, not patronizing; and since children are smaller, it helps to get down to their level so they can be eye to eye. Just as in any reference interview, do not assume that you know what the child wants. Don't lead them and let them tell you, to the best of their ability, what it is they are looking for. For example, is there an assignment sheet that you can look at? Do they need to use certain sources such as books, encyclopedias, or the Internet? If at all possible, encourage the child to ask and answer the questions, not the parent. This is not always easy—parents mean well, but the child needs to develop the skills to interact with library staff on his own.

We do such a good job of making the library friendly and comfortable for children that libraries have become a safe haven for those who go directly to the library after school until their parents get home. Many such children are well behaved and quietly read or do their homework, but there may be others who take advantage of their "freedom" and need supervision or who get hurt while acting out. Afterschool homework clubs or tutoring by peers or teens are good ways to engage both groups—but the library cannot be expected to act in loco parentis, in the place of the parent. Libraries must have policies in place that address unattended children and spell out the parents' responsibilities—including for those children who are not picked up by closing time.

A sampling of policies from public libraries around the country regarding unattended children is remarkably similar. The following textbox is an amalgam of these policies:

SAMPLE UNATTENDED CHILDREN POLICY

1. The library provides a welcoming environment for children and families.
2. Children under the age of eight must have a parent/caregiver (over the age of fourteen) on the premises. The library is not an alternative to daycare.
3. If children under the age of eight are found to be unattended, attempts will be made to contact the parents. If the parents' cannot be located, the library is authorized to call the police.
4. The library staff are available to help children with their homework needs but are not responsible for children left unattended. Staff are busy and often unaware of what children are doing.
5. Children who are left in the library must be engaged in homework, book selection, or be attending a program.
6. Children are expected to observe the rules of conduct. If a child and parent/caregiver violates the code, they will be reminded of the rules. If it continues, the family may be asked to leave.
7. If a child appears to be at risk or is left alone at closing time, the library will contact the parents. If the parents cannot be located, the library is authorized to call the police.
8. Library staff are not responsible for children left outdoors after closing, socializing or waiting for rides.

Children's librarianship is a **microcosm** of adult librarianship in that everything done for adults is also done for children but at their level. The librarian (or the LSS) is responsible for collection development, material selection, collection maintenance, reference services, and reader's advisory. They are also responsible for program planning, marketing, public relations, and publicity for whatever goes on in the children's department. Only by recognizing the importance of all of the aspects of library customer service can we then provide the best possible library service to children.

SERVICE TO TEENS

According to the Young Adult Library Services Association of ALA (YALSA), young adults (YA) or teens generally fall into the age range of twelve to eighteen, although this can be adjusted up or down depending on the individual. Just as we saw with children, the LSS who serves teens must understand the mind of a teen and how teens think at different stages of their development. They generally need emotional support and social engagement; they are novelty-seeking and creative. Also common to teen behavior is a skewed risk-versus-reward system of motivation.[9] Teens are unique, and their needs are legitimate and must be recognized and addressed.

Teens often have a reputation for being difficult and causing trouble in the library—and unfortunately that attitude is too often communicated to the teen. A group of YAs comes into the library and the first reaction of many staff members is to expect the worst. Understanding what resources the library has for that age group is imperative; instead of seeing the teens as the enemy, they must be seen as a unique group of patrons with unique needs. Just as we buy picture books for toddlers and large-print books for seniors, so should books and materials that appeal to teens be actively sought and added to the collection.[10] Many teen collections include computers, gaming software, graphic novels, music (CDs and other emergent technologies), downloadable books and video resources, quiet study spaces, and print materials that support their interests and curriculum. Engaging teens in tutoring or mentoring children is another option that may interest them.

Another way to make teens welcome is to offer activities that appeal to them. Particularly effective in middle school media centers but equally appealing in the public library are contests and active games, themed programs, and live demonstrations (especially if it involves animals). Creative book lists can capture the interest of this age group as well, such as horror books (all titles must have the word *horror*, *death*, or *terror* in it) or Shades of Grey (all titles must have the word *grey* in it). The possibilities are endless.[11]

YAs need their own space as well, and it helps to get their input as to what would meet their needs. Empowering them gives them a sense of ownership and pride.

Not every library has the room or the finances to create such a teen space, but any area that can be isolated or carved out of existing space goes a long way toward recognizing the needs of this population. Ideally, it affords privacy (though it must still be monitored) and some sort of noise control. Just like children who have been cooped up all day in a classroom, teens need to blow off some steam when they come into the library after school. If the YA room is private or soundproofed, this may not be much of a problem. They can usually be quieted with a gentle warning, although there was

TEEN SPACE GUIDELINES

- Convey that the space is teen-owned and maintained.
- Be sure it is comfortable, inviting, open and has a vibrant and teen-friendly look and feel.
- It should accommodate individuals as well as group use for socializing and learning.
- Include colorful and fun accessories selected by teens. Include up-to-date and teen friendly décor.
- Allow for ample display of teen print, artistic and digital creations.
- Allow food and drink in the space.
- Contribute to a sense of teen belonging, community involvement, and library appreciation.
- Be sure it is appealing to both users and non-users, and provide resources for customers from diverse social groups, backgrounds and interests.
- It should be easy to navigate with clear signage and distinct areas for socializing, entertainment, teen print/digital collections and study and quiet areas.
- Make sure it is easily navigable for teens with wheelchairs, walkers and other assistive devices.

Source: American Library Association, "National Teen Space Guidelines," Young Adult Library Services Association, last modified May 2012, accessed December 10, 2014, http://www.ala.org/yalsa/sites/ala.org.yalsa/files/content/guidelines/guidelines/teenspaces.pdf.

Used with permission from the American Library Association

at least one time that I asked a small but vocal—and cooperative—group of teens to go outside one beautiful day and run around the building a couple of times. Since they were "regulars" and were familiar with the staff and library, they actually welcomed the suggestion. Not all libraries have that option, and unfortunately, it is not uncommon for libraries to employ monitors to keep patrons—of all ages—in line.

The best customer service the LSS can provide to teens is to be approachable, nonjudgmental, tolerant, patient, and respectful. Talk with them to find out what they are interested in, what books, magazines, or technology they are using. The LSS already has great customer service skills—now is the time to tailor them to a specific audience and find out how they can be improved.

SOCIAL MEDIA AMONG CHILDREN AND TEENS

Communication among children and teens has come a long way from passing notes in school when the teacher isn't looking. Now electronic communication, through which users create online communities to share information, ideas, and personal messages, has become the norm.[12] This is **social media**.

In the beginning, there was Web 1.0. This was static, electronic computer content that was essentially "read only." Then along came Web 2.0, which is interactive. It allows the user to share content with a site and with other people. It is no surprise

Figure 8.2. "Teenscape" Teen Room. *Photograph courtesy of the Groton Public Library*

that children and teens have adopted social media and other technologies. In her 2014 book *It's Complicated: The Social Lives of Networked Teens*, danah boyd says, "Over the past decade social media has evolved from being an esoteric jumble of technologies to a set of sites and services that are at the heart of contemporary culture. Teens turn to a plethora of popular services to socialize, gossip, share information, and hang out."[13] Libraries have responded to this by developing websites, blogs, wikis, Facebook pages, and Twitter accounts, for example. By using social media, libraries can connect with their constituents—including teens—in ways with which they are both familiar and comfortable.

Besides providing social media sites to reach out to all patrons, this is also a great resource for homeschool families, who rely heavily on libraries for curriculum support and programs.

LSS that work with children and teens have a lot of tools on hand to engage these kids in-house. They can encourage young adults to become lifelong library users by helping them to discover what libraries offer, how to use library resources, and how

Figure 8.3.   "Teenscape" Teen Room Interior. *Photograph courtesy of the Groton Public Library*

libraries can assist them with their growth and development. By empowering them to create content by and for the library, children and teens become partners in the creation and maintenance of social media. The LSS can develop and supervise youth participation, such as teen advisory groups, recruitment of teen volunteers to build and maintain library webpages and blogs, or partner with seniors to teach computer skills and website navigation. LSS are teaching teens to produce podcasts, videos, and YouTube content, providing opportunities for future employment as well as building assets in youth in order to develop healthy, successful young adults.[14]

Social media is not without its issues. Children and teens tend to reveal a lot about themselves, including personal information, photographs, and contact information, although they also feel they are doing a good job of protecting their privacy by using available privacy settings.[15] In a Pew Internet Research project of Facebook use measured in both 2006 and 2012,

- 91% post a photo of themselves, up from 79% in 2006.
- 71% post their school name, up from 49%.
- 71% post the city or town where they live, up from 61%.
- 53% post their e-mail address, up from 29%.
- 20% post their cell phone number, up from 2%.[16]

This information may or may not be surprising, but it is certainly thought provoking. These "digital natives" are often "digital naives" who would benefit from more digital literacy education, including understanding the dangers, real and imagined, that their online presence might incur—including sexual predators, cyberbullying, and Internet addiction.[17] While teens want their privacy, and creating an online presence achieves that, parents want to know that their kids are safe. They worry about how their children are presenting themselves online and to whom. Many choices of parental monitoring software are on the market that allow parents to have control over what their teens see and do on websites, social media, gaming, and chat. However, as we will see in further chapters, these applications may be imperfect, and teens themselves can be creative in outsmarting them.

CHAPTER SUMMARY

Service to children and young adults is the gateway to library use and literacy for the whole family. Remembering that "kids are patrons, too" requires that all young people be treated with respect, using the concepts and skills of customer service, and recognizing that their needs are as legitimate as those of adults. Understanding the development of the young brain requires adjusting that service to the child's or teen's level of comprehension so that service to that population is both appropriate and thorough. They will be able to recognize and respond to diversity in user needs and preference for resources and services. Social media is a big part of their lives, and it is the responsibility of the LSS to stay current with emergent technologies. Libraries have an obligation to do all that they can to facilitate this access in a safe, nonthreatening environment.

DISCUSSION QUESTIONS AND ACTIVITIES

1. There is little doubt that libraries are important for children.
    a. How can this provide a gateway to adult library use?
2. When school budgets are tight, the library budget and media specialist position are often the first to be cut.
    a. Do you think that school libraries can be run successfully by teachers, LSS, or volunteers?
    b. Explain your answer.
3. If your community has adopted Common Core Standards in its schools, interview a local children's librarian.
    a. Find out if it has affected their collection policies.
    b. If so, how?
4. As the LSS tasked with creating a teen space in your library:
    a. How can you make the library more teen friendly?
    b. What specifically would you do?
5. The use of social media by children and teens can be problematic.
    a. What can the LSS do to promote its positive use?

NOTES

1. Common Core State Standards Initiative, "About the Standards," Common Core State Standards Initiative: Preparing America's Students for College and Career, http://www.core standards.org/about-the-standards/.

2. Carolyn Miller, Kathryn Zickuhr, Lee Rainie, and Kristen Purcell, "Parents, Children, Libraries, and Reading," Pew Internet and American Life Project, last modified May 1, 2013, http://libraries.pewinternet.org/2013/05/01/parents-children-libraries-and-reading/.

3. Karen Muller, "First School Library?," *karenmuller's blog*, American Library Association, http://www.ala.org/tools/first-school-library.

4. Kay Bishop and Anthony Salveggi, "Responding to Developmental Stages in Reference Service to Children," *Public Libraries*, October/November 2001, 354–58.

5. Jennifer Wallender, "The Common Core State Standards in American Public Education: Historical Underpinnings and Justifications," *Delta Kappa Gamma Bulletin* 80, no. 4 (Summer 2014): 7–11, http://search.ebscohost.com/login.aspx?direct=true&db=mfi&AN=96688858&site=eds-live.

6. Olga Nesi, "The Public Library Connection: The New Standards Require That Public and School Librarians Pull Together on Common Core," *School Library Journal* 58, no. 12 (December 2012): 20.

7. Betsy Diamant-Cohen, *Mother Goose on the Loose: A Handbook and CD-ROM Kit with Scripts, Rhymes, Songs, Flannel-Board Patterns, and Activities for Promoting Early Childhood Development* (New York: Neal-Schuman, 2006).

8. Judith Rovenger, "The Bottom Line: Reflections on the Role of Youth Services Librarian," *School Library Journal* 49, no. 12 (December 2003): 42–43.

9. Allyson Evans, "How Understanding Teen Brain Development Can Help Improve YA Reference Services," *Young Adult Library Services* 12, no. 3 (2014): 12–14.

10. Patrick Jones, "Connecting Young Adults and Libraries in the 21st Century," *APLIS* 20, no. 2 (June 2007): 12–14.

11. Karen Cornell Gomberg, *Books Appeal: Get Teenagers into the School Library* (Jefferson, NC: McFarland, 1987).

12. "Social Media," in *Merriam-Webster Online: Dictionary and Thesaurus*, http://www.merriam-webster.com/.

13. danah boyd, *It's Complicated: The Social Life of Networked Teens* (New Haven, CT: Yale University Press, 2014), 6.

14. American Library Association, "YALSA's Competencies for Librarians Serving Youth: Young Adults Deserve the Best," Young Adult Library Services Association, last modified January 2010, http://www.ala.org/yalsa/guidelines/yacompetencies2010.

15. Sarah Bayliss, "Teen Social Media Use Rising," *Library Journal* 38, no. 11 (June 15, 2013): 28.

16. Mary Madden, Amanda Lenhart, Sandra Cortesi, Urs Gasser, Maeve Duggan, Aaron Smith, and Meredith Beaton, "Teens, Social Media, and Privacy," Pew Research Center, last modified May 21, 2013, http://www.pewinternet.org/2013/05/21/teens-social-media-and-privacy/.

17. boyd, *It's Complicated*, 22.

REFERENCES, SUGGESTED READINGS, AND WEBSITES

American Library Association. "National Teen Space Guidelines." Young Adult Library Services Association. Last modified May 2012. http://www.ala.org/yalsa/sites/ala.org.yalsa/files/content/guidelines/guidelines/teenspaces.pdf.

———. "YALSA Fact Sheet." Young Adult Library Services Association. http://www.ala.org/yalsa/aboutyalsa/yalsafactsheet.

———. "YALSA's Competencies for Librarians Serving Youth: Young Adults Deserve the Best." Young Adult Library Services Association. Last modified January 2010. http://www.ala.org/yalsa/guidelines/yacompetencies2010.

Barack, Lauren. "Using Social Media to Engage Teens in the Library." *The Digital Shift*, July 10, 2013.

Bayliss, Sarah. "Teen Social Media Use Rising." *Library Journal* 38, no. 11 (June 15, 2013): 28.

Bishop, Kay, and Anthony Salveggi. "Responding to Developmental Stages in Reference Service to Children." *Public Libraries*, October/November 2001, 354–58.

boyd, danah. *It's Complicated: The Social Life of Networked Teens*. New Haven, CT: Yale University Press, 2014.

Braun, Linda W. "Who Is the Customer?" *YALSA Blog*. Last modified August 15, 2008. http://yalsa.ala.org/blog/2008/08/15/who-is-the-customer/.

Common Core Standards. http://www.corestandards.org/.

Common Core State Standards Initiative. "About the Standards." Common Core State Standards Initiative: Preparing America's Students for College and Career. http://corestandards.org/about-the-standards.

Diamant-Cohen, Betsy. *Mother Goose on the Loose: A Handbook and CD-ROM Kit with Scripts, Rhymes, Songs, Flannel-Board Patterns, and Activities for Promoting Early Childhood Development*. New York: Neal-Schuman, 2006.

Eberhart, George, ed. *The Whole Library Handbook*. 5th ed. Chicago: American Library Association, 2013.

Evans, Allyson. "How Understanding Teen Brain Development Can Help Improve YA Reference Services." *Young Adult Library Services* 12, no. 3 (2014): 12–14.

Gromberg, Karen Cornell. *Books Appeal: Get Teenagers into the School Library*. Jefferson, NC: McFarland, 1987.

Hofschire, Linda, and Meghan Wanucha. "Public Library Websites and Social Media." *Computers in Libraries* 34, no. 8 (October 2014): 4–9.

Jones, Patrick. "Connecting Young Adults and Libraries in the 21st Century." *APLIS* 20, no. 2 (June 2007): 48–54.

Madden, Mary, Amanda Lenhart, Sandra Cortesi, Urs Gasser, Maeve Duggan, Aaron Smith, and Meredith Beaton. "Teens, Social Media, and Privacy." Pew Research Center. Last modified May 21, 2013. http://www.pewinternet.org/2013/05/21/teens-social-media-and-privacy/.

Miller, Carolyn, Kathryn Zickuhr, Lee Rainie, and Kristen Purcell. "Parents, Children, Libraries, and Reading." Pew Internet and American Life Project. Last modified May 1, 2013. http://libraries.pewinternet.org/2013/05/01/parents-children-libraries-and-reading/.

Muller, Karen. "First School Library?" *karenmuller's blog*, American Library Association. http://www.ala.org/tools/blog/419.

The National. "Think Time: Teens and Social Networks." YouTube. https://www.youtube.com/watch?v=7QWoP6jJG3k.

Neary, Lynn. "Talk, Sing, Read, Write, Play: How Libraries Reach Kids before They Can Read." National Public Radio. December 30, 2014. http://www.npr.org/2014/12/30/373783189/talk-sing-read-write-play-how-libraries-reach-kids-before-they-can-read.

Nesi, Olga. "The Public Library Connection: The New Standards Require That Public and School Librarians Pull Together on Common Core." *School Library Journal* 58, no. 12 (December 2012): 20.

Quenk, Rachel, and Wilda W. Williams. *Do It Right! Best Practices for Serving Young Adults in School and Public Libraries*. New York: Neal Schuman, 2001.

Rockefeller, Elsworth. "Effectively Managing Teen Services Departments in Public Libraries: Basic Steps for Success." *Young Adult Library Services* 12, no. 1 (Fall 2013): 16–19.

Rovenger, Judith. "The Bottom Line: Reflections on the Role of Youth Services Librarian." *School Library Journal* 49, no. 12 (December 2003): 42–43.

"Social Media." In *Merriam-Webster Online: Dictionary and Thesaurus*. http://www.merriam-webster.com.

TopTenREVIEWS. "2015 Best Parental Software Reviews: Reviews and Comparisons." Top-TenREVIEWS. http://parental-software-review.toptenreviews.com/.

Wallender, Jennifer. "The Common Core State Standards in American Public Education: Historical Underpinnings and Justifications." *Delta Kappa Gamma Bulletin* 80, no. 4 (Summer 2014): 7–11. http://search.ebscohost.com/login.aspx?direct=true&db=mfi&AN=96688858&site=eds-live.

Wittig, Corey, Jack Martin, and Adrienne Stock. "Library Service for Teens: Who Are We? What Are We? And, Where Are We Going?" *Young Adult Library Services* 13, no. 1 (Fall 2014): 4–6.

YALSA1957. "YALSA Academy: Creating a Great Space for Teens." YouTube. https://www.youtube.com/watch?v=u48E_lJriP8.

CHAPTER 9

Customer Service to Older Adults

Library support staff (LSS) will know the basic concepts and skills of customer service. They will be able to recognize and respond to diversity in user needs and preference for resources and services. (ALA-LSSC Competencies #9, #11)

Topics Covered in This Chapter:

- The Older Adult
- Resources for the Active Older Patron
- Older Adults and Internet Use
- Services to the Homebound
- Outreach to Assisted Living and Nursing Homes

Key Terms:

Active older adults: Active older adults are those individuals (usually fifty-five and older) who have little or no physical or cognitive impairment and maintain a healthy and active lifestyle.

Baby boomers: "Baby boomers" is the name given to those born between 1946 and 1964. They are so named because of the increase in births in the years following World War II. As of 2012, they made up close to one quarter of the U.S. population.

Bi-Folkal kits: Bi-Folkal kits are themed multisensory kits designed to encourage older people to reminisce and create connections. This is just one of the ways that libraries can provide outreach to the older adult or the elderly.

Homebound: The homebound are those who, for reasons of infirmity or lack of mobility, cannot come to the library. Libraries then must consider strategies to reach this segment where they live, be it home, a retirement community, or a nursing facility.

Older adults: Older adults are people generally considered to be of retirement age, usually sixty-five and older. They make up an important library demographic as they may have more time to spend using the library.

THE OLDER ADULT

Who is an "older adult"? There is no single answer to this question, and the older one is, the higher that elusive number seems to get. The American Association of Retired Persons (AARP)[1] considers the answer to be age fifty, but very few people are actually retired at that age—nor would they consider themselves an "older adult." The senior center in my town considers it to be fifty-five. Depending on what year one was born, the Social Security Administration deems it to be sixty-six, the age at which one is entitled to full retirement benefits. However, one can apply for benefits as early as age sixty-two.

Some years ago I offered the senior center newsletter to a very dignified eighty-plus-year-old woman, who thanked me but refused it, saying that the senior center was for old people! Older adults can be identified more by their interests and abilities than their ages. There are a plethora of articles debating whether sixty is the new forty, but the fact is that "in 2011, the first of the baby boomers reached what used to be known as retirement age. And for the next 18 years, boomers will be turning 65 at a rate of about 8,000 a day."[2] Many people in their fifties, sixties, seventies, and beyond are active and productive members of society and are also library users. Age may be a state of mind for many, but that doesn't mean that their needs aren't changing. It's up to the library to anticipate ways in which we can meet those needs. "Libraries are in a position to offer something that few other institutions are providing: intellectual stimulation and forums for sharing thoughtful ideas. We've seen that lifelong learning opportunities don't have to stop when you retire. In fact, lifelong learning becomes more important than ever when people have the luxury of more time."[3]

RESOURCES FOR THE ACTIVE OLDER PATRON

As was mentioned in a previous chapter, a library must be familiar with its demographic before it can make any plans for resources and services. Providing for the needs of older adults is probably not a priority for special, academic, or school libraries but will certainly be a priority for public libraries. As the population ages, these needs will become evident. In 2012, *Library Journal* produced a multipart study called "Patron Profiles." Their statement "as baby boomers age, the 61–80 cohort will be expanding for the next decade"[4] is predictive of how libraries must plan to provide for the older adult.

It is important that the LSS not stereotype older patrons. Age alone does not automatically confer infirmity or prevent patrons from driving or walking to the library. This is what is meant by **"active" older adults**. They are perfectly capable of using

TARGETED SERVICES FOR OLDER ADULTS

1. Ensure that the special needs and interests of older adults in your community are reflected in the library's collections, programs, and services.
2. Make the library's collections and physical facilities safe, comfortable, and inviting for all older adults.
3. Consider providing at least one wheelchair in the library for public use.
4. Make the library a focal point for information services to older adults.
5. Cooperate with local agencies on aging, senior nutrition programs, senior volunteer programs, and others in this service provider network by advertising their services and making their publications and other information more readily accessible.

the library and have little or no physical or cognitive impairment. In fact, the first thing the library may want to consider when planning outreach to older adults is to ask them what they want. Just as we have created teen advisory groups, why not create one for older adults? Let them decide on the services that would make their library use more convenient.

We should take a good look at the spaces used by all patrons but particularly those used by older adults. Be sure that there are chairs placed where they may need to sit while browsing and tables or other clear surfaces for them to place their books. One of my pet peeves in the grocery store is that displays of new products are often placed on the outer edges of the aisles where people are walking with shopping carts. It makes navigating those aisles difficult. Now think about the aisles in the library. Anything that impedes access for the older adult may discourage them from even using that part of the library. We will address issues of mobility and disabilities in depth in another chapter.

Evaluate your shelving as well. Traditional shelves require that books and other materials be placed at very high or very low levels, requiring bending or lifting. While you may not be able to avoid this arrangement, be aware of your patrons' abilities to reach these materials, especially in the large-print collection. Having stepstools or ladders may be fine for younger patrons but can present a hazard for older patrons. This is where the LSS can provide excellent customer service by being aware of what the patrons are looking for and being available to assist them.

Even the most active of older adults may have some impairment of vision, hearing, or mobility. Signage should be clearly printed and well placed. Take a look at the spine labels on the materials—are they large enough to be read without magnification? Figure 9.1 shows regular-size spine labels next to larger labels on large-print books.

At the reference desk, be sure to have pencil and paper in order to better communicate with the patron who may have some hearing impairment. Be patient with the patron who may not be walking as quickly as others. An arthritic hip or a bum knee may slow a person down but does not detract from their status as valued and, yes, active older patrons. Some of my favorite patrons over the years were older women,

Figure 9.1.   Regular and Large-Print Spine Labels. *Photograph courtesy of the Bill Memorial Library*

some in their nineties, who drove themselves to the library and read voraciously. One such gracious lady brought us tiny bouquets from her garden of the first lily of the valley of the season; another baked gingerbread men for us every Christmas. (That they were inedible was beside the point.)

Such active older adults are a valuable resource for the library. They are frequent library visitors and have a great appreciation for the staff, collection, and the library in general. Figure 9.2 shows the level of satisfaction of older adults compared to other age groups.

There are dozens of great programming ideas that would appeal to the active older adult population. My experience has been that some older people prefer not to drive at night—this is certainly something to take into consideration when planning activities for this age group. Depending on the time of year, early evening programs can be over with before dark, but afternoons are a good alternative in order to offer a diverse range of programs. The Reference Services Section of the American Library Association, in a posting called "Library Services to an Aging Population," offers "21 Ideas for the 21st Century" suitable for senior patrons (see textbox on page 116).[5]

It's helpful if the library has adequate program space for these activities, although some can take up little to no room. Just as we have created teen spaces, why not explore a dedicated "senior" area? Few libraries have the luxury of extra space, but a little creativity can co-opt an existing space. If your library has a community room, perhaps it can be booked for a specific time for these activities.

Another avenue to explore for the active older adult is gaming. Assuming that your library is successful in attracting this age group to other programs and events,

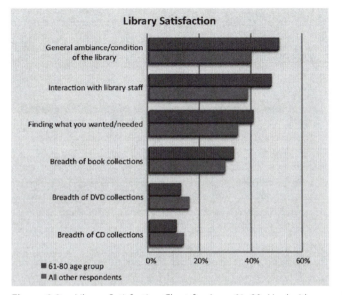

Figure 9.2. Library Satisfaction Chart for Ages 61–80. *Used with permission from* Library Journal Patron Profiles *July 2012*

gaming offers yet another option. Gaming provides stress relief and sociability. "Gaming has many documented benefits for seniors: it can engage their interests, get their competitive juices flowing, facilitate computer proficiency and work their muscles both mentally (Brain Age) and physically (WiiFit)."[6] Games such as *Wii Fit Plus, Big Brain Academy: Wii Degree, Wii Sports Resort*—even *Dance, Dance Revolution* or *Dancing with the Stars* can appeal to active older adults. A library in my community offers a regular Wii bowling league.

Board games are also popular and mentally stimulating. They run the gamut from the classics—checkers, chess, cribbage, and card games—to designer board games that can be thematic or strategic and encourage tactical decision making. "Designer board games promote creativity, invoke multi-generational interaction, increase social engagement, and have the potential to be thought-provoking, challenging and, of course, fun. But even more than that, designer board games build a culture of positive interaction between sometimes disparate ages and social groups."[7] Ideas can be found at the local game store, toy store, or by sharing ideas with colleagues in other libraries.

Offering such programs can be rewarding but can also be a drain on staff time. Friends of the Library and other volunteers are a good source of personnel; engaging older children and teens creates instant intergenerational programs as well.

OLDER ADULTS AND INTERNET USE

As we saw in chapter 1, library users tend to fall into two categories: digital natives and digital immigrants. The older adult certainly falls into the latter category, but we saw that many have become technologically fluent and have adapted to all that

TWENTY-ONE IDEAS FOR THE 21ST CENTURY

- Host a class on internet resources. Class ideas could include:
  - Basic web searching
  - Genealogy on the internet
  - How to avoid internet "scams"
  - Financial information on the web
  - Become a Secret Shopper
- Offer medical programming done by medical professionals.
- Sponsor an intergenerational community history project.
- Provide Senior Adult "storytimes" at senior centers, nursing homes, retirement communities, etc.
- Initiate a quilting program—create a historical/commemorative quilt.
- Sponsor an intergenerational photo contest.
- Offer programs on Burma Shave signs, local trivia, music boxes, WWII.
- Start an oral history project.
- Have a musical program: outdoor band concert, big band music, local school group.
- Contact someone to start a discussion group for seniors or caregivers.
- Offer the library as a place for support groups to meet.
- Sponsor a home safety program.
- Provide programs on Social Security, Medicare, taxes.
- Host a Mad Hatter's Tea.
- Offer a consumers series.
- Have a show of wedding fashions from the 30s and 40s.
- Start a recipe exchange.
- Sponsor a "sock hop" with live music or a DJ and a dance instructor.
- Provide library space for displays of crafts and hobbies, and for recreational activities.
- Host tax counseling services for seniors.—Call the IRS or AARP to set it up.
- Establish Senior Day in your community.

Used with permission from the American Library Association

technology has to offer. A Pew Research project conducted in 2012 found that half of those over the age of sixty-five were using e-mail or the Internet and it has become part of their daily routine (see figures 9.3 and 9.4).

Of this age group, one in three were using social media like Facebook and LinkedIn (figure 9.5). Their reasons are primarily to stay in touch with family, as opposed to younger people who reach out to friends.

Older adults own and use cell phones as well, although smartphone use is not as prevalent, and all use drops after age seventy-five. Still, these findings are very encouraging for libraries as it reinforces the idea that libraries can reach all age groups in appropriate ways.[8]

Internet use by age group, 2000-2012

% of American adults age 18+ who use the internet

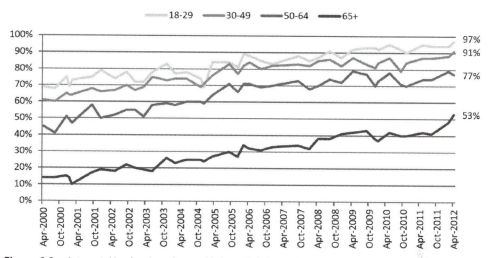

Figure 9.3. Internet Use by Age Group. *Kathryn Zickuhr and Mary Madden, "Older Adults and Internet Use," Pew Research Center, last modified June 6, 2012, accessed December 21, 2014, http://pewinternet.org/ Reports/2012/Older-adults-and-internet-use.aspx. Used with permission from the Pew Research Center*

Email use by age group

% of adult internet users in each age group who use email

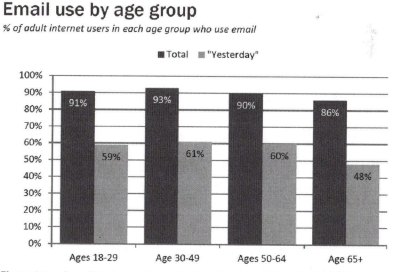

Figure 9.4. E-mail Use by Age Group. *Kathryn Zickuhr and Mary Madden, "Older Adults and Internet Use," Pew Research Center, last modified June 6, 2012, accessed December 21, 2014, http://pewinternet.org/Reports/2012/Older-adults-and-internet-use.aspx. Used with permission from the Pew Research Center*

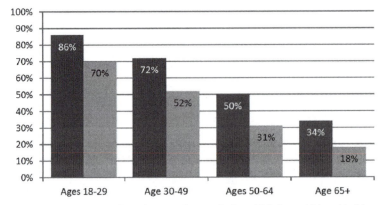

Social networking site use by age group

% of adult internet users in each age group who use social networking sites

■ Total   ▨ "Yesterday"

Figure 9.5.   Social Networking by Age Group. *Kathryn Zickuhr and Mary Madden, "Older Adults and Internet Use," Pew Research Center, last modified June 6, 2012, accessed December 21, 2014, http://pewinternet.org/Reports/2012/Older-adults-and-internet-use .aspx. Used with permission from the Pew Research Center*

SERVICE TO THE HOMEBOUND

There are patrons who cannot physically get to the library. Some may not have transportation, and the library is not within walking distance or is not on the bus line. Some may have health issues that prevent them from leaving their homes, including physical disabilities. Not to be confused with remote users who are technologically capable and who choose to use library services from home, these people are truly **homebound**. Their physical status should not, however, deprive them of the use of library services.

Many older adults fall into this category. For as many seventy-, eighty- and ninety-year-olds who are still driving, there are just as many who must rely on others to transport them. They may have family or friends who can drive them to doctor appointments, the grocery store, the pharmacy, and so on, and these friends may also be able take them to the library. However, many older people do not want to impose on their friends for anything other than the basics. For this reason, many libraries provide service to the homebound.

This service, quite simply, consists of delivering materials to patrons. It can be a formal program of the Friends of the Library group or other volunteers that follows a schedule of who drives on various days of the week and to which parts of town. It also can be as informal as a staff member dropping a book off on the way home to a patron in the neighborhood. The number of patrons who need this service will dictate how the program is run in any given library. In my former library, we only had two or three patrons at any given time who needed this service. For some patrons, it was a matter of dropping off a book or CD that came up on reserve for them. Other patrons routinely called in with a list of titles that they would like to read, including those that needed to be obtained through interlibrary loan (ILL).

Their ages and states of health did not impact their desire to read some of the most interesting books that have come across our desks. That they welcomed a visit from the library representative is an added bonus for both the LSS and the patron.

Service to the homebound is not without its problems. Some libraries refuse to issue library cards unless the patron can appear in person with a valid form of ID—impossible for some. The confidentiality rules in some libraries may prevent adult children from creating and accessing their elder parents' library accounts. Libraries need to realize that serving an ageing population requires revisiting arbitrary rules and coming up with creative ways to get materials into the hands of homebound seniors.

Some older patrons may be homebound by choice. They may begin to feel uncomfortable leaving home, insecure about driving, or fearful of the traffic that they encounter crossing streets on the way to the library. They may prefer to have their children—boomers themselves—do their errands for them. In a research project conducted by Wendy Robbins, a Canadian librarian, she found that

> participants in my study generally didn't accompany their elderly relatives and friends to the library. Instead, they became mediators for the library experience. They registered elders for services, and they borrowed and returned elders' books and CDs. One consulted reference librarians and used the library's Internet access for querying government departments on behalf of a parent. One placed online audiobook holds for a vision-impaired friend; the friend then walked to a branch to pick them up. Study participants appreciated being able to have access to their elders' library accounts, and were pleased to find reference librarians who could help with parents' tax and pension issues.[9]

Not all homebound patrons are isolated. Many have Internet access to the library's catalog and databases and are able to take care of their own accounts, research their own questions, and can participate in electronic communication and social media. But for the truly homebound older patron with limited contact with the outside world, home delivery can be a lifesaver.

OUTREACH TO ASSISTED LIVING AND NURSING HOMES

Those in assisted living communities are not necessarily homebound; many residents keep their cars and their mobility. Many assisted living communities also include a nursing home component, and independent skilled nursing facilities exist as well for those residents who can no longer live alone or who develop more serious health issues. Some of these facilities may have well-tended and well-stocked libraries. The administrators of such facilities often welcome a partnership arrangement with the local library in order to augment their collections and to provide programs to the residents. Public libraries can and do create circulating collections that are checked out to a nursing home for a period of time, say three months, for example. These library books are marked and identified as belonging to the local public library, and they circulate among the residents until it's time to return that particular collection for a set of new titles. Libraries can offer **Bi-Folkal kits**, which are multisensory programming kits, as well as books by mail, talking books, and Braille services. Details of these services will be addressed in the chapter on serving patrons with special needs.

The libraries of these facilities also may appreciate the donation of gently used books and audiobooks that may have been donated to the library but that cannot be used, or still-serviceable library discards, particularly large-print books. Another way LSS can reach out to assisted living and nursing homes is by volunteering to spend time reading to the residents. Being read to is a joy we never outgrow, and for the older adult or senior whose eyesight has failed, it can be a special gift.

This venue is yet another intergenerational opportunity for children and teens to pair with seniors to teach them computer skills, how to use Skype, how to download music, how to use a smartphone, or to simply visit. As suggested by Amanda Cavaleri, CEO of Capable Living, a holistic lifestyle concierge service that connects millennials with elders who need companionship, "One of the problems we're trying to solve is how to get high school and college grads to work with elders, at least for a couple of years, so the younger people can get the benefit of the elders' experience."[10] What a great model for LSS to create programs that bring young library patrons into assisted living and nursing home facilities. Studies show that both kids and seniors benefit from these interactions.[11]

The Reference Services Section of the American Library Association posting called "Library Services to an Aging Population," referenced earlier in this chapter,[12] offers a number of programming ideas that LSS can bring to a nursing home. Providing an adult story time would be of benefit, particularly to those whose cognitive skills may have deteriorated. The assisted living facility is the perfect venue for starting a program on journaling or an oral history project on a variety of topics. Bring in LSS from the local history section of the library to gather these oral history stories before they are lost. They can also begin a book discussion group or a discussion on current events or other topics of choice.

In an ideal world, there would be enough staff to do outreach and create every kind of program for our older adult population. The reality, of course, is that library resources are usually stretched quite thin for staff and resources. However, it is important to remember that older adults are still our library patrons, and we must make every effort to bring library services to them as best we can.

CHAPTER SUMMARY

Older adults make up a large segment of library users. Age does not imply infirmity, and the number of active older adults offers libraries a chance to develop programming specific to this population. Active older adults, in fact, can serve as a bridge to the homebound or nursing home residents. Including the library's children and teen patrons also provides an opportunity for intergenerational outreach and programing. Older adults are often loyal users; as such, they need to be accommodated and encouraged to remain patrons of the library. It is the job of the library and LSS to understand the basic concepts and skills of customer service. LSS able to recognize and respond to diversity in user needs and preference for resources and services can make sure that all available resources are explored so that outreach to the older adult becomes a regular part of library service.

DISCUSSION QUESTIONS AND ACTIVITIES

1. Examine the practices of your library or one you frequent toward serving the older patron.
   a. What are they doing well, and what could they be doing better?
2. What are some ways the LSS can make it easier for the older patron in the library?
3. Design a (hypothetical) intergenerational program for your local library and take into consideration:
   a. the library's resources, and
   b. the library's space limitations.

NOTES

1. American Association of Retired Persons, "Baby Boomers Turning 65," AARP.org, last modified November 12, 2014, http://www.aarp.org/personal-growth/transitions/boomers_65/.
2. American Association of Retired Persons, "Baby Boomers Turning 65."
3. Kathleen Mayo, "The Challenges and Opportunities of Serving America's Elders," American Library Association, last modified 2009, http://www.ala.org/offices/olos/olospro grams/jeanecoleman/index2.
4. Steve Paxhia and John Parsons, "Media Consumption and Library Use," *Library Journal, Patron Profiles* 1, no. 4 (July 2012): 22. Bold emphasis added.
5. Reference and User Services Association, "Library Services to an Aging Population: 21 Ideas for the 21st Century," American Library Association, http://www.ala.org/rusa/sections/rss/rsssection/rsscomm/libraryservage/ideas21stcentury.
6. Liz Danforth, "Kleiman on Gaming for Seniors," *Library Journal* 135, no. 15 (September 15, 2010): 44.
7. John Pappas, "Older Adults and Seniors," Webjunction.org, last modified December 30, 2013, http://www.webjunction.org/explore-topics/older-adults.html.
8. Kathryn Zickuhr and Mary Madden, "Older Adults and Internet Use," Pew Research Center, last modified June 6, 2012, http://pewinternet.org/Reports/2012/Older-adults-and-internet-use.aspx.
9. Wendy Robbins, "Baby Boomers, Their Elders and the Public Library," *Feliciter* 57, no. 6 (2011): 233–34.
10. Claire Martin, "Millennial Entrepreneur Makes a Career of Improving Life for Elders," *Denver Post*, last modified November 6, 2014. http://www.denverpost.com/lifestyles/ci_26874296/millennial-entrepreneur-makes-career-improving-life-elders.
11. Corita Brown and Nancy Henkin, "Building Communities for All Ages: Lessons Learned from an Intergenerational Community-Building Initiative," *Journal of Community & Applied Social Psychology* 24, no. 1 (January/February 2014): 61–68.
12. Reference and User Services Association, "Library Services to an Aging Population."

REFERENCES, SUGGESTED READINGS, AND WEBSITES

American Association of Retired Persons. "Baby Boomers Turning 65." AARP.org. Last modified November 12, 2014. http://www.aarp.org/personal-growth/transitions/boomers_65/.
Bi-Folkal Productions. http://www.bifolkal.org/.

Brown, Corita, and Nany Henkin. "Building Communities for All Ages: Lessons Learned from an Intergenerational Community-Building Initiative." *Journal of Community & Applied Social Psychology* 24, no. 1 (January/February 2014): 61–68.

Burek Pierce, Jennifer. "An Old Friend in the Library." *American Libraries* 43, no. 9/10 (September/October 2012): 16.

Capable Living. http://capableliving.com/.

Danforth, Liz. "Kleiman on Gaming for Seniors." *Library Journal* 135, no. 15 (September 15, 2010): 44.

Mabry, Celia Hales. "Serving Seniors: Dos and Don'ts at the Desk." *American Libraries* 34, no. 11 (December 2003): 64–65.

Martin, Claire. "Millennial Entrepreneur Makes a Career of Improving Life for Elders." *Denver Post*, last modified November 6, 2014. http://www.denverpost.com/lifestyles/ci_268742 96/millennial-entrepreneur-makes-career-improving-life-elders.

Mayo, Kathleen. "The Challenges and Opportunities of Serving America's Elders." American Library Association. Last modified 2009. http://www.ala.org/offices/olos/olosprograms/ jeanecoleman/index2.

National Library for the Blind and Physically Handicapped. http://www.loc.gov/nls/.

Pappas, John. "Older Adults and Seniors." Webjunction.org. Last modified December 30, 2013. http://www.webjunction.org/explore-topics/older-adults.html.

Paxhia, Steve, and John Parsons. "Media Consumption and Library Use." *Library Journal, Patron Profiles* 1, no. 4 (July 2012): 22–26. *Patron Profiles, Understanding the Behavior and Preferences of U.S. Public Library Users* is a four-part series published by *Library Journal* in 2012. Each volume concerns a different aspect of this study. Analysis by Steve Paxhia and John Parsons; Rebecca T. Miller, *Patron Profiles* series editor.

Reference and User Services Association. "Library Services to an Aging Population: 21 Ideas for the 21st Century." American Library Association. http://www.ala.org/rusa/sections/rss/ rsssection/rsscomm/libraryservage/ideas21stcentury.

Robbins, Wendy. "Baby Boomers, Their Elders and the Public Library." *Feliciter* 57, no. 6 (2011): 233–34.

Young, Scott H. "15 Steps to Cultivate Lifelong Learning." *Lifehack* (blog). http://www.life hack.org/articles/lifestyle/15-steps-to-cultivate-lifelong-learning.html.

Zickuhr, Kathryn, and Mary Madden. "Older Adults and Internet Use." Pew Research Center. Last modified June 6, 2012. http://pewinternet.org/Reports/2012/Older-adults-and -internet-use.aspx.

CHAPTER 10

Customer Service to Patrons with Special Needs

Library support staff (LSS) will know the basic concepts and skills of customer service. They will be able to recognize and respond to diversity in user needs and preference for resources and services. (ALA-LSSC Competencies #9, #11)

Topics Covered in This Chapter:

- The Americans with Disabilities Act
- Practical Applications
- Adaptive Technology

Key Terms:

Adaptive technology: Adaptive technologies are methods of making visually or audibly delivered materials available to individuals with those impairments, such as magnified screens, closed-captioning, and enhanced telecommunications devices. It also relates to provisions for physical disabilities.

Disability: A disability is a physical or mental impairment that substantially limits one or more major life activities of such individuals, such as having difficulties with mobility, speech, or hearing.

Discrimination: Discrimination means limiting, segregating, or classifying someone in a way that adversely affects the opportunities or status of that person. LSS must learn to treat all individuals equally, regardless of ethnicity, physical ability, or economic status.

Handicap: A handicap is a situation or barrier imposed by society or the environment, such as too-narrow doorways or curbs that are too high for a wheelchair, doors that are difficult to open, or signage that is too small to read.

THE AMERICANS WITH DISABILITIES ACT

The Americans with Disabilities Act, or the ADA, was passed in 1991 as an act of Congress and bans **discrimination** against the approximately fifty-seven million Americans—19 percent of the population—who are hearing impaired, legally blind, epileptic, paralyzed, developmentally disabled, speech impaired, mentally impaired, and HIV positive. It applies to anyone with a condition that substantially limits one's life actions.[1]

Most of these provisions went into effect in 1992, which meant that businesses were required to remove physical barriers and assist communication and that new buildings had to be totally physically accessible. It was amended in 2008 to shift the focus from whether an employee had a **disability** to whether the employer had made reasonable accommodations. Exceptions are made for existing businesses with fewer than fifteen employees. An employer is required to make a

> reasonable accommodation to the known disability of a qualified applicant or employee if it would not impose an undue hardship on the operation of the employer's business. Reasonable accommodations are adjustments or modifications provided by an employer to enable people with disabilities to enjoy equal employment opportunities. Accommodations vary depending upon the needs of the individual applicant or employee. Not all people with disabilities (or even all people with the same disability) will require the same accommodation.[2]

Examples of this would include a deaf applicant requiring an interpreter for an interview, a diabetic employee needing breaks to monitor blood sugar, or an employee with cancer needing time off for treatments. However, as mentioned above, an employer does not have to provide reasonable accommodations if it imposes undue hardship relative to the size of the business or the number of employees.

There are no specific remedies, penalties, or guidelines in the law itself. Complaints may be made to the Equal Employment Opportunity Commission, or the employee may file a lawsuit against the offending business. Businesses are then required to make reasonable efforts, but changes requiring "undue hardship," such as significant difficulty or expense, may not be required. If, however, the law finds in favor of the employee, they may then be entitled to reinstatement, back pay, attorney's fees, and other costs. Intentional violation of the law may incur financial penalties or other punitive damages to the offending business.[3]

PRACTICAL APPLICATIONS

One of the most important changes brought about by awareness of the ADA is in our language. The textbox on page 125, adapted from an information sheet produced by the Pacer Center: Champions for Children with Disabilities in Minnesota,[4] illustrates these changes.

Not every disability is physical or easily identifiable. LSS must learn considerations in meeting everyone's needs effectively. Everyone should be spoken to directly and normally; one should never "talk down" to someone. Provide clear signage and good lighting and keep aisles clear, as was mentioned earlier. Other suggestions follow on page 126.

IT'S THE PERSON FIRST, NOT THE DISABILITY

What do you see first: the wheelchair, the cane, the person? If you saw someone in a wheelchair unable to get up the stairs into a building, would you say "there is a handicapped person unable to find the ramp," or would you say "there is a person with a disability who is handicapped by an inaccessible building"?

Consider how you introduce someone who doesn't have a disability. You would say "this is my friend Jane Doe, she lives in my neighborhood and likes movies and going out to lunch." Why say it differently for a person with disabilities? Everyone has characteristics—mental and physical—and few want to be identified only by their ability to play tennis, or by the mole on their face. Those are just parts of us.

Here are a few tips for improving your language related to disabilities:

1. Speak of the person first, then the disability.
2. Emphasize abilities, not limitations.
3. Do not label people as part of a group—"the disabled"—rather, "people with disabilities."
4. Don't give excessive praise or attention to a person with a disability—in other words, don't patronize them.
5. Choice and independence are important: let the person speak for herself.
6. A *disability* is a functional limitation that interferes with a person's ability to walk, talk, hear, etc. Use *handicap* to describe a situation or barrier.

Say this:	*Instead of this:*
Person with a disability	Disabled or handicapped person
Person with cerebral palsy	Palsied, or spastic
Person without speech, nonverbal	Mute or dumb
Person with emotional disorder or mental illness	Crazy, insane
Person who is deaf or hard of hearing	Deaf and dumb
Person who uses a wheelchair	Confined to a wheelchair
Person with retardation	Retarded
Person with epilepsy	Epileptic
Person with Down syndrome	Mongoloid
Person who has a learning disability	Is learning disabled
Person who is nondisabled	Normal, healthy
Person who has a physical disability	Crippled
Person with a congenital disability	Birth defect
Person with a condition	Disease
Person who has seizures	Fits
Person who has a cleft lip	Harelip
Person who has a chronic illness	Sickly
Person who is paralyzed	Invalid or paralytic
Person of short stature	Midget, dwarf

Reprinted with permission from PACER Center, Minneapolis, MN

When speaking with a person with retardation:

- be positive;
- speak slowly and distinctly;
- show and explain;
- treat the adult patron as an adult with a need for simplified materials.

When speaking with a person who stutters:

- relax and give them time;
- do not try to complete the person's words, sentences, or thoughts;
- listen carefully.

When speaking with someone who speaks a foreign language:

- be familiar with the cultures in your area, their values and traditions;
- become familiar with easy phrases to help you converse;
- determine who on the staff or in the community can help if so needed;
- listen carefully for words that sound like their English equivalents;
- do not raise your voice—speaking louder won't make the patron understand you better.

When speaking with a person with a hearing impairment:

- speak clearly and do not mumble;
- speak in a normal voice and avoid shouting;
- face the patron so that he or she can see your face and lips;
- try using different words or phrases as some pitches and timbres are easier for some to hear;
- keep paper and pencil handy.

When speaking with someone with limited vision:

- have magnifiers available;
- provide good lighting;
- offer to read pertinent information out loud.

When speaking with someone who is blind:

- introduce yourself and get the patron's name;
- use the patron's name so it is clear that you are speaking to him or her;
- avoid gestures and use words instead;
- do not touch or guide them without their permission;
- if you receive such permission, offer your arm and walk a half step ahead and warn of barriers.

The best way to meet everyone's needs effectively is to treat them as you would want to be treated.

ADAPTIVE TECHNOLOGY

The LSS must be able to assist all patrons in finding resources in the library. It is helpful to look around the facility through the eyes of someone with limitations. Do the doors open in or out? Is there an automatic door opener? Buildings should have doorways without thresholds that are wide enough for a wheelchair to pass through. Public restrooms should have enough room to navigate a wheelchair or other equipment and have grab bars. The aisles in the library need to be wide enough to accommodate wheelchairs, barriers should be removed, and the circulation and information desks need to be at a height that works for everyone; some desks may have a lower surface for people of short stature or who use a wheelchair. For those patrons who have hearing impairments, it is helpful to provide pencil and

Figure 10.1. Adaptive DVD Box. *Photograph courtesy of the Groton Public Library*

paper to assist communication. Drive-up returns and Redbox-style DVD services are also helpful to the patron with disabilities.

Older library buildings are more likely to have structural barriers. The building that I worked in for many years was built in 1890. The front doors opened in rather than out, there were raised thresholds in every doorway, and the bathroom was barely accessible even to the nondisabled. As inaccessible as it was, this library was exempt from ADA compliance because it employed fewer than fifteen people. However, when an addition was built in 1994, all of the renovations were then subject to ADA approvals. Fortunately, it had generous doorways that did not need any remediation. The thresholds were allowed to stay because they were low and a wheelchair could navigate them. The restroom was expanded in order to accommodate equipment and grab bars. Because of the physical structure, it was impossible to turn the doors around to open outward, but these were "grandfathered" (exempt from new regulations) because it was a historic structure. Shelving was rearranged in order to create wider aisles, and a ramp was installed in order to provide building access for those with mobility issues. Since the upper floor was not used by the public, the library did not have to install an elevator. Because of the historical nature of the building, some access issues remain, but the library staff does a wonderful job of making sure that all users are accommodated to the best of their ability.

Besides the condition and adaptations of the physical plant, there are other resources the LSS must be aware of in order to help patrons with special needs. We call these assistive or **adaptive technologies**. "They are applied to aids that either assist the user in accessing a library resource or adapt that resource in such a way that it becomes usable."[5]

For the visually impaired patron, one of the first things that comes to mind is large-type materials. These are books, newspapers, and magazines that use a readable font made up of straight lines with a type size of eighteen or larger.[6] Libraries will usually have a collection of books on CD as well, in which a work of fiction or nonfiction is narrated and dramatized for the reader to listen to. For those who have hearing impairments, adaptive technology provides closed-captions or subtitles for television and movies in DVD and Blu-ray.

The Library for the Blind and Physically Handicapped is another valuable resource.

> The Library for the Blind has over 60,000 titles of general reading material, much the same as a public library, in both audio and braille formats. The service is sponsored by the Library of Congress, National Service for the Blind and Physically Handicapped at no cost of any kind to the patron. Equipment and books are loaned to the patron and usually delivered by the U.S. Postal System as Free Matter for the Blind.[7]

Talking books require a special playback device, and even materials downloadable through the National Library Service (NLS) Braille and Audio Reading Download (BARD) must be transferred to one of these machines (see figure 10.2). Materials are generally current and bestselling titles and are available for all age groups.[8] Other available equipment includes handheld video magnifiers such as the Ruby Reader and several types of binocular spectacles (see figures 10.3 and 10.4).

As noted, materials are also available in Braille, a system of raised dots that represent letters, numbers, and punctuation marks (see figure 10.6). Created by Louis Braille, who lost his sight as a child in nineteenth-century France, it is not a separate language but a code that allows an alternative way to read and write. Materials in Braille can also be downloaded through BARD.

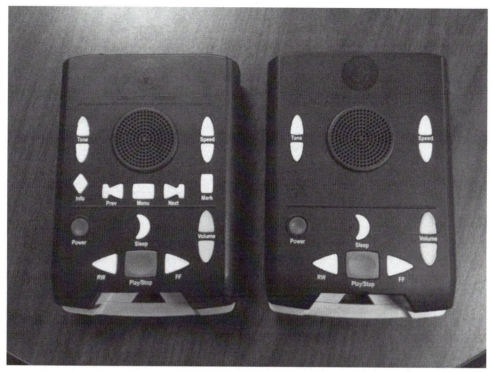

Figure 10.2. Digital Talking-Book Machines. *Used with permission from the CT Library for the Blind and Physically Handicapped*

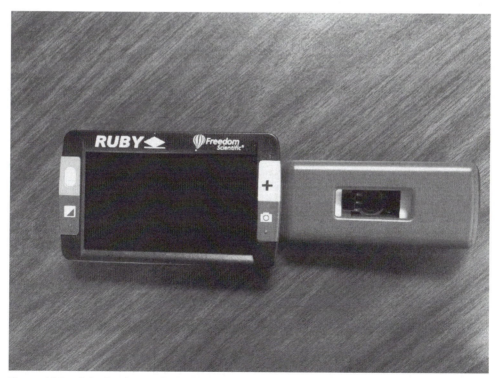

Figure 10.3. Ruby Reader Handheld Magnifier. *Used with permission from the CT Library for the Blind and Physically Handicapped*

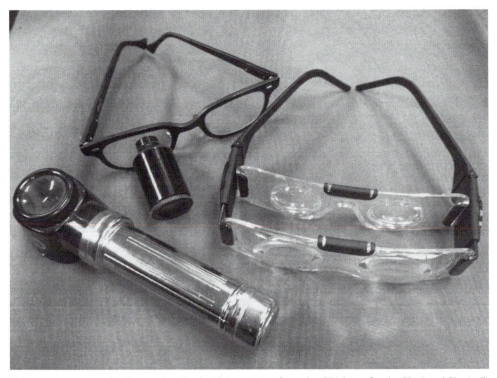

Figure 10.4. Binocular Spectacles. *Used with permission from the CT Library for the Blind and Physically Handicapped*

Programs can be purchased for screen magnification, for example, JAWS, Window Eyes, Zoom-Text, and BigShot magnification software. Text-to-speech devices—Kurzweil, Natural Reader, ReadSpeaker, and Yakitome—are also useful, as they can convert any written text, webpage, or e-mail, for example, to spoken word. Physical screen magnifiers can also be placed over the monitor for amplification of text up to one and a half times. Low-vision aids, from hand magnifiers to spectacle magnifiers to standing

Braille Alphabet

| | a | b | c | d | e | f | g | h | i | j |

The six dots of the braille cell are arranged and numbered: (1 4 / 2 5 / 3 6)

| | k | l | m | n | o | p | q | r | s | t |

The capital sign, dot 6, placed before a letter makes a capital letter. (1 4 / 2 5 / 3 6)

| | u | v | w | x | y | z | Capital Sign | Number Sign | Period | Comma |

The number sign, dots 3, 4, 5, 6, placed before the characters a through j, makes the numbers 1 through 0. For example: a preceded by the number sign is 1, b is 2, etc.

National Library Service for the Blind and Physically Handicapped
LIBRARY OF CONGRESS

Figure 10.5. The Braille Alphabet. *Used with permission from the CT Library for the Blind and Physically Handicapped*

magnifiers, can also be provided to help the low-vision patron. However, similar free options are variously built into both the Mac OS X and the Windows 8 platforms and magnify or adjust the size and background of text on a computer screen and the size or color of the cursor. They also provide speech-to-text and text-to-speech or narrator options, onscreen keyboards, slow keys (a feature that allows the user to specify how long a key needs to be held down), sticky keys (a shortcut that allows the user to press and release a modifier key, such as Shift, Ctrl, Alt, and have it remain active until any other key is pressed), and several other accessibility options. (The Mac OS X also provides for Braille displays without a BARD download and playback device.)

For those without computer access, the Federal Communications Commission (FCC) offers free services for the hearing impaired that include:

Telecommunications Relay Service (TRS)—a telephone service that allows a person with hearing or speech disabilities to place and receive telephone calls. TRS uses operators, called communications assistants (CAs), in order to facilitate telephone calls between people with hearing and speech disabilities and other individuals. A TRS call may be initiated by either a person with a hearing or speech disability or a person without such a disability. When a person with a hearing or speech disability initiates a TRS call, the person uses a teletypewriter (TTY) or other text input device to call the TRS relay center and gives the CA the number of the party that he or she wants to call.

Text-to-Voice TTY-based TRS—With this type of "traditional" TRS, a person with a hearing or speech disability uses a TTY to call the communications assistant at the relay center. TTYs have a keyboard and allow people to type their telephone conversations. The text is read on a display screen and/or a paper printout. A TTY user calls a telephone relay center and types the number of the person he or she wishes to call. The CA at the relay center then makes a voice telephone call to the other party and relays the call back and forth between the parties by speaking what the text user types and typing what the voice telephone user speaks.

Voice Carry Over (VCO)—a type of TRS that allows a person with a hearing disability, but who wants to use his or her own voice, to speak directly to the called party and receive responses in text from the CA. No typing is required by the calling party. This service is particularly useful to senior citizens who have lost their hearing but who can still speak.

Hearing Carry Over (HCO)—a type of TRS that allows a person with a speech disability, but who wants to use his or her own hearing, to listen to the called party and type his or her part of the conversation on a TTY. The CA reads these words to the called party, and the caller hears responses directly from that party.

Speech-to-Speech (STS) Relay Service—This form of TRS is used by a person with a speech disability. A CA (who is specially trained in understanding a variety of speech disorders) repeats what the caller says in a manner that makes the caller's words clear and understandable to the called party. No special telephone is needed.

Shared Non-English Language Relay Services—Due to the large number of Spanish speakers in the United States, the FCC requires interstate TRS providers to offer Spanish-to-Spanish traditional TRS.

Captioned Telephone Service—Captioned telephone service, like VCO, is used by individuals with a hearing disability but still who still retain some residual hearing. It uses a special telephone that has a text screen to display captions of what the other party is saying. A captioned telephone allows the user, on one line, to speak to the called party and to simultaneously listen to that party and read captions of what he or she is saying.

Video Relay Service (VRS)—This Internet-based form of TRS allows people whose primary language is American Sign Language (ASL) to communicate with the CA in ASL using video-conferencing equipment. The CA speaks what is signed to the called party and signs the called party's response back to the caller.

Internet Protocol (IP) Relay Service—IP Relay is a text-based form of TRS that uses the Internet rather than traditional telephone lines for the leg of the call between the person with a hearing or speech disability and the CA. Otherwise, the call is generally handled just like a TTY-based TRS call.

Figure 10.6. Adaptive Self-Checkout Station. *Photograph courtesy of the Groton Public Library*

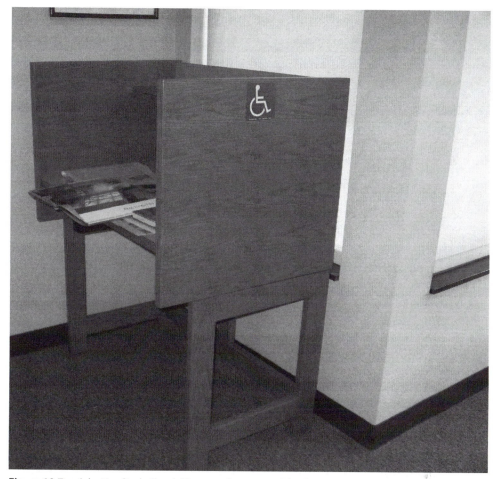

Figure 10.7. Adaptive Study Carrel. *Photograph courtesy of the Groton Public Library*

> *IP Captioned Telephone Service*—IP captioned telephone service, one of the newest forms of TRS, combines elements of captioned telephone service and IP Relay.
> *711 Access to TRS*—Just as you can call 411 for information, you can dial 711 to connect to certain forms of TRS anywhere in the United States. Dialing 711 makes it easier for travelers to use TRS because they do not have to remember TRS numbers in every state.[9]

LSS must be aware that those with physical disabilities must have technologies available to them as well. Using a public computer can pose a challenge for the person who uses a wheelchair. Desks and tables should be adjustable in order to accommodate the patron so that the desktop is at the correct height (see figure 10.7). A moveable arm for adjusting the monitor, ergonomic keyboards, oversized keyboards, on-screen keyboards, trackballs, and joysticks are useful for people with limited dexterity.[10]

Another example of an adaptive technology is the installation of automatic door openers. Think about how the patron who uses a wheelchair, cane, or crutches would open a heavy door without an automatic option, especially if he or she is carrying books or bags.

As we have seen, LSS are conscientious about making services accessible to patrons with many kinds of special needs. Another segment of the library population that must be considered is the obese patron. "With obesity rates rising, libraries need to meet the needs of larger patrons and staffers."[11] We need to be ready to accommodate the plus-size patron. According to the most recent data, more than one-third of adults and 17 percent of youth in the United States are obese.[12] With this in mind, chairs with armrests should be thirty-six inches across—better yet, get chairs without armrests. Benches, sofas, and loveseats are good choices that can accommodate all. Chairs with fixed armrests in conference or classrooms can be difficult for large people, including children. Remembering that some heavy patrons have trouble walking long distances, having appropriate seats strategically placed would be considerate. In the restroom, toilets should be placed in the center of the stall rather than off to one side in order to allow extra hip room. Restrooms designed for the disabled are often larger and more accommodating for an obese person. Make sure that stepstools are labeled for weight, elevators are large enough to accommodate an emergency that might require extra personnel or a stretcher, and that important phone numbers are posted throughout the library in case of a health emergency.[13]

A final note on patrons with special needs: Not all disabilities are visible. Patrons may have dyslexia, memory issues, or aphasia. Some may wear prosthetic devices or have temporary disabilities such as broken bones, recent surgery, or injuries that may cause impairment. Some other related issues will be discussed in the following chapter on challenging patrons.

CHAPTER SUMMARY

The role of the LSS is to understand the concepts and skills of customer service. They will be able to recognize and respond to diversity in user needs and preference for resources and services in order to treat all patrons with consideration and to treat them as the LSS would want to be treated. The Americans with Disabilities Act is specific about what accommodations and adaptations are required. Special needs and disabilities span a wide range for which we must be prepared with a range of assistive and adaptive technologies.

DISCUSSION QUESTIONS AND ACTIVITIES

1. Team up with a colleague for this exercise.
    a. Put on a pair of noise-cancelling headphones, then proceed to communicate with each other.
    b. What strategies must be used in order for the "hearing impaired" to understand what the other is trying to communicate?
2. Partnering with a colleague for safety, take turns wearing a blindfold and then proceed to navigate the library as a visually impaired patron would have to.
    a. What barriers or obstacles do you find?

3. Under the provisions of the ADA, what must you do to make your library accessible if you have ten employees?
4. What is adaptive technology?
   a. Name several examples.
   b. Why does the LSS need to know about it?

NOTES

1. U.S. Census, "Anniversary of Americans with Disabilities Act: July 26," *Profile America: Facts for Features*, last modified July 25, 2012, https://www.census.gov/newsroom/releases/archives/facts_for_features_special_editions/cb12-ff16.html.

2. U.S. Equal Opportunity Employment Commission, "Facts about the Americans with Disabilities Act," U.S. Equal Opportunity Employment Commission, http://www.eeoc.gov/eeoc/publications/fs-ada.cfm.

3. QuickCounsel, "The Americans with Disabilities Act," Association of Corporate Counsel, last modified June 15, 2009, http://www.acc.com/legalresources/quickcounsel/tawda.cfm.

4. Pacer Center: Champion for Children with Disabilities, "It's the 'Person First' Then the Disability," Pacer Center Action Information Sheet, last modified 2005, http://www.pacer.org/parent/php/php-c31.pdf.

5. John J. Burke, "Assistive-Adaptive Technologies," *American Libraries* 44, no. 11/12 (November/December 2013): 44–46.

6. J. Elaine Kitchel, "APH Guidelines for Print Document Design," American Printing House for the Blind, Inc., http://www.aph.org/edresearch/lpguide.htm.

7. Library of Congress, "That All May Read," National Library Service for the Blind and Physically Handicapped, http://www.loc.gov/nls/.

8. Library of Congress, "That All May Read."

9. Federal Communications Commission, "Telecommunications Relay Service (TRS)," Federal Communications Commission, last modified October 17, 2014, http://www.fcc.gov/guides/telecommunications-relay-service-trs.

10. Barbara Mates, "Twenty Years of Assistive Technologies," *American Libraries* 41, no. 10 (October 2010): 40–42.

11. Lori L. Smith, "Is Your Library Plus-Size Friendly?," *American Libraries* 44, no. 9/10 (September/October 2013): 44–46.

12. Cynthia L. Ogden et al., "Prevalence of Childhood and Adult Obesity in the United States, 2011–2012," *JAMA* 311, no. 8 (February 26, 2014): 806–814.

13. Smith, "Is Your Library Plus-Size Friendly?," 44–46.

REFERENCES, SUGGESTED READINGS, AND WEBSITES

American Foundation for the Blind. "Technology Resources for People with Vision Loss." American Foundation for the Blind. http://www.afb.org/info/living-with-vision-loss/using-technology/12.

Americans with Disabilities Act. "Introduction to the ADA." Americans with Disabilities Act. Last modified July 26, 1990. http://www.ada.gov/ada_intro.htm.

Americans with Disabilities homepage. http://www.ada.gov.

Apple, Inc. "Accessibility." Apple, Inc. https://www.apple.com/accessibility/osx/#motor-skills.

Booth, Char. "Accessibility Makes Incremental Gains." *Library Journal* 138, no. 16 (October 1, 2013): 42–43. http://search.ebscohost.com/login.aspx?direct=true&db=aph&AN=90381808&site=eds-live.

Burke, John J. "Assistive-Adaptive Technologies." *American Libraries* 44, no. 11/12 (November/December 2013): 44–46. http://search.ebscohost.com/login.aspx?direct=true&db=f5h&AN=91782533&site=eds-live.

Federal Communications Commission. "Telecommunications Relay Service (TRS)." Federal Communications Commission. Last modified October 17, 2014. http://www.fcc.gov/guides/telecommunications-relay-service-trs.

Kitchel, J. Elaine. "APH Guidelines for Print Document Design." American Printing House for the Blind, Inc. http://www.aph.org/edresearch/lpguide.htm.

Library of Congress. "That All May Read." National Library Service for the Blind and Physically Handicapped. http://www.loc.gov/nls/.

Mates, Barbara. "Twenty Years of Assistive Technologies." *American Libraries* 41, no. 10 (October 2010): 40–42. http://search.ebscohost.com/login.aspx?direct=true&db=f5h&AN=54358396&site=eds-live.

Microsoft. Ease of Access Center. Microsoft. http://windows.microsoft.com/en-us/windows/make-computer-easier-to-use#1TC=windows-7.

National Library for the Blind and Physically Handicapped. http://www.loc.gov/nls/.

———. *Digital Talking Book Player Models DS1 and DA1: Library Guide*. Washington, DC: Library of Congress, February 2009. http://www.loc.gov/nls/transition/DTBM-Library-Manual-0.63.pdf.

Ogden, Cynthia L., Margaret D. Carroll, Brian K. Kit, and Katherine M. Flegel. "Prevalence of Childhood and Adult Obesity in the United States, 2011–2012." *JAMA* 311, no. 8 (February 26, 2014): 806–14.

Pacer Center: Champion for Children with Disabilities. "It's the 'Person First' Then the Disability." Pacer Center Action Information Sheet. Last modified 2005. http://www.pacer.org/parent/php/php-c31.pdf.

QuickCounsel. "The Americans with Disabilities Act." Association of Corporate Counsel. Last modified June 15, 2009. http://www.acc.com/legalresources/quickcounsel/tawda.cfm.

Silver Linings Technologies. http://silverliningvision.com/index.html.

Smith, Lori L. "Is Your Library Plus-Size Friendly?" *American Libraries* 44, no. 9/10 (September/October 2013): 45–46. http://search.ebscohost.com/login.aspx?direct=true&db=f5h&AN=90183115&site=eds-live.

U.S. Census. "Anniversary of Americans with Disabilities Act: July 26." Profile America: Facts for Features. Last modified July 25, 2012. https://www.census.gov/newsroom/releases/archives/facts_for_features_special_editions/cb12-ff16.html.

U.S. Equal Opportunity Employment Commission. "Facts about the Americans with Disabilities Act." U.S. Equal Opportunity Employment Commission. http://www.eeoc.gov/eeoc/publications/fs-ada.cfm.

CHAPTER 11

Customer Service to Challenging Patrons

Library support staff (LSS) will know the basic concepts and skills of customer service. They will be able to recognize and respond to diversity in user needs and preference for resources and services. (ALA-LSSC Competencies #9, #11)

Topics Covered in This Chapter:

- Service to the Poor
- Service to the Homeless
- The Disruptive Patron
- Security of Personnel

Key Terms:

Disruptive patron: A disruptive patron is one whose behavior interferes with the use of the library by other patrons or interferes with a staff member's completion of his or her duties; one who interferes with the normal functioning of the library.

Diversity: Diversity is the state of people of more than one nationality, race, gender, color, sexual orientation, and socioeconomic status. It encourages acceptance of these differences and the uniqueness of each individual. Libraries are an example of a place where diversity is encountered on a regular basis, and libraries must strive to make their services acceptable and sensitive to the demographic.

Homelessness: The homeless are those who, through lack of employment, poverty, mental illness, substance abuse, or other factors, are without permanent housing. This includes those who live in transitional housing or shelters, either temporarily or chronically. The homeless are frequent library users because libraries provide shelter from the weather.

Poverty: Poverty is the circumstance of having little or no money to purchase goods and services or lacking a means of financial support. This can impact a patron's liabilities if he or she gets a library card: paying fines or being responsible for lost materials.

Security risk management: Security risk management means being aware of your immediate physical environment and identifying potential problem areas in the library—including areas where one can hide and inadequate lighting in the parking lot, as well as knowing who has keys to the library.

Service attitude: The service attitude is how LSS behave toward patrons: a positive attitude shows warmth, friendliness, and helpfulness; a negative attitude may show disinterest, disdain, or annoyance. Both can affect return visits to the library.

SERVICE TO THE POOR

Poverty is an economic condition—people and families are poor when they have little or no money to purchase goods and services.[1] The federal poverty level is determined annually by the Department of Health and Human Services and is used to determine eligibility for benefits and programs. The textbox below shows the federal poverty guideline for 2015.

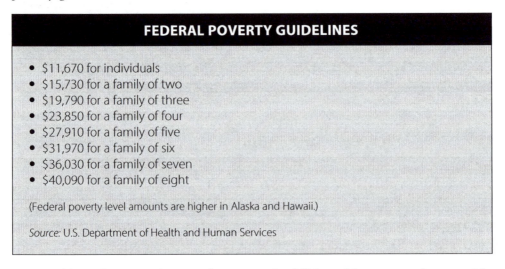

FEDERAL POVERTY GUIDELINES

- $11,670 for individuals
- $15,730 for a family of two
- $19,790 for a family of three
- $23,850 for a family of four
- $27,910 for a family of five
- $31,970 for a family of six
- $36,030 for a family of seven
- $40,090 for a family of eight

(Federal poverty level amounts are higher in Alaska and Hawaii.)

Source: U.S. Department of Health and Human Services

Every library has a contingent of patrons who fall into this category. It goes without saying that all that we have learned about excellent customer service applies to all patrons, regardless of economics. Although poverty may be many things, including homelessness or lack of employment, poverty may be impossible to discern from a patron's appearance.

The poor may not want to get library cards for fear of amassing fines or losing books for which they cannot pay. Reviewing and clarifying fine policies can give the LSS the authority to waive fines or fees or to offer patrons creative ways to "work off" their fines. LSS can also make sure there are comfortable areas in the library where patrons can simply sit and read, rather than check material out. If your library requires a library card to access the public computers, then consider having free day passes for these patrons, for example.[2]

The American Library Association (ALA) has a policy statement on "Library Services to the Poor," which recommends, among other things,

- promoting the accessibility of print and nonprint materials that address issues of poverty and deal with the poor in a respectful way;
- promoting the inclusion of low-income programs and services as part of the regular library budget;
- promoting equity in funding adequate library services in terms of materials, facilities, and equipment;
- promoting public awareness of poverty-related resources;
- training and sensitizing staff about issues that affect the poor; and
- promoting the collection of food and clothing donations.[3]

Many people and families fall into the category of the "working poor"—that is, they have a job, they have a home, but they may not have enough money for all of their living expenses, especially food. Three libraries in the area where I worked had an annual Food for Fines drive every fall prior to Thanksgiving. Patrons were urged to donate nonperishable goods to each library in lieu of fines for a period of two weeks, and the food was then given to the local social service agency. After several years of this successful effort, the library where I worked decided that since poverty and hunger is not just a seasonal problem, we would collect these items all year, regardless of fines. We obtained a very large basket and posted a sign that said "The Need Is Always There." Patrons appreciate having a convenient place to bring donations, and the agency is grateful for year-round contributions. Another area library held a Halloween costume drive and donated the many costumes collected to those who could not afford them. Gloves, scarves, hats, coats—all have been collected by libraries to donate to local agencies in order to help those in need.

Having a "gift tree" during the December holiday season is another way that libraries can encourage the community to help the poor. The library can hang tags on the tree with the names of needed items; patrons then take the tag and return it with the item, which in turn goes to the agency that is coordinating the distribution of gifts. The same can be done for monetary donations. Social service agencies can encourage the library to "adopt a family" by making public a list of clothing, toys, and personal items that patrons can bring in. This kind of interagency cooperation allows for the anonymous collection of needed items to benefit the poor in that community. These are all low- or no-cost library initiatives to help the poor in the community with minimal effort but maximum impact.

It is important to assess what needs and services the library can address for the poor in your area within the mission of the library, such as building the collection of resume and job manuals, providing access to computers without having a library card, or providing story times and other programs. Consult with the local social service department for staff training in how to help those who are in obvious need. The social service agency can provide local or federal resources, referrals, and lists of food pantries, soup kitchens, clinics, and other free services that LSS can make available to the patron. Create flyers or handouts with relevant information and post them on a community bulletin board or place them on a table with other local information.

SERVICE TO THE HOMELESS

People are **homeless** for a variety of reasons. Many may be homeless due to alcohol or drug abuse. The reality is that many people are on the verge of becoming homeless due to job insecurity, unemployment, underemployment, domestic violence, or other dire situations. The working poor may be homeless, going from their day job to a friend's couch, their car, or an emergency shelter at night. According to the Department of Housing and Urban Development (HUD),[4] there are four federally defined categories under which individuals and families may qualify as homeless:

1. Literally homeless
2. Imminent risk of homelessness
3. Homeless under other Federal statutes
4. Fleeing/attempting to flee domestic violence

The homeless have a profound effect on the library. For many, the public library is their refuge or even their safe haven during the day. That they may be dirty, smelly, or otherwise offensive can be a problem for staff and patrons. They may be discouraged, through policy or physical barriers, from using the facilities to wash, shave, or change clothes. Because libraries require proof of address in order to obtain a library card, it is difficult, if not impossible, for the homeless to do so. As we noted previously, the library can still offer a multitude of programs and services for those who do not have library cards, such as computer access, comfortable places to sit and read, and readily available information on where to go for food, shelter, and showers.

SAMPLE CODE OF CONDUCT

Patrons are welcome to use the library as long as they:

- Do not interfere with another person's use of the library or with library staff in the performance of their duties.
- Do not disturb or annoy others with loud or unreasonable noise, including electronic equipment at a volume that disturbs others.
- Keep audible cell phone ringers turned off.
- Do not use profanity or abusive or threatening language.
- Do not steal, damage, or inappropriately use library property within facilities or on library grounds.
- Are not under the influence or possession of alcohol or illegal drugs.
- Do not use restrooms for bathing, shampooing, doing laundry, or changing clothes.
- Do not litter.
- Do not disturb others through poor personal hygiene resulting in offensive and pervasive body odor.
- Supervise all children.

Having patron conduct or behavior policies is essential. Such documents may include rules about eating or drinking in the building, talking loudly, disruptive use of electronic devices, profanity, hygiene issues, and so on. Such policies ensure that behaviors are not disruptive to other patrons and can be used to justify asking a patron to modify his or her behavior or to leave the premises. While it is uncomfortable to tell a patron that their body odor is offensive, they can be spoken to quietly or handed a note to that effect. This spares the patron that embarrassment.

Possibly the best-known case of discrimination against a homeless man was the lawsuit *Kreimer v. Bureau of Police for the Town of Morristown* (New Jersey) in 1992.[5] Richard Kreimer, a homeless man, sued the public library for violation of his First Amendment rights for evicting him from the library due to his appearance, hygiene, and behavior problems. The case went back and forth through the courts several times as the legality of his claim was challenged. Ultimately, he won a settlement but not before library policy was examined and rewritten to be more accommodating. Library policies have to make sure that they do not discriminate.

> The most important thing to remember when designing lists of unacceptable behavior is that policies must be written in such a way to ensure equal enforcement. This means that if sleeping is prohibited, it cannot be enforced only against the homeless; it must be enforced against all patrons, including children, teenagers, the elderly, prominent community members, and so on. Furthermore, patrons must be fully informed of inappropriate conduct and given the opportunity to argue their case. Only behavior that infringes on other patrons' rights should be considered.[6]

A formerly homeless man named Michael Brennan, in his article "All I Really Need to Know I Learned in the Library,"[7] was reminded of the Kreimer case when he tried to concentrate on his work while sitting near an apparently homeless woman who disturbed him with her muttering. The judge in the Kreimer case, H. Lee Sarokin, wrote, "If we wish to shield our eyes and noses from the homeless, we should revoke their condition, not their library cards." Brennan was remorseful when recalling his own homelessness and how offensive he must have been to others. His article on this experience is an eloquent first-person account from both sides of the issue. Although this article is old, its relevance is timeless, and I highly recommend reading it.

We already know that the "Library Services to the Poor" policy statement ethically obligates us to ensure accessibility and equality of all services. As we learned in a previous chapter, it is important to get to know your demographic. The homeless population that uses the library will come in all ages, genders, and races. Find out specific information about their information needs. Many overnight shelters are closed during the day; investigate the hours of the available day shelters so that programs can be planned accordingly.[8]

When planning programs for this population, it isn't enough to use traditional media sources and in-house advertising. Outreach means just that: find the shelters in your area and make sure that they get promotional materials—posters or by e-mail—for programs that target this population and might be of interest to them. Some examples that might be useful include programs on health, rental assistance, job training and resume writing, and applying for government benefits. All programs should be offered free of charge.[9]

Libraries in Denver, Colorado, and San Francisco, California, go one step further. At Denver Public Library, staff members visit a women's shelter twice a year to teach interviewing skills and provide library cards. In 2009, the San Francisco Public Library placed a psychiatric social worker on staff to provide outreach to the more than 15 percent of the library's visitors who are homeless. Much of what the social worker's job entails includes providing information to people about services like free meals, temporary shelters, and legal aid. She can also do clinical assessments of people with more urgent needs.[10] Not everyone is supportive, of course, but city librarian Luis Herrera says, "Urban libraries are one of the most democratic intuitions that we can have, and we welcome everybody; 99 percent of the individuals come in here, use the library respectfully, for its intended purpose, but we're always going to have that small percentage that has some problems or some issues."[11]

Homelessness has a ripple effect. It is an enormous problem that affects the library, the community, the town, the state, and the nation. To date only three states, Rhode Island, Connecticut, and Illinois (as of this writing, California is still pending), have passed a Homeless Bill of Rights.[12]

THE HOMELESS BILL OF RIGHTS

The Homeless Bill of Rights gives the homeless the right to:

1. use and move freely in public spaces, including public sidewalks, parks, transportation, and buildings, among other spaces;
2. equal treatment by government agencies;
3. be free of discrimination while seeking or maintaining equipment;
4. receive emergency medical care;
5. vote, register to vote, and receive documentation necessary for voting;
6. have personal records and confidential information not disclosed; and
7. have a reasonable expectation of privacy over personal property to the same extent as one would have in a permanent residence.

Source: Law eCommons

Much of what the LSS can do for the poor can be extended to the homeless. No doubt it is challenging—but the fact that we have the resources for outreach to these populations makes us powerful and has the potential to create the refuge that is so dearly sought by the chronically underserved.

THE DISRUPTIVE PATRON

LSS who work at the circulation or information desks are often the first people that someone sees when they walk into the library. These frontline employees represent the entire organization, and it is their job to present the library as a welcoming place, to project an air of helpfulness and interest. If staff members treat everyone fairly as an individual with important needs, it will garner good public relations. There are, however, some users who do not respond to courteous treatment and efficient service. They may be individuals with contentious personalities or bad attitudes; to them, any attempt at fair treatment is unappreciated, and reasonable library service is insufficient. It is important *not* to get into the habit of considering all library patrons with problems as "problem patrons." Users often have valid criticisms, and to treat them as problem patrons reflects a negative **service attitude**. It can also be contagious—branding someone as a problem patron reinforces that opinion so that soon everyone who sees him coming will automatically think poorly of him.

This is not to say, though, that there aren't difficult patrons; we prefer to refer to them as "disruptive." A **disruptive patron** is *anyone who interferes with the normal functioning of the library*. Some people may suffer from "library anxiety"—those unfamiliar with a library may be overwhelmed or intimidated and it reflects in their behavior. There are patrons who are impatient, confused, or angry for other reasons, including

- those with medical problems,
- those using alcohol or illicit drugs, and
- those who may be emotionally unstable or disturbed.

Public libraries have been impacted by the deinstitutionalization and mainstreaming of such people, as well as the homeless, who may, in fact, be part of that population. Nonmainstream people can have real and legitimate reasons for using the library, and their request for help should be treated with the same respect given to anyone else.

Patrons can be uncomfortable with someone because of their appearance or eccentric behavior; the previous sections on the poor and the homeless have already shown us this. Library policy should be clear on what behaviors are allowed and what the consequences are for violating policy. This applies across the board, to mainstream and nonmainstream patrons alike.

There are other "problem patrons." Some are extremely talkative and may try, unwittingly, to monopolize your time. Every staff member should have the ability to terminate such conversations effectively but with grace. It helps for LSS to be observant, particularly if there are patrons known for this behavior. A strategic "phone call" or summons to another part of the library can help extricate a staff member trapped by the overly talkative. Some patrons are unknowingly offensive—but so are some staff members. (Remember that customer service is both external and internal.) They may wear too little deodorant or too much aftershave or have annoying personal traits such as humming or obsessively straightening shelves. The library's code of conduct can be used for reference.

A Canadian professional by the name of Guy Robertson refers to some of these patrons as "sub-problem" patrons—those whose annoyances are not worth dealing with. Among his pet peeves are the Babbler (constant talkers), Mobile Mums (always on their cell phones), the Gum Ghost (who places chewed gum under tables), the Feeders (who leave trash around), and Romeo and Juliet, the amorous couple who show up in just about every library at some point. He fantasizes about what he'd really like to say to some of them but ultimately realizes that using good customer service skills, including eye contact and being firm, resolves the problem.[13]

In my experience as a library director, we had our share of disruptive patrons, ranging from the harmless—a man who spent a lot of time laughing to himself about whatever he was reading and who let us know we wouldn't see him for a while because he would be going up in an alien spaceship—to the potentially dangerous, such as the flasher who came by just before the elementary school next door dismissed for the day. We had people who slept on the outdoor benches, made peanut butter sandwiches on the library's front steps, and washed their hair in the bathroom sink. Whether they pose a threat, violate a policy, or are just a nuisance is a judgment call that the library has to make. As the previously mentioned Professor Robertson says, some annoyances are not worth dealing with.

On the other hand, a person who, without provocation, becomes verbally abusive or tries to intimidate or otherwise interfere with library function is considered to be disruptive. There need to be procedures in place to deal with any escalating situations. The disruptive patron should be

- firmly warned (quietly) that his or her behavior is not appropriate for the library;
- reminded of library policy;
- given a choice to follow rules and stay or choose to leave. This gives the person *control* over his or her situation.

Documentation should be kept of any incidents or repeated incidents involving a particular patron.

While all library policy should be posted, a short, clear list of rules in printed form can be available to show or give to the patron. This goes a long way toward avoiding making the patron feel that he or she is being singled out. Reciting library policy is more effective than a personal challenge.

Be aware of irrational behavior. Referring back to what we've learned about customer service, the following textbox is a list of suggestions for dealing with disruptive patrons:

DEALING WITH DISRUPTIVE PATRONS

- Be assertive but not aggressive.
- Speak in a clear, firm voice.
- Sound in control of yourself and the situation.
- Establish good eye contact: this helps ground the person being addressed.
- Present a helpful face.
- Model good behavior.
- Construct your statements around what you want done (e.g., If you'll wait here, I'll be back to assist you in five minutes).
- Be very specific with statements or promises.
- Reinforce positive behavior with verbal praise when appropriate.

One of our "regulars" was a man with a chronically bad attitude. If there was anything to complain about, he would. He occasionally became confrontational and often bragged about how many other libraries he had been banned from. The LSS consistently used the previous suggestions to deal with his aggression; in fact, they went out of their way to be nice to him by greeting him pleasantly, asking how he was, and showing him courtesy that he apparently was not used to. In time, this man became more reasonable and there were far fewer incidents.

SECURITY OF PERSONNEL

Be aware of your surroundings, exits, and alarms and be able to identify potential problem areas. LSS who work throughout the library are in the best position to identify problems. This is **risk management**, and it is an ongoing process. It is critical for safety in case of an emergency.

Although we hope it never happens, plans need to be in place in case disruptive patrons become security or safety issues.

- Know and have a good relationship with your local police.
- Have signals known by all staff to alert them to emergencies.
  - One technique is to have an agreed upon word or phrase: when someone asks for the "blue folder," for example, everyone knows that there is an emergency.
- Know when to call the police or use a silent alarm, if the library has one.
- Always have at least two staff members on duty, especially at night. There is safety in numbers.

When dealing with a disruptive patron, *do not*

- threaten,
- raise your voice,
- make a promise and break it,
- name call,
- invade personal space without permission,
- show visible anger,
- show fear,
- accompany the patron to out of the way place or stacks without notifying a colleague,
- turn your back on a patron.

If you are threatened or approached by a disruptive patron:

- Don't relinquish your safety area.
- Create a barrier, such as a desk or chair.
- Deescalate the situation by using the model behaviors we have learned.
  - People will address you in the same tone of voice with which you speak to them, so keep your voice moderated.

- ○ Be diplomatic: use phrases such as "I understand; let me see what I can do."
- ○ Hold eye contact.
- ○ Maintain an open face.
- If you need a weapon, use items such as a stapler, books, electrical cords, or coffee mugs.
- Use a code word as was previously mentioned.
  - ○ Screaming for help may agitate the attacker.

If you are attacked, there are three options:

- Fight—if you choose to fight, it needs to be aggressive, immediate, and intentional. You want to create pain and also a diversion.
  a. Pepper spray—if you choose to use this, buy two: examine one for the distance of spray, taste, and other effects. You need to know *what it will do*, and don't be afraid to use it.
- Flight—if you choose to flee, know the library's escape routes and be aware of your own physical capabilities.
- Passive resistance—drop to the ground, become dead weight.[14]

Having good policies won't stop a disruptive patron who is out of control. Know when to call the police, and do not hesitate to do so if patrons exhibit threatening behavior to persons or physical property, if they refuse to leave, or if you witness drug use or indecent acts. The safety and security of the staff and other patrons comes first.

CHAPTER SUMMARY

In this chapter, we reinforced the basic concepts and skills of customer service as they apply to challenging patrons. The LSS can understand the basic concepts and skills of customer service. They can recognize and respond to diversity in user needs and preference for resources and services, including service to the poor, the homeless, and the disruptive patron, all of whom may pose a challenge to traditional customer service. We emphasized the need to identify the resources and services available to these various groups of people, both within the library and in the greater community. We also discussed safety for library personnel and patrons and ways to deal with situations that may become security or safety issues.

DISCUSSION QUESTIONS AND ACTIVITIES

1. How would you propose to provide borrowing privileges to patrons with no permanent address?
2. A patron complains to you that someone at the next table is muttering and laughing to herself.
   a. What is your response?
   b. How do you back it up?

3. Review the Homeless Bill of Rights.
   a. Do you think it is a reasonable document?
   b. If so, why do you think that so few states have adopted it?
4. What procedures does your library have in place to deal with potentially violent patrons?
   a. If you do not work in one, ask to see what your local library has posted or on file.
5. What are some useful behaviors that you might use with a patron who is being difficult or disruptive?

NOTES

1. Leslie Edmonds Holt, *Public Library Services for the Poor: Doing All We Can* (Chicago: American Library Association, 2010).

2. Holt, *Public Library Services for the Poor*, 51.

3. American Library Association, "ALA Policy Statement: Library Services to the Poor," American Library Association, http://www.ala.org/offices/extending-our-reach-reducing-homelessness-through-library-engagement-7.

4. U.S. Federal Government, "Homelessness Assistance," U.S. Department of Housing and Urban Development, http://portal.hud.gov/hudportal/HUD?src=/program_offices/comm_planning/homeless.

5. H. Lee Sarokin, *Richard R. Kreimer, Plaintiff, v. Bureau of Police for the Town of Morristown, et al., Defendants*, United States District Court, District of New Jersey, last modified May 22, 1991, http://www.ahcuah.com/lawsuit/federal/kreimer1.htm.

6. Amy Mars, "Library Service to the Homeless," Public Libraries Online, last modified April 26, 2013, http://publiclibrariesonline.org/2013/04/library-service-to-the-homeless/.

7. Michael Brennan, "All I Really Need to Know I Learned in the Library," *American Libraries* 23, no. 1 (January 1992): 38–39.

8. Mars, "Library Service to the Homeless."

9. American Library Association, "Extending Our Reach: Reducing Homelessness through Library Engagement," American Library Association, http://www.ala.org/offices/sites/ala.org.offices/files/content/olos/toolkits/poorhomeless_FINAL.pdf.

10. PBS, "From Nurses to Social Workers, See How Public Libraries Are Serving the Homeless," *PBS NewsHour*, January 28, 2015 (originally aired January 28, 2015), narrated by Cat Wise.

11. PBS, "From Nurses to Social Workers."

12. Jonathan Sheffield, "A Homeless Bill of Rights: Step by Step from State to State," *Law eCommons* 19, no. 1 (2013): 8–17.

13. Guy Robertson, "Into Every Professional Life, a Little Moon Will Shine: Dealing with Sub-problem Patrons," *Feliciter* 59, no. 1 (2012): 27–30.

14. Roger Beaupre, "Personal Safety in a Public Place" (lecture, Middletown Library Service Center, Middletown, CT, May 26, 2004).

REFERENCES, SUGGESTED READINGS, AND WEBSITES

American Library Association. "ALA Policy Statement: Library Services to the Poor." American Library Association. http://www.ala.org/offices/extending-our-reach-reducing-home lessness-through-library-engagement-7.

———. "Extending Our Reach: Reducing Homelessness through Library Engagement." American Library Association. http://www.ala.org/offices/sites/ala.org.offices/files/content/olos/toolkits/poorhomeless_FINAL.pdf.

Beaupre, Roger. "Personal Safety in a Public Place." Lecture, Law Enforcement Resource Center, Meriden, CT, May 26, 2004.

Brennan, Michael. "All I Really Need to Know I Learned in the Library." *American Libraries* 23, no. 1 (January 1992): 38–39. http://search.ebscohost.com/login.aspx?direct=true&db=eric&AN=EJ439908&site=eds-live.

Calvin, Beatrice. "Workplace Violence." *Library Worklife*, November 2013. http://ala-apa.org/newsletter/2013/11/12/workplace-violence-are-you-prepared-to-manage-a-crisis-situation/.

CPI. "Promoting a Safe and Respectful Workplace." PrepareTraining.com. Accessed January 7, 2015. http://www.crisisprevention.com/Specialties/Prepare-Training.

Creating and Maintaining a Respectful Workplace. http://study.com/academy/lesson/creating-maintaining-a-respectful-workplace.html.

Federal Poverty Guidelines for FFY 2015. LIHEAP Clearing House. Last modified July 30, 2014. http://www.liheapch.acf.hhs.gov/profiles/povertytables/FY2015/popstate.htm.

Hill, Nanci Milone. "Public Libraries and the Homeless." *Public Libraries*, November/December 2011, 13–22.

Holt, Leslie Edmonds. *Public Library Services for the Poor: Doing All We Can*. Chicago: American Library Association, 2010.

Mars, Amy. "Library Service to the Homeless." Public Libraries Online. Last modified April 26, 2013. http://publiclibrariesonline.org/2013/04/library-service-to-the-homeless/.

National Coalition for the Homeless. http://nationalhomeless.org/.

PBS. "From Nurses to Social Workers, See How Public Libraries Are Serving the Homeless." *PBS NewsHour*. January 28, 2015 (originally aired January 28, 2015). Narrated by Cat Wise.

Robertson, Guy. "Into Every Professional Life, a Little Moon Will Shine: Dealing with Sub-problem Patrons." *Feliciter* 59, no. 1 (2012): 27–30. http://search.ebscohost.com/login.aspx?direct=true&db=f5h&AN=85444933&site=eds-live.

Sarokin, H. Lee. *Richard R. Kreimer, Plaintiff, v. Bureau of Police for the Town of Morristown, et al., Defendants*. United States District Court, District of New Jersey. Last modified May 22, 1991. http://www.ahcuah.com/lawsuit/federal/kreimer1.htm.

Sheffield, Jonathan. "A Homeless Bill of Rights: Step by Step from State to State." *Law eCommons* 19, no. 1 (2013): 8–17.

U.S. Federal Government. "Federal Poverty Level (FPL)." HealthCare.gov. https://www.healthcare.gov/glossary/federal-poverty-level-FPL/.

———. "Homelessness Assistance." U.S. Department of Housing and Urban Development. http://portal.hud.gov/hudportal/HUD?src=/program_offices/comm_planning/homeless.

CHAPTER 12

Library Programming and Public Relations

Library support staff (LSS) will be able to communicate and promote the library's values and services to staff, volunteers, users, and the community. (ALA-LSSC Competency #10)

Topics Covered in This Chapter:

- Programming
- Public Relations
- Marketing and Branding
- Display

Key Terms:

Art release: The art release is the creation of a design or a graphic that can be used for posters, flyers, and handouts. It is included in a newsletter or other sources to advertise a library event.

Branding: Branding is the process involved in creating a unique name and image in the consumer's mind for a product (or library) through advertising campaigns with a consistent theme.

Marketing: Marketing is based on thinking about the library in terms of customer needs and satisfaction. It relies on designing the library's offering in terms of those needs and on using effective communication to inform and motivate them.

Press release: The press release uses the "5 Ws"—*who, what, when, where,* and *why,* plus *how*—to create a narrative that can be distributed to multiple media outlets in order to advertise a library event.

Programming: Programming is the offering of events, classes, and other programs to the variety of library patrons in any given community. It serves to bring people to the library, as well as to create community spirit.

Word-of-mouth marketing (WOMM): Word-of-mouth marketing is a powerful marketing tool that consists of people talking and listening to each other and spreading the word about library services and activities.

PROGRAMMING

Libraries are many things to many people in a community. They offer books, media, and periodicals; they offer information on a variety of topics such as health, education, and business. They offer services such as Internet access, databases, resume writing and job search help, and copy and fax machines. They also offer programs, which can be broken down into three types: *educational*, *recreational*, and *outreach*.[1] We offer programming for tangible reasons: it brings people into the library. We do it for intangible reasons: to expose patrons to art, music, and the humanities. We do it, also, for the sake of community spirit and connections.

Educational programs can include offering lifelong learning opportunities. Using public library resources and services in collaboration with educators in the community can provide a wealth of programs. Examples include classes on foreign languages, finance, health and fitness, nutrition and aging, and more. Many libraries offer lectures on a variety of topics relevant to the community, such as local history, nutrition, medical issues, and health insurance. Most libraries do not charge for programs, although there may be a materials fee in some cases for books or equipment. Another good resource offered through colleges and community adult education programs are online classes on virtually any subject through Ed2Go, a fee-based online learning environment.

For those who have limited reading or language skills, the library can offer classes in literacy by partnering with Literacy Volunteers, or English as a Second Language (ESL) tutors. For the poor, homeless, or otherwise underserved, classes on resume writing and interviewing are invaluable, as are classes on life skills, how to manage a budget, or how to apply for local, state, or federal aid.

For children, teens, the newly literate, or GED candidates, the library can offer homework help by partnering with schools or student mentors. This is a great opportunity for teens needing community service hours or for retired teachers and older adults. For the college bound, informational programs are popular to help with the universal application or writing the college essay or assisting parents with issues of financing and student support.

Recreational programs are an important part of library service. Less structured, perhaps, than educational programming, they are no less instructive. Libraries fortunate enough to have the space can offer musical events, from a simple piano performance to large outdoor concerts. Book discussions, a staple of library programming, offer an opportunity for stimulating thought and can be on any topic, such as science fiction and fantasy, history, political novels, or any number of themes. There is no shortage of teachers or other professionals who would be happy to lead a discussion about something from their area of expertise.

Also included as recreational programming are summer reading programs for children that reinforce reading skills while out of school and promote reading-related activities. Many reading programs are reward based and track how many books are read. Consider whether your reading programs are inclusive to children with special needs, and if not, what can be done to improve them. Adult reading programs have become popular as well. Similar to children's programs, they may offer incentives to read and conclude with a program or prizes. Many states collaborate and offer themes and supporting materials to libraries, as well as online programs with components for children, teens, and adults. For example, the 2014 theme for many U.S. libraries was "Fizz Boom Read," a science-themed program for children. The teen component was "Spark a Reaction," and the adult version was "Literary Elements." Programs and reading lists were then built around those themes.[2]

Gaming, as we referred to in previous chapters, is also a popular recreational offering for all ages, ranging from board games and scavenger hunts to mentally and physically challenging interactive computer games for all ages. Also falling into the category of recreational programming are exhibits that consist of new books or other library materials on a theme; personal collections such as political buttons, postcards, or vintage dolls; and displays related to local events or holidays. If your library is going to provide space for personal collections, it is imperative that the display space be secure.

Films are always popular, but it is important to know that if movies are shown the library must obtain a public performance license, available from a variety of vendors. This is an umbrella license that covers a number of film studios and allows for the free showing of anything in their catalog. (More information is available from the websites provided at the end of this chapter.) Ideally, all programs reinforce the value of the library and the services that it provides. When planning a movie night, for example, rather than just setting up the equipment and leaving the room, plan to discuss the movie when it is done. Perhaps set up a display of books and other materials that relate to the theme of the film. Choose movies that have name recognition and model your event after Sundance, Cannes, and the Oscars. Be aware of your target audience so that you can guarantee to fill at least a few seats.[3] As with all programs, even when your target is spot on, be prepared for low attendance. There is a lot going on these days, and the time of day, weather, and conflicting activities can all impact the audience that you get.

Any activities that take place at the library, whether library sponsored or by an outside group, need to adhere to the library's meeting room policy. As we will see in a later chapter on intellectual freedom and censorship, meeting room policies must be comprehensive, inclusive, and very specific as to what is or is not allowed.

Outreach programming can include library service to the homebound, nursing homes, or daycare centers, for example, sending books or volunteer readers to these locations. As we saw in a previous chapter, outreach to homeless shelters can provide needed information about community services available to that population, resume writing help, and interview coaching. Outreach also refers to bookmobiles, a boon to rural communities and those without regular access to a library. A 2007 book by Masha Hamilton, *The Camel Bookmobile*,[4] is a novel based on the true events of book delivery by camel to far-flung villages in Africa. While this is an extreme example of outreach, it does serve to illustrate the need to get library materials to those who cannot physically come to a library.

Outreach does not necessarily mean off the premises. Providing multicultural collections and materials in other languages is also a means of reaching underserved populations. Having a display of brochures and flyers about community services and activities falls into this category, as do lists of food and shelter sources and contact information to social service agencies.

Most, if not all, of the suggested programs can be obtained at little or no cost. Your community has a wealth of doctors, chiropractors, naturopaths, lawyers, master gardeners, florists, teachers, and authors who are happy to work with the library on a program. The local music school or high school music groups, dance and yoga teachers, and book appraisers are great sources for programs. Check with the local bar or medical associations for their speaker's bureau, and don't overlook your county extension services. Many potential presenters will do it for free or only require a small stipend or a donation to their organization.

Other sources for programs, besides those previously mentioned, include local authors, new businesses in town that would like to present their services, and local radio and television personalities, to name only a few. Network with your colleagues to see what they have done lately and if it was successful. If you are fortunate enough to have a programming budget—and many large libraries do—then your choices expand to professional performers, nature centers, magicians, theatrical groups, and more. Some states may have a public programming catalog that lists available performers and their fees, or they may host a performance showcase that highlights performers in your area. The list of program ideas is only limited by your imagination.

So you have decided on a terrific program for your target audience. That was the easy part! Now you have to begin the process of making it happen. There are a number of "first things" you have to do. Make sure that you agree on a date and time, ensuring that there are no other conflicts in the library or meeting space, and then book it. Particularly if your library meeting space is available to outside groups, be sure that you get your event on the calendar. If you know what's going on in your community or nearby libraries, it doesn't hurt to check those for conflicts as well. Anything else that takes place at the same time can potentially affect your audience. Create a checklist, a sample of which follows on page 153.

By creating and filling in such a form, you can check off as you go along to be sure that nothing is left out. Know who your speaker or performer is and what his or her formal name or title is. Agree on when the event begins and ends. Make sure you know that your speaker has the event on his calendar as well and what fees he requires, if any. Determine who this event is for so that you can create your marketing to target that audience, and then carry out your public relations campaign. It is helpful to take preregistration, as this not only gives you an idea of how many to expect, but it also gives you information that you can use to invite the attendees to future events.

In spite of all of your efforts, sometimes a program just bombs. It could be due to bad weather, conflicting activities, or poor timing. Sometimes there is no apparent reason. I still remember every program my library ever gave that had poor attendance, in spite of our best efforts. Warn your presenter if you are unsure of your

---

PROGRAM CHECKLIST

Name/title of program

_____

Duration

_____

Dates

_____

Confirm speaker and fees, if any

_____

Confirm the room requirements and equipment needed

_____

Determine target audience

_____

Public relations: media, flyer, lists

_____

Preregistration

_____

Other

_____

---

audience. While it is disappointing, it is a learning experience, and perhaps the next time you'll know what to avoid.

Given all of the above, programming in libraries is very labor intensive. Some may argue that the time and costs—both overt (paper, ink, fees) and hidden (staff time start to finish)—make it questionable. Every library has to look long and hard at why they do it in order to determine if it is worth it to their institution.

PUBLIC RELATIONS

Once you have determined that you are having a program, it's the job of the LSS to get the word out. It can be the best program you ever offered, but if no one knows about it, no one will come. Most libraries can't afford billboards or signs on buses, but they can do a media campaign. This means sharing your information with as many media outlets as you can identify:

- Newspapers
- Radio stations
- Local television
- The library website

- Social media
- Other libraries
- The senior center and other local organizations, clubs, and community centers
- Schools and colleges

There are two components to the media campaign: the **press release** and the **art release**—and they are free. For a press release, gather all of the facts, or what is referred to as the 5 Ws, and sometimes H:

- *Who* will be speaking or presenting?
- *What* is the primary topic?
- *Where* will it take place?
- *When* will it take place?
- *Why* are you having this program?
- *How* did it happen?

The LSS will use these elements when writing a press release. The time-tested "inverted pyramid-style" structure is a good model (figure 12.1). Following this structure, the "base" of the pyramid—the most fundamental facts—appear at the top of the story, in the lead paragraph. Nonessential information appears in the following paragraphs in order of importance. Editors cut from the bottom up, and while all of the information in your press release is important, the most critical news needs to be first.

Identify and develop a contact within each media outlet that is used, and keep this list updated, as personnel can change or be reassigned. Find out how each outlet wants the press release delivered—most will want an e-mail or an electronic form. Know when the deadlines are for each one; a minimum of two weeks is what

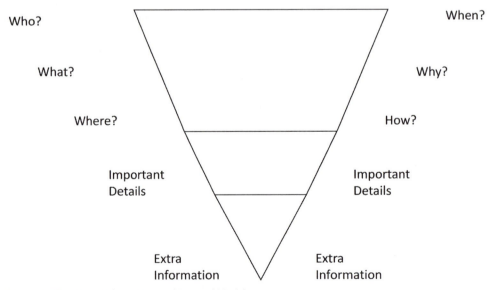

Figure 12.1. Press Release Inverted Pyramid Model

SAMPLE PRESS RELEASE

Contact: Susan Smith
Phone (123) 456-7890: Fax (123) 456-7891
E-mail: s.smith@anytownpl.org

FOR IMMEDIATE RELEASE

Outdoor Art Show at Anytown Public Library

Enjoy the soft summer breezes as you experience inspiring works of art at the first annual Anytown Public Library Outdoor Art Fair on Saturday, July 18, from 11 a.m. to 4 p.m. Families and art lovers are invited to come and make a day of it by exploring the grounds, picnicking in a lovely setting, watching an artist at work, or purchasing a beautiful original piece of art. There will be something fun for everyone in the family.

This event is free and open to the public. The Anytown Public Library is located in the heart of the historic district at 46 Main Street, Anytown, USA. Parking is free and refreshments will be available for sale. For more information, please call the library at (123) 456-7890 or check us out on the web at anytownlibrary.org.

---

most media outlets require, but don't assume that they are all alike. Follow up with a phone call to make sure that they received your information. Think of it from their point of view: there are a lot of organizations with events, and they may be inundated at any given time with hundreds of press releases from schools, libraries, and local businesses and organizations. Make sure that yours has been received and acknowledged. If possible, include a photo with your press release to a newspaper (or on your webpage or newsletter). Try to establish a relationship with the photography department at the local paper; they will be more likely to send a photographer to cover your event if they know who you are.

For the art release, create a design that can be used for posters, flyers, handouts, and graphics for inclusion in a newsletter. The design can be done in-house with Microsoft Publisher, downloaded images, clipart, or scanned images and can include a graphic or a picture. When designing your art release, keep the fonts and graphics as simple as possible. Use no more than two different fonts, and keep the design uncluttered—it needs to be readable from a distance.

Use the art release or the design on the library's webpage and mailing lists to patrons, past program attendees, or a target group. If it is a very special event and the budget permits, you can place a paid ad in your local newspaper. Most newspapers include all press releases and paid ads in their digital version as well, so that increases the ad's visibility. However, it can be quite expensive, as newspapers charge by the column inch—the larger the ad, the higher the price. The rate for a nonprofit in my local paper is $33.00 per column inch for a weekday ad. The price increases to $38.00 for the Sunday paper. This is for a circulation of only about twenty-nine thousand subscribers. As you can imagine, this can be a costly venture but one worth considering depending on your event and your budget.

Public relations (PR) is an ongoing job. We've been talking about it in terms of a specific program, but ultimately, *all* libraries want to maintain a high profile in the community. Good PR supports the library's resources and collections. Libraries must prove their value to their funders. The greater the numbers of people who are aware of the library, the more people will use it, promote it, and support it. This is particularly important at budget time when the library may be competing with other town departments for limited dollars.

We know that competition for money is not the only threat to the viability of libraries: the Internet has made it easier for people to think that everything they need can be found on the web. It is incumbent upon us to reinforce that we are the proponents of information literacy, and that the LSS can direct patrons to quality information from reliable resources. We need to do everything we can to increase our visibility and remain relevant.[5]

MARKETING AND BRANDING

Marketing is part of any library's public service. Besides wanting to bring attention to programs or services, libraries are in competition with so many other options, including bookstores and the Internet. There are those, of course, who predict the end of libraries, but we are finding that libraries are still relevant both as a place to find materials and services and as the "third place"—the social area separate from home and work. People are living increasingly more isolated lives, as evidenced by the upswing in social networking. Libraries are often the social center of a community.

Marketing for libraries is based on thinking about customers' needs and their satisfaction. It consists of an effort to discover, create, and satisfy customer needs. In other words, marketing has less to do with getting customers to "buy" a product than it does developing a demand for that product and thus fulfilling the customer's needs.[6] This is done all the time on television and in magazines—products and services are designed to meet a need, to let the potential market know that these products are available and in turn influence our behavior. In effect, they suggest that we have needs we didn't know we had! QVC, the Home Shopping Network, and product infomercials even let you call in *right now* before you can change your mind. Marketing relies heavily on designing the library's offering in terms of the target market's needs and desires and on using effective communication in order to inform and motivate. We want the public to know what we offer and to come in *right now* to get it before it's gone! It is "necessary to help nonprofits promote their values, accomplish their mission, and develop increased resources to address a wide range of compelling concerns."[7] Libraries have been slow to come to the marketing table. After all, we're libraries and everyone knows what we do. Or do they? Libraries have changed so much that it is no longer good enough to rest on our former reputation. If we don't let the public know what we are about these days, who will? As we saw above, libraries have a product, and we need to make the public aware of that product—and aware that the library is the best place to get it. We need to get our patrons to think of the library as a place not just for books or a meeting space but as a place of cultural preservation of information in its various formats.

That assumption has been tested, though. The popularity of bookstores has had an impact on libraries in recent years. Typically, bookstores have a good selection, good hours, comfortable amenities, and coffee shops. However, they don't have a good classification system, knowledgeable customer service, or decent pay—which leads to high staff turnover and inconsistent service. Libraries can and do offer reference assistance, pressure-free browsing, and free Internet access—and you don't have to buy anything. But libraries are expensive to run, and they have limited hours, particularly on nights and weekends.

One strategy that libraries have adopted is to mimic the services of a bookstore.[8] As we touched on in chapter 4, many libraries are borrowing the best of bookstores by offering more comfortable seating, coffee bars, face-out shelving, and more staff on the floor. Some are even choosing to do away with traditional library cataloging in favor of subject cataloging or grouping like topics together. According to the Maricopa County Library District in Arizona, "The library was designed to be customer-centric. That emphasis included placing low shelving at the entrance to draw people into the collection, tripling the number of lounge chairs, creating reading nooks, and adding signage to help patrons navigate."[9] Variations of this theme are being used in libraries all over the country.

Figure 12.2. Seating Area. *Photograph courtesy of the Mystic and Noank Library*

Besides changing the layout of the library, other marketing methods are being used to showcase library services in an ever-more competitive market. "The advertising arena has changed. Today there are so many more choices and so much clutter . . . the average person is exposed to 3,000 advertising messages a day."[10] That is a lot of information, and with those odds, we have to make sure that our message doesn't get lost in the barrage. However, although we may be hit with a lot of advertising, we usually remember what a friend tells us—especially if it's positive. This is a concept called **word-of-mouth marketing** (WOMM). It's personal, immediate, honest, and free. As we mentioned several times in previous chapters, the LSS at the front desk are the first people encountered when someone walks through the door. It starts with them—they should be greeting patrons and telling them what's new today. Staff, trustees, town officials, and other patrons should be talking about the library. Word of mouth is a powerful marketing tool that all libraries should be using. "There is no more powerful communication technique than one person talking with and listening to another, whether it's on social media (good) or live and in person (best). WOMM tops the chart."[11]

Social media is an invaluable marketing tool as well. Facebook, blogs, Twitter, Instagram, Tumblr, e-mail, and texts are great tools to get the word out, particularly these days when most people are constantly connected to their mobile devices. Be sure that you know who your target audience is, find out what their needs are, and market to them. As we referred to in previous chapters, libraries have a diverse clientele. It's up to the library to recognize this, target their needs, and then get the word out in the most appropriate way for each group.

Another way to increase your visibility is by **branding**. Branding is not the same as marketing; rather, it is an important first step and part of the "marketing mix." Branding is part of the marketing *strategy*, while promotion and publicity are part of the marketing *tools*.[12] Branding is the process involved in creating a unique name and image for a product in the consumer's mind through advertising campaigns with a consistent theme. Branding aims to establish a presence in the market that attracts and retains loyal customers. It's making your library known for something.

Think about commercial brands. You see an image or logo and instantly think of what it represents. In business, the brand is for a product, but in libraries, it is for a service. "Within a service profession the staff's relationships and interactions with customers play a pivotal role in influencing brand quality and brand values."[13] That is the purpose behind branding a library. It can be an image, a logo, a tagline, or anything that makes the library instantly recognizable. Using the library's brand in all marketing and public relations reinforces its value to the community. Examples of library branding can include an eye-catching logo as well as a tagline, such as Waterford Public Library in Connecticut: "Discovery Begins Here"; Curtis Memorial Library in Maine: "A World of Possibility"; and the Cuyahoga County Public Library in Ohio: "Browsing Is Just the Beginning."

Possibilities for branding are limitless, but it can be a challenging process that takes a lot of time and energy. Having an objective facilitator for a series of brainstorming sessions is helpful, as she can keep the group on task and mediate if necessary. It can be an emotional process, but the end result can go a long way toward making your marketing strategy more effective.

DISPLAYS

Part of the marketing strategy includes displays. Think of the grocery or drug store: magazines and candy are displayed at the checkout, and there are aisle endcap displays of sales and specials. By highlighting inventory and making it available, the store draws attention to something it wants you to buy. These items are displayed for precisely that reason. The same can be true in the library—we want to get your attention, and it begins at the entrance.

Imagine someone new to the community walking into the library for the first time. One of the first things they might see is the circulation desk with people behind it—do they look approachable? They might see some basic informational signs. They'll see patrons, all of whom seem to know what they are doing. Perhaps there is a guard on duty. This could intimidate the patron and cause him to wonder if he needs permission to enter or if he needs to show his ID or library card. Some or all of these things may confuse or disturb a patron. No one likes to walk into an unfamiliar place, and each library differs in its arrangement. This patron may feel uneasy because he hasn't been in a library since childhood or because he doesn't know what he wants or how to ask for help. He has no idea of how the library is arranged, and he may wander into the wrong room or feel confused that everyone else seems to know where they are going and what they are doing. There may be all kinds of information he needs, but it may be hard to ask.

Now imagine this same scenario with displays and signage that clearly identify the information desk; the children's, teen, and reference rooms; the computers;

Figure 12.3. Example of Library Display. *Photograph courtesy of the Bill Memorial Library*

Figure 12.4. Example of Library Display. *Photograph courtesy of the Groton Public Library*

newspapers and magazines; and the restrooms. Maybe there is an interesting display, which, at the very least, gives him an excuse to loiter while he tries to get his bearings. There are different kinds of signage and displays with different purposes:

- Directional signage can provide a floor plan and a guide to the rooms within the library, such as the reference room, children's room, or restrooms.

- Location indicators on shelving can direct the patron to the content of the collection and can also be used to cross-reference parts of the collection.
- Library informational policies should be prominently displayed, such as the circulation policy, the code of conduct, and rules for Internet use.
- There may be displays on topics of interest or new materials.

The opportunity exists for any number of special displays—thematically linked to a holiday, season, or subject. Examples of such displays include putting flower pots, trowels, gloves, and gardening books in a small wheelbarrow during spring; pumpkins and hay in a small wagon with fall books; highlighting cookbooks by creating a display with pots, pans, and wooden spoons or place settings. The school library displays can "sell" books. Using—or reusing—items found in the classroom or library can create excitement. Be sure that all displays use bright, clean paper and items; in my former library, we were liberal with strings of lights, which can immediately brighten a display and call attention at the same time.[14]

There are also non-library-related displays: most libraries will have a community bulletin board or shelving with a variety of local events information and resources. Libraries are the go-to place for tax forms and voter registration cards. If they have the space, many libraries will also host art exhibits of local artists or school children. Other proven marketing ideas include providing passes to your patrons for local museums and other attractions (although this can become costly, as the library has to purchase them). These are nonrelated in the sense that they are not directly related to library service, but they tie the library to the community. This connection can "sell" services and functions so that the taxpayer and library funders can see where their dollars are going.

CHAPTER SUMMARY

In this chapter, we looked at the ways in which libraries can provide programs and services to patrons in three categories: educational, recreational, and outreach. As it isn't enough to merely create programs, the topic of public relations or publicity is an important component in getting the word out to the public in order to promote the library's values and services to staff, volunteers, users, and the community. This can be achieved in a number of ways: by writing and distributing press releases to all available media outlets; creating posters, flyers, and other forms of art releases in the library and in the community; and using all available social network sites as well. Finally, branding your library and using that in your marketing plan creates and sustains the library's profile and its many services.

DISCUSSION QUESTIONS AND ACTIVITIES

1. Please name the three sections into which library programming can be broken down.
   a. Do you feel that they are equally important and worth doing, given the costs?
2. Using your local print or online newspaper and social media sites, find five examples of library press releases.
   a. Do they tell you all that you need to know?
   b. Is there any pattern that makes them similar?

3. It is almost impossible to escape the barrage of advertising in the media.
   a. What makes you pay attention to any particular ad?
   b. How would you adapt that for library marketing?
4. Do you think it is necessary for libraries to create a brand?

NOTES

1. G. Edward Evans and Thomas L. Carter, *Introduction to Library Public Services*, 7th ed., Library and Information Science Text (Westport, CT: Libraries Unlimited, 2009), 307–8.

2. Collaborative Summer Library Program, accessed February 4, 2015, http://www.csl-preads.org/.

3. Alan Jacobson, "How to Offer More Than a Movie," *American Libraries* 42, no. 7/8 (July/August 2011): 43–45.

4. Masha Hamilton, *The Camel Bookmobile* (New York: Harper Collins, 2007).

5. Anita Rothwell Lindsay, *Marketing and Public Relations Practices in College Libraries*, CLIP Notes 34 (Chicago: American Library Association, 2004).

6. "Marketing," in *BusinessDictionary.com*, http://www.businessdictionary.com.

7. Amy Shaw and Peter Deekle, *Outstanding Library Public Relations: 60 Years of the John Cotton Dana Award* (Chicago: American Library Association, 2007), 4.

8. Steve Coffman, "What If You Ran Your Library Like a Bookstore?," *American Libraries* 29, no. 3 (March 1998): 40.

9. Barbara Fister, "The Dewey Dilemma," *Library Journal* 134, no. 16 (October 1, 2009): 22.

10. Peggy Barber, "The Power of Word-of-Mouth Marketing," *American Libraries* 40, no. 11 (November 2009): 36.

11. Peggy Barber, "Contagious Marketing," *American Libraries* 45, no. 1/2 (January/February 2014): 34.

12. Elisabeth Doucette, "Branding for Public Libraries," Lyrasis, last modified December 8, 2009, http://www.slideshare.net/conniemassey/branding-for-public-libraries.

13. Rajesh Singh, "Branding in Library and Information Context: The Role of Marketing Culture," *Information Services & Use* 24, no. 2 (2004): 94.

14. Gayle Skaggs, *Look, It's Books! Marketing Your Library with Displays and Promotions* (Jefferson, NC: McFarland, 2008), 7.

REFERENCES, SUGGESTED READINGS, AND WEBSITES

American Library Association. "Promotion Guide." American Library Association. http://www.ala.org/programming/promotion-guide.

Association of College and Research Libraries. "Marketing @ Your Library." Association of College and Research Libraries. http://www.ala.org/acrl/issues/marketing.

Barber, Peggy. "Contagious Marketing." *American Libraries* 45, no. 1/2 (January/February 2014): 32–35. https://search.ebscohost.com/login.aspx?direct=true&db=aph&AN=93362375&site=ehost-live&scope=site.

———. "The Power of Word-of-Mouth Marketing." *American Libraries* 40, no. 11 (November 2009): 36–37. https://search.ebscohost.com/login.aspx?direct=true&db=aph&AN=45315135&site=ehost-live&scope=site.

Coffman, Steve. "What If You Ran Your Library Like a Bookstore?" *American Libraries* 29, no. 3 (March 1998): 40. https://search.ebscohost.com/login.aspx?direct=true&db=aph&AN=3065 38&site=ehost-live&scope=site.

Collaborative Summer Library Program. Accessed February 4, 2015. http://www.cslpreads .org/.

Doucette, Elisabeth. "Branding for Public Libraries." Lyrasis. Last modified December 8, 2009. http://www.slideshare.net/conniemassey/branding-for-public-libraries.

Evans, G. Edward, and Thomas L. Carter. *Introduction to Library Public Services.* 7th ed. Library and Information Science Text. Westport, CT: Libraries Unlimited, 2009.

Fister, Barbara. "The Dewey Dilemma." *Library Journal* 134, no. 16 (October 1, 2009): 22–25. https://search.ebscohost.com/login.aspx?direct=true&db=aph&AN=44468055&site=eh ost-live&scope=site.

Hamilton, Masha. *The Camel Bookmobile.* New York: HarperCollins, 2007.

Jacobson, Alan. "Building Displays That Move the Merchandise." *American Libraries* 43, no. 1/2 (January/February 2012): 42–44. https://search.ebscohost.com/login.aspx?direct=true &db=aph&AN=70708060&site=ehost-live&scope=site.

———. "How to Offer More Than a Movie." *American Libraries* 42, no. 7/8 (July/August 2011): 43–45. https://search.ebscohost.com/login.aspx?direct=true&db=aph&AN=64028544&sit e=ehost-live&scope=site.

James, Geoffrey. "How to Write a Press Release, with Examples." CBS News. November 10, 2010. http://www.cbsnews.com/news/how-to-write-a-press-release-with-examples/.

John Cotton Dana Library Public Relations Award. http://www.ebscohost.com/academic/ john-cotton-dana.

Library Displays. http://librarydisplays.org/.

Lindsay, Anita Rothwell. *Marketing and Public Relations Practices in College Libraries.* CLIP Notes 34. Chicago: American Library Association, 2004.

"Marketing." In *BusinessDictionary.com.* http://www.businessdictionary.com.

Motion Picture Licensing Corporation. http://www.mplc.org/.

Movie Licensing USA. http://www.movlic.com/.

Murphy, Sarah Anne. "Info Pro: Adopting Tools from the World of Business Consulting." *American Libraries* 42, no. 1/2 (January/February 2011): 36–39. https://search.ebscohost .com/login.aspx?direct=true&db=aph&AN=57186040&site=ehost-live&scope=site.

Shaw, Amy, and Peter Deekle. *Outstanding Library Public Relations: 60 Years of the John Cotton Dana Award.* Chicago: American Library Association, 2007.

Singh, Rajesh. "Branding in Library and Information Context: The Role of Marketing Culture." *Information Services & Use* 24, no. 2 (2004): 93–98. https://search.ebscohost.com/ login.aspx?direct=true&db=aph&AN=13547222&site=ehost-live&scope=site.

———. "Engaging Your Library Community through Effective Brand Advocacy: STEPPS to Success." *Feliciter* 60, no. 3 (June 2014): 27–29. https://search.ebscohost.com/login.aspx? direct=true&db=aph&AN=97207090&site=ehost-live&scope=site.

Skaggs, Gayle. *Look, It's Books! Marketing Your Library with Displays and Promotions.* Jefferson, NC: McFarland, 2008.

PART III

Access to Information: A Fundamental Right

CHAPTER 13

Intellectual Freedom and Censorship

An Overview

Library support staff (LSS) will know the ethics and values of the profession, including an understanding of the Library Bill of Rights, the ALA Code of Ethics, the freedom of information, confidentiality of patron records, and privacy issues. (ALA-LSSC Competency #2)

Topics Covered in This Chapter:

- The First and Fourth Amendments
- Library Bill of Rights
- Intellectual Freedom
- Censorship

Key Terms:

Bill of Rights: The Bill of Rights is the first ten amendments to the Constitution that were written in response to calls from several states for greater constitutional protection for individual liberties. Ratified in 1791, they are the basis for the Library Bill of Rights.

Censorship: Censorship is the "suppression of ideas and information that certain persons—individuals, groups or government officials—find objectionable or dangerous."[1] Censorship of materials is a major issue in libraries.

First Amendment: The First Amendment to the U.S. Constitution is that part of the Bill of Rights that prohibits the making of any law "respecting an establishment of religion or prohibiting the free exercise thereof; or abridging the freedom of speech, or of the press, or of the right of the people peaceably to assemble."[2] Thus, libraries can purchase whatever materials they deem relevant to their collections and can make their meeting and exhibit space available to the public without restriction.

Fourth Amendment: The Fourth Amendment to the U.S. Constitution is that part of the Bill of Rights that prohibits unreasonable searches and seizures. This protects the privacy of library patrons from having their reading or Internet searching history accessed without their permission.

Intellectual freedom: Intellectual freedom is the right of everyone to seek and receive information from all points of view without restriction. It encourages free access to all ideas and is protected under the First Amendment. Libraries provide a variety of materials so that users can choose the information that suits their needs.

Privacy: Privacy is the right to be left alone and free from surveillance; the right to determine whether, when, how, and to whom one's personal information, including any history or records of library materials borrowed or Internet sites accessed, is to be revealed.

THE FIRST AND FOURTH AMENDMENTS

Any discussion of intellectual freedom and censorship must begin with an examination of the U.S. Constitution. In 1789, several states felt that the Constitution did not go far enough to protect the rights of individual citizens.

The Bill of Rights is a list of limits on government power. For example, what the Founders saw as the natural right of individuals to speak and worship freely was protected by the First Amendment's prohibitions on Congress from making laws establishing a religion or abridging freedom of speech. For another example, the natural right to be free from unreasonable government intrusion in one's home was safeguarded by the Fourth Amendment's warrant requirements.[3]

The First Amendment reads, "Congress shall make no law respecting an establishment of religion, or prohibiting the free exercise thereof; or abridging the freedom of speech, or of the press, or the right of the people peaceably to assemble, and to petition the Government for a redress of grievances."[4] *"Abridging the freedom of speech, or of the press, or the right of the people peaceably to assemble"* are the key terms that ensure that citizens of the United States are entitled to express themselves freely without interference by the government, including through their choice of reading materials, exhibits, and meetings held on library property. There are those who would suppress and remove from public access information that they judge inappropriate or dangerous so that no one else has the chance to read or view the material and make up their own minds about it.

The Fourth Amendment reads,

Search and arrest warrants. The right of the people to be secure in their persons, houses, papers, and effects, against unreasonable searches and seizures, shall not be violated, and no Warrants shall issue, but upon probable cause, supported by Oath or affirmation, and particularly describing the place to be searched, and the persons or things to be seized.[5]

This means that citizens of the United States have the right to have their personal information protected. Privacy is an important concept protected by the Fourth

Amendment but is being undermined daily. We trade off a level of privacy for convenience in many of our daily digital transactions.[6] Web searches, phone calls, e-mails, and texts—our daily communications—are subject to exposure. When a product or subject is researched online, related ads often pop up when navigating to a different page. We have the options of adjusting our privacy settings on our computers, but we are not completely immune, as Internet cookies are often left behind. "A cookie is a piece of text that a Web server can store on a user's hard disk. Cookies allow a Web site to store information on a user's machine and later retrieve it."[7] The cookie identifies you as a user that has visited a site and what your interests or shopping preferences may be. A potential danger is that a company can sell your information to other companies with similar products and track your movements across multiple sites. This can feel a lot like spying.[8]

THE LIBRARY BILL OF RIGHTS

These constitutional amendments provide the basis for the Library Bill of Rights. Because the federal government requires no restrictions on speech and stringent restrictions on privacy, in 1939, the American Library Association (ALA) adopted the Library Bill of Rights. (It has been amended several times since then.) It affirms that all libraries are forums for information and ideas and provide for free access to all information regardless of background, origin of author, or views of those contributing to its creation. The association and its state affiliates urge that all governing bodies of individual libraries adopt the Library Bill of Rights as their own policy statement.

We will see how these rights form the foundation for the principles of intellectual freedom and censorship.

INTELLECTUAL FREEDOM

Intellectual freedom is the right of everyone to seek and receive information from all points of view without restriction. It provides for free access to all ideas and is protected under the First Amendment of the U.S. Constitution.

At its basic level, it means that everyone has the right to use the library, regardless of age, origin, background, or personal views, and that the library will provide material on all points of view. There will always be controversial subjects, and if a library collects materials offering one point of view, it must also provide materials that offer the opposing point of view. Collection development requires balance regardless of the politics or creed of the materials buyer. For example, if I am the book selector and I come across a review for a book that endorses a philosophy with which I disagree, I cannot let my personal bias influence my selection choices. If it is well reviewed, meets the criteria of the library's selection policy, and fills a need in the collection, then it will be chosen regardless of my personal feelings.

The ALA publishes the *Intellectual Freedom Manual*, an essential resource for librarians. Currently in its eighth edition, it includes intellectual freedom guidelines, policies, and interpretations of the Library Bill of Rights as it applies to public, school, academic, and special libraries. It addresses how intellectual freedom principles and practices have adapted in this age of electronic access. Also included are guidelines and interpretations regarding public library Internet use, user behavior, filtering software, the freedom to read, and challenges to materials.

The Freedom to Read Statement, published by the ALA and included in the *Intellectual Freedom Manual*, says that "the freedom to read is guaranteed by the Constitution. Those with faith in free people will stand firm on these constitutional guarantees of essential rights and will exercise the responsibilities that accompany these rights."[9] It further asserts, in part, that it is in the public interest for librarians to make available the widest diversity of views and expressions, including those that are controversial or distasteful. We know that librarians do not endorse every idea or opinion presented by the material in the library. It is not in the public interest for librarians to deny access to writings on the basis of the personal or political beliefs of the author. Further, it is the responsibility of librarians to resist those seeking to impose their own beliefs upon the community.[10]

Intellectual freedom does not apply only to the written word or visual materials. Libraries that make exhibit spaces, bulletin boards, and meeting rooms available to the public they serve should make such facilities available on an equitable basis, regardless of the beliefs or affiliations of individuals or groups requesting their use. Article 6 of the Library Bill of Rights makes this clear:

THE SIXTH ARTICLE OF THE LIBRARY BILL OF RIGHTS

VI. Libraries which make exhibit spaces and meeting rooms available to the public they serve should make such facilities available on an equitable basis, regardless of the beliefs or affiliations of individuals or groups requesting their use.

Used with permission from the American Library Association

It is necessary that the library has a well-worded policy available to all who use these facilities that makes clear that library meeting spaces, if publicly funded, are available to the general public for non-library-sponsored events. It cannot exclude any group based on the subject matter that the group espouses. If the library allows use by nonprofits and clubs, it cannot exclude political or religious groups. The library must be sure to post a notice that it does not endorse or support the viewpoints of any groups that use the meeting space. Use inclusive, rather than exclusive, wording, for example, "the library's facilities are open to organizations engaged in educational, cultural, intellectual, or charitable activities" is an inclusive statement of the limited uses to which the facilities may be put.[11]

Still, adherence to policy doesn't guarantee that there will not be conflict. Matt Hale, the white supremacist leader of the World Church of the Creator, took advantage of these policies to book library meeting rooms around the country in the early 2000s. While there were no problems in Salt Lake City, Utah, or Peoria, Illinois, in two cases (in Wallingford, Connecticut, in 2001[12] and in Wakefield, Massachusetts, in 2002[13]), advance publicity brought in protestors, riots, and the police. Physical damage to the properties occurred, and people were hurt. In cases where a known group causes

---

SAMPLE MEETING ROOM POLICY

1. The purpose of the library's meeting rooms is to provide space for library programs and events and civic, cultural, educational, and informational meetings.
2. Requests for use of the meeting room may be made in person, by telephone, or in writing. Requests will be honored on a first-come, first-served basis.
3. Use of the meeting rooms does not imply library endorsement of ideas expressed in the meetings or of the goals and objectives of the organizations using the facilities.
4. Meeting rooms are available during regular library hours. Some rooms may be available earlier than library opening hours, but meetings may not go beyond library closing time.
5. All meetings held at the library must be free of charge.
6. Sales or solicitation in the library's meeting rooms are prohibited except for events that benefit the library.
7. Rooms are not available for private parties.
8. Tables and chairs are provided, as well as a screen and lectern. Groups are responsible for returning the room to the way in which it was found. Groups will be charged to cover the cost of resetting the room, damage to the room or library equipment, or extraordinary cleaning that results from use.
9. Food and nonalcoholic beverages may be served. Groups are responsible for cleanup.
10. The library's rules of conduct apply to the use of the meeting rooms.

---

damage and incites confrontation, Judith Krug, then head of the ALA's Office for Intellectual Freedom, said, "Given the record of violent demonstrations, libraries are justified in closing the public spaces."[14] Libraries can choose to restrict their meeting spaces to only library-related activities if they feel that a wider policy would invite conflict.

That librarians and the ALA have always held these beliefs, however, is historically inaccurate. Most professional librarians wholeheartedly support the concepts, if not the exact wording, expressed in the Library Bill of Rights. But have the profession, libraries, and their trustees always felt this way? Surprisingly, no.

CENSORSHIP

In 1908, in his inaugural speech titled "The Librarian as Censor," newly elected ALA president Arthur Bostwick advocated that librarians carefully censor their selection of literature. Literature, especially popular novels, was considered frivolous and, therefore, immoral. Bostwick said, "Books that distinctly commend what is wrong, that teach how to sin and tell how pleasant sin is, sometimes with and sometimes without the added sauce of impropriety, are increasingly popular, tempting the author to imitate them, the publishers to produce, the bookseller to exploit. Thank Heaven they do not tempt the Librarian."[15]

The popular books of the day were largely historic fiction, Christian fiction, and Westerns.

Through the latter part of the nineteenth century and well into the twentieth, society expected the new library profession to exercise censorship. Anthony Comstock, founder of the New York Society for the Suppression of Vice (the first federal antipornography law of 1873 was named for him), sought to limit the use of sexual speech in written materials in the United States.[16] This represented the "community standards" of the time. There was a much more uniform understanding of morality and depravity, and people generally agreed on what should be excluded from libraries. A librarian selecting books today, especially for a small- to medium-sized library, doesn't have that consensus to rely on. Libraries must select from a much wider variety of possible publications and media—and for a vastly diverse population. By contrast, bestsellers from the *New York Times'* 2015 list of combined print and e-book titles include erotic fiction, self-help, military history, and crime novels.

The adoption of the Library Bill of Rights in 1939 and its further amendments redefined how we think about these issues today. According to the ALA, censorship is the "suppression of ideas and information that certain persons—individuals, groups or government officials—find objectionable or dangerous. It is no more complicated than someone saying, 'Don't let anyone read this book, or buy that magazine, or view that film, because I object to it!'"[17] The *Intellectual Freedom Manual* states, "Censorship . . . means not only deletion or excision of parts of published materials but also efforts to ban, prohibit, suppress, proscribe, remove, label, or restrict materials."[18]

NOVELS OF 1908–1909

1. *When a Man's a Man*, by Harold Bell Wright
2. *The Little Shepherd of Kingdom Come*, by John Fox Jr.
3. *The Winning of Barbara Worth*, by Harold Bell Wright
4. *The Valley of the Giants*, by Peter B. Kyne
5. *Their Yesterdays*, by Harold Bell Wright
6. *The Heart of the Hills*, by John Fox
7. *If Winter Comes*, by A. S. M. Hutchinson
8. *The Mysterious Rider*, by Zane Grey
9. *The Virginian: A Horseman of the Plains*, by Owen Wister
10. *At the Foot of the Rainbow*, by Gene Stratton-Porter
11. *When Knighthood Was in Flower*, by Edwin Caskoden
12. *The Log of a Cowboy: A Narrative of the Old Trail Days*, by Andy Adams
13. *To Have and to Hold*, by Mary Johnston
14. *A Knight of the Cumberland*, by John Fox Jr.
15. *Green Light*, by Lloyd C. Douglas

Source: Publishers Weekly/Wikipedia

BESTSELLERS OF 2015

The Life-Changing Magic of Tidying Up, by Marie Kondo
10-Day Green Smoothie Cleanse, by J. J. Smith
What to Expect When You're Expecting, by Heidi Murkoff and Sharon Mazel
Fifty Shades of Grey, by E. L. James
Obsession in Death, by J. D. Robb
Big Little Lies, by Liane Moriarty
Killing Patton, by Bill O'Reilly and Martin Dugard
Upstairs at the White House, by J. B. West with Mary Lynn Kotz
American Sniper, by Chris Kyle with Scott Mcewen and Jim Defelice
Private Vegas, by James Patterson and Maxine Paetro

There are four basic motivational factors that underlie the censor's actions:

- Family Values
  - The censor may feel threatened by changes in the accepted, traditional way of life.
- Religion
  - The censor may view explicitly sexual works and politically unorthodox ideas as attacks on religious faith.
- Political Views
  - The censor may view a work that advocates radical change as subversive.
- Minority Rights
  - The censor has been joined by groups who want their own special values recognized.
  - Ethnic minorities and women struggling against long-established stereotypes, for example, are anxious to reject materials viewed as perpetuating those stereotypes.[19]

Censors, who may have the highest of motives, may pressure public institutions like libraries to suppress and remove from public access information that they judge inappropriate or dangerous so that no one else has the chance to read or view the material and make up their own minds about it. They seldom see themselves as censors or "the bad guys"; rather, they are sincerely concerned individuals who believe that censorship can improve society, protect children, and restore values.

Censors can be both internal and external. The source of *internal* censorship that libraries are likely to face include members of the trustees or governing bodies, library staff members, and library management. All of these individuals are involved in activities and groups outside of the library that may influence their judgment. A staff member may subtly censor by neglecting to select materials on a particular topic, causing an unbalanced collection. Restrictive circulation and cataloging can also keep materials from the public. Library trustees or other governing agents may pressure the librarian to restrict what they perceive to be offensive topics.

The *external* censors are often individuals, parents, religious groups, political groups, and ethnic groups. What they may object to are references to sex and drugs, profanity, witchcraft and the occult, racism, health or sexual education, or materials that they perceive as being inappropriate for children at a particular age. Another source of external censorship comes from national organizations, such as Family Friendly Libraries headed by Karen Jo Gounaud (now called Citizens for Community Values, or CCV), Safe Libraries, and Parents Against Bad Books in Schools. Their shared missions are to promote emphasis on the traditional family, Judeo-Christian values, and local authority over school and public libraries. They oppose the policies and philosophies of the ALA. They can be effective in working together in order to put pressure on libraries to restrict access to what they find objectionable and to organize locally in order to coordinate challenges and pressure local officials.

In subsequent chapters, we will continue with the concepts of book banning and media and Internet challenges, as well as the processes of relying on policies and procedures to respond to specific challenges.

CHAPTER SUMMARY

This chapter introduced the concepts of intellectual freedom and censorship. As they are based on the U.S. Constitution, the Library Bill of Rights, the ALA Code of Ethics, and the Freedom to Read Statement provide a framework for libraries to promote equal access to all materials in all formats without restriction. They address opposition to the censorship of materials that are perceived by some to be offensive or inappropriate. They endorse confidentiality of patron records and privacy issues and proscribe unauthorized access to one's reading or Internet search history.

DISCUSSION QUESTIONS AND ACTIVITIES

1. In what ways do the First and Fourth Amendments to the U.S. Constitution influence the Library Bill of Rights?
2. Privacy is the key to intellectual freedom and censorship.
   a. What expectations should library patrons have regarding their right to privacy?
3. Do you feel that using the Internet compromises your privacy?
   a. If so, in what ways?
4. Are there any instances in which you feel censorship may be justified?
5. Several national organizations disagree with the ALA's policies.
   a. Is there anything in the Freedom to Read Statement that you find objectionable?
6. Google yourself or a family member.
   a. Are you surprised by what you find?

NOTES

1. American Library Association, "What Is Censorship?," American Library Association, http://www.ala.org/advocacy/intfreedom/censorshipfirstamendmentissues/ifcensorshipqanda.

2. Constitution Facts, "Learn about the United States Bill of Rights," Constitution Facts, http://www.constitutionfacts.com/us-constitution-amendments/bill-of-rights/.

3. James Madison, "Bill of Rights of the United States of America (1791)," Bill of Rights Institute, http://billofrightsinstitute.org/founding-documents/bill-of-rights/.

4. Constitution Facts, "Learn about the United States Bill of Rights."

5. Constitution Facts, "Learn about the United States Bill of Rights."

6. Rebecca T. Miller, "Protect Thy Patrons," *Library Journal* 138, no. 16 (October 1, 2013): 6.

7. Marshall Brain, "How Internet Cookies Work," How Stuff Works, http://computer.howstuffworks.com/cookie1.htm.

8. Brain, "How Internet Cookies Work."

9. American Library Association, "The Freedom to Read Statement," American Library Association, http://www.ala.org/advocacy/intfreedom/statementspols/freedomreadstatement.

10. American Library Association, *Intellectual Freedom Manual*, 8th ed. (Chicago: ALA Editions, 2010), 211–13.

11. American Library Association, *Intellectual Freedom Manual*, 170–71.

12. Paul Zielbauer, "Shouts and Scuffles at White Supremacy Rally," *New York Times*, last modified March 11, 2001. http://www.nytimes.com/2001/03/11/nyregion/shouts-and-scuffles-at-white-supremacy-rally.htm.

13. Norman Oder, "Racist Group Takes Advantage of PL Meeting Room Policies," *Library Journal* 127, no. 17 (October 15, 2002): 14.

14. Oder, "Racist Group Takes Advantage."

15. Arthur E. Bostwick, "The Librarian as Censor," *Library Journal* 33, no. 7 (July 1908): 257–64.

16. Barnum Museum, "The Comstock Act," Barnum Museum, http://www.barnum-museum.org/.

17. American Library Association, "What Is Censorship?"

18. American Library Association, *Intellectual Freedom Manual*, 13.

19. American Library Association, "The Censor: Motives and Tactics," American Library Association, http://www.ala.org/bbooks/challengedmaterials/preparation/censor-motives-and-tactics.

REFERENCES, SUGGESTED READINGS, AND WEBSITES

American Library Association. "The Censor: Motives and Tactics." American Library Association. http://www.ala.org/bbooks/challengedmaterials/preparation/censor-motives-and-tactics.
———. "The Freedom to Read Statement." American Library Association. http://www.ala.org/advocacy/intfreedom/statementspols/freedomreadstatement.
———. *Intellectual Freedom Manual*. 8th ed. Chicago: ALA Editions, 2010.
———. "Library Bill of Rights." American Library Association. http://www.ala.org/advocacy/intfreedom/librarybill.
———. "What Is Censorship?" American Library Association. http://www.ala.org/advocacy/intfreedom/censorshipfirstamendmentissues/ifcensorshipqanda.
———. Office for Intellectual Freedom. http://www.ala.org/offices/oif.
Barnum Museum. "The Comstock Act." Barnum Museum. http://www.barnum-museum.org/.
Bostwick, Arthur E. "The Librarian as Censor." *Library Journal* 33, no. 7 (July 1908): 257–64.
Brain, Marshall. "How Internet Cookies Work." How Stuff Works. http://computer.howstuffworks.com/cookie1.htm.
Constitution Facts. "Learn about the United States Bill of Rights." Constitution Facts. http://www.constitutionfacts.com/us-constitution-amendments/bill-of-rights/.

"David McCullough Interview: Intellectual Freedom." YouTube. https://www.youtube.com/watch?v=yb39W3lBmVo.

Gounaud, Karen Jo. "Family Friendly Libraries." Citizens for Community Values. http://www.ccv.org/issues/harmful-to-children/family-friendly-libraries/.

Kleinman, Dan. "Editorial Supports Family Friendly Libraries in Greensboro, NC, and Bandwidth Shapers Help." *Safe Libraries* (blog). November 21, 2009. http://safelibraries.blogspot.com/2009/11/editorial-supports-family-friendly.html.

LibraryThing. "Book Awards: Top Ten List of Bestselling Novels for 1908 and 1909." Library Thing. http://www.librarything.com/bookaward/Top+ten+list+of+Bestselling+novels+for+1908+and+1909.

Madison, James. "Bill of Rights of the United States of America (1791)." Bill of Rights Institute. http://billofrightsinstitute.org/founding-documents/bill-of-rights/.

Miller, Rebecca T. "Protect Thy Patrons." *Library Journal* 138, no. 16 (October 1, 2013): 8. https://search.ebscohost.com/login.aspx?direct=true&db=aph&AN=90381745&site=ehost-live&scope=site.

Oder, Norman. "Racist Group Takes Advantage of PL Meeting Room Policies." *Library Journal* 127, no. 17 (October 15, 2002): 14. http://search.ebscohost.com/login.aspx?direct=true&db=aph&AN=7521055&site=eds-live.

Parents Against Bad Books in Schools. http://www.pabbis.com/.

Zielbauer, Paul. "Shouts and Scuffles at White Supremacy Rally." *New York Times*, last modified March 11, 2001. http://www.nytimes.com/2001/03/11/nyregion/shouts-and-scuffles-at-white-supremacy-rally.html.

CHAPTER 14

The Freedom to Read

Library support staff (LSS) will know the ethics and values of the profession, including an understanding of the Library Bill of Rights, the ALA Code of Ethics, the freedom of information, confidentiality of patron records, and privacy issues. They will also know and understand the principles of intellectual freedom and censorship. (ALA-LSSC Competency #2)

Topics Covered in This Chapter:

- Challenged Materials
- Selection Policies
- When the Censor Comes
- The USA PATRIOT Act and Libraries

Key Terms:

Banned books: A banned book is one that is subject to objection and/or is physically removed from the library shelf on the basis that it is in some way offensive to someone. In so doing, it is made unavailable to anyone.

Censorship: Censorship is the "suppression of ideas and information that certain persons—individuals, groups or government officials—find objectionable or dangerous."[1] Censorship of materials is a major issue in libraries.

Challenged materials: A challenge to materials is a formal, written complaint requesting the restriction or removal of a book based on the objections of a person or group. The majority of these people are parents, and the location is often the school library.

The USA PATRIOT Act: This is the acronym made by the Uniting and Strengthening America by Providing Appropriate Tools Required to Intercept and Obstruct Terrorism Act.

Created by Congress in the wake of 9/11, it substantially expanded the authority of U.S. law enforcement for the stated purpose of fighting terrorism in the United States and abroad. It expanded the authority of the FBI to gain access to library records, including stored electronic data and communications.

CHALLENGED MATERIALS

We ended the previous chapter with a discussion of censorship. As we recall, **censorship** is the suppression of ideas and information that certain people find objectionable or dangerous. This in and of itself can be a personal matter, but when it is brought to the attention of others, it becomes a public issue. Censorship is not a new concept. Originally it was largely religiously based; one of the first noted instances was in 1235 when Pope Gregory IX established the Inquisition in order to patrol and enforce Catholicism. Several centuries of censure were related to religious heresy; it then evolved to censor sedition (the encouragement of the people to disobey the government). It wasn't until the seventeenth century that books began to be selected for this "honor" for obscene, lewd, and indecent content.[2] In the centuries to come, all three of these reasons for censorship would reappear and do so today. Censorship has not been confined to books, however; speech, film, and art were and are equally maligned.

We already know the reasons why people want books to be censored. But they often go one step further and either challenge a title or request that it be banned. There is a difference between **challenging** and **banning** a book: banning a book means the physical removal of the item. A challenge, however, is a formal, written complaint requesting the restriction or removal of a book based on the objections of a person or group. The majority of these people are parents, and the location is usually the school library. According to a position statement by the National Council of Teachers of English (NCTE) titled the Student's Right to Read, "American schools have been pressured to restrict or deny students access to books or periodicals deemed objectionable by some individual or group on moral, political, religious, ethnic, racial, or philosophical grounds."[3] The NCTE asserts, as does the American Library Association's (ALA) Freedom to Read Statement, that the right to read is basic to a democratic society. These statements agree that the library does not endorse the viewpoint of every author and acknowledge that some materials may be found objectionable to some—but it is the library's responsibility to provide for a wide range of materials. After all, parents can choose *not* to borrow materials that are counter to their beliefs, but they do not have the right to decide that no one else should borrow them either.

There are lists upon lists of books that have been challenged or banned over the years, and they run the gamut from classic literature (*Ulysses*—sexual themes) to picture books (*In the Night Kitchen*—nudity). Each year the ALA publishes a top-ten list of frequently challenged books, most of which are objected to because of sexually explicit material, offensive language, unsuitability to an age group, violence, and homosexuality.[4] Among the most frequently and perpetually challenged titles are the Captain Underpants series, by Dav Pilkey; *The Absolutely True Diary of a*

Part-Time Indian, by Sherman Alexie; *The Hunger Games*, by Suzanne Collins; *The Chocolate War*, by Robert Cormier; and *The Bridge to Terabithia*, by Katherine Paterson. The entire Harry Potter series also makes the list. Objections to these titles include offensive language, violence, racism, the occult, and, of course, sex. This does not imply that these titles have no merit. On the contrary, many of these titles are popular, well reviewed, recommended, and have value as literature. That they were challenged only means that someone found something objectionable that someone else may not even have noticed.

Typically, a child will bring home a reading list or a book assigned to the entire class. A parent may have "heard" that the book is objectionable, or they may read it themselves and find reasons to not want their child to read it. A local library had a patron with a high school–aged son; she would routinely bring in his class reading list and ask the staff to tell her which ones had sex in them so that she could cross them off of the list. She was encouraged to find the books on the shelves and look them over herself or bring her son with her. The fact that she was doing this for her son instead of letting him choose what interested him was problematic but not, unfortunately, unusual.

It is not uncommon for books in school libraries to be challenged because some parents feel that the content is inappropriate to that age group. "Many contemporary novels for adolescents focus on the real world of young people—drugs, premarital sex, alcoholism, divorce, high school gangs, school dropouts, racism, violence, and sensuality."[5] A former patron was so offended by the content of her daughter's middle school library that she withdrew her from public school and placed her in a parochial school that had a library collection with which she was more comfortable.

Places I Never Meant to Be: Original Stories by Censored Writers is a collection of short stories by authors whose works have been challenged or banned. Judy Blume, who edited the book, points out that "if you ask a dozen people what censorship means, you'll get twelve different answers."[6] All of the authors in this collection have been challenged—and puzzled by it on many occasions. Harry Mazer's book *The Last Mission* is about war. Shouldn't it use the language of soldiers? Another contributor, David Klasse, says of his book *Wrestling with Honor*, "How can we expect teen-agers to read books if we avoid real-life situations?"[7] These authors did not intend to create controversy; they just wrote books for young adults that reflect the lives of that age group. From their points of view, a challenge can be an opportunity to start a discussion. Sanitizing a book in order to avoid offending someone is, in itself, offensive, but that is the position in which many of these authors find themselves.

As long as books are written, music is composed, and art is created, there will be someone who will object to the content. We can't prevent people from censoring, challenging, or attempting to ban, but we do have tools to work with in order to create options.

SELECTION POLICIES

It is essential that libraries adopt and adhere to a *materials selection policy* based on the Library Bill of Rights and the Freedom to Read Statement. The policy should be fairly detailed about the scope of the library's collection. The sample selection policy in chapter 2 contains the elements of such a document.

As you can see, it should contain a statement about weeding—the removal of books and materials from the collection and under what condition a book would *not* be removed in order to differentiate between regular collection maintenance and the removal of material under censorship pressure.

A selection policy for a school media center would be similar but would include a statement about materials chosen to support the educational goals and curriculum on all levels of difficulty and variety of viewpoints and formats. It would follow the format for the public library in that it would include a statement of responsibility, criteria of selection (including review sources), procedures for selection (including removal or replacement of worn materials), and reconsideration of materials. For an academic library, the policy follows a similar format but would include criteria for electronic resources, subject guidelines, and possibly interdisciplinary indexes.[8]

If a patron asks for a book to be removed, a procedure must be followed before any materials are taken off of the shelf. There are the steps to take under these circumstances. Offer the patron a Request for Reconsideration form, an essential part of the selection policy. Such a form can be found on page 181.

In the many years that I was a public librarian, I received comments and complaints, but no one ever filed a formal request for reconsideration. In one case, a young mother was offended by the nudity of a little boy in *Tommy Takes a Bath*, by Gunilla Wolde (currently out of print). She made sure that I was aware of it but did not ask for anything to be done about it. On another occasion, a complaint came in from a mother whose daughters had brought home a graphic novel from the teen room that had offensive language. She couldn't understand why we'd allow something like this on the shelf. After explaining our policy and her options, I thanked her for being concerned and suggested that perhaps she could come with them to choose books together. Again, she was offered the means to register a complaint but chose not to. Sometimes allowing the patron to vent is all that is needed. I was fortunate never to have a challenge escalate but that cannot be said for many

STEPS TO FOLLOW WHEN ASKED TO REMOVE A BOOK

1. Greet the patron with a smile—communicate your openness to talk.
2. Ask if they've read the book.
3. Ask to what they particularly object.
4. Practice "active listening"—take time to acknowledge the person's concern (I'm sorry you're upset; I understand your concern).
5. Stay calm and courteous.
6. Know your selection policy and give facts—not personal opinions.
7. Be prepared to give a clear and nonintimidating explanation of library procedure, registering a complaint, and about when a decision will be made.
8. Do not remove material until the complaint is resolved.

REQUEST FOR RECONSIDERATION

1. Name_____

2. Date_____

3. Address_____

4. Phone_____

5. E-mail_____

6. Resource on which you are commenting:

   a. Book

   b. DVD

   c. Magazine

   d. Program

   e. Newspaper

7. Title, author, publisher_____

8. What brought this to your attention?_____

9. Have you read/examined this item?_____

10. What is your concern?_____

11. Do you represent

    a. Yourself_____

    b. Group_____

public and school libraries in this country. Challenging and book banning are all too prevalent. Links to several examples can be found at the end of this chapter.

The ALA celebrates Banned Books Week annually at the end of September. This is a national collaborative effort among librarians, authors, publishers, teachers, and concerned readers to bring attention to the freedom to read. By focusing on efforts to ban, challenge, or restrict books, it draws attention to the harm of censorship. Libraries often plan programs around the subject, including author events, group readings, book discussions, and signage and displays.[9]

Having a policy and filing a complaint never stopped an incident from occurring and doesn't protect a library from an initial complaint or from the unpleasantness that can follow. Sometimes the very existence of a policy and the fact that the patron has to write a complaint is enough to diffuse the situation. Giving the patron options gives him or her control. The handling of a complaint in an established, consistent, officially approved way shows that due process has been followed and provides a body of evidence on which a court case could be built, should it come

Figure 14.1.   Banned Books Display. *Photograph Courtesy of the Bill Memorial Library*

to that. This is about the larger principle of the freedom to read, not the subjective merit of an individual book.

WHEN THE CENSOR COMES

When a parent or group of parents act spontaneously to question a textbook or library material, the national groups we referred to in the previous chapter (Citizens for Community Values [CCV], Parents Against Bad Books in Schools [PABBIS], Safe Libraries, and others) may contact them and send in their literature, lists of other books that the parent should be aware of, and advice. For example, CCV's "10 Ways to Create a Family Friendly Library"[10] include finding facts on local public library systems (collection policies and funding), contacting local officials and studying their voting records, sharing the findings with local community groups, and using petitions and flyers to inform the public of that which the group finds to be harmful. These groups can and do try to become active in local politics by recommending the election of moral and ethical leaders to public office, governing agencies, and even the library board. While wanting ethical leadership may be commendable, it becomes a problem if it is done in order to influence selection policies. The literature from these groups will suggest that the parents organize and that they also review the local library for questionable titles. The result of this activity is that, whereas at one time a censorship incident would be over one book, now an incident may spread to a whole list of objectionable titles. They are particularly suspicious of the ALA and their "licentious political and cultural agenda."[11] As they sincerely believe in their cause, they may also involve the media.

If the media does get involved, there are some strategies that can help. First, have one spokesperson for the library and make sure that everyone knows who that person is. Know the message that you want to deliver—most likely related to the library's policies. It's easy to become intimidated by the press, but try to stay positive, not defensive. It helps to get others involved, too, such as the Friends of the Library, board members, and other community supporters. Remember to keep it professional and simple. Use real words, not jargon, and reference the freedom of choice for all patrons. Other tips for dealing with the media include:

TIPS FOR DEALING WITH THE MEDIA

- Be clear on whom you represent—you or the library.
- Know your audience so that you can focus your remarks.
- Make your own statements: don't be manipulated by questions such as "Isn't it true that your library . . . ?"
- Don't be afraid to admit it if there is something that you don't know.
- Avoid saying "no comment"; rather say, "I'm sorry, I can't answer that."
- Remember—nothing is ever "off the record."

Also remember that it isn't just what you say but how you present yourself. Look and sound professional, dress appropriately, and show enthusiasm for all of the good things that the library does.

People who try to censor or who organize or affiliate with a national organization such as CCV or PABBIS truly believe that they are supporting traditional family values and protecting children. What they fail to understand is that they are making this value judgment for everyone—taking away the very freedom of choice that the First Amendment guarantees.

THE USA PATRIOT ACT AND LIBRARIES

In the wake of the events of September 11, 2001, then U.S. attorney general John Ashcroft asked Congress for additional powers needed to fight terrorism. What many see as a serious breach of the Fourth Amendment to the U.S. Constitution (the prohibition of unreasonable searches and seizures) became the **USA PATRIOT ACT**, or the Uniting and Strengthening America by Providing Appropriate Tools Required to

Intercept and Obstruct Terrorism Act. It substantially expanded the authority of U.S. law enforcement for the stated purpose of fighting terrorism in the United States and abroad. The PATRIOT Act became law on October 26, 2001, without any hearings by congressional committees. It expanded the definition of terrorism to include "domestic terrorism," enlarging the number of activities to which these powers could be applied. It amended more than fifteen federal statutes, including

> the laws governing criminal procedure, computer fraud and abuse, foreign intelligence, wiretapping, immigration, and the laws governing the privacy of student records. These amendments expanded the authority of the Federal Bureau of Investigation and law enforcement to gain access to business records, medical records, educational records and library records, including stored electronic data and communications. It also expanded the laws governing wiretaps and "trap and trace" phone devices to Internet and electronic communications. These enhanced surveillance procedures pose the greatest challenge to privacy and confidentiality in the library.[12]

The Foreign Intelligence Surveillance Act (FISA) of 1978 prescribes procedures for requesting judicial authorization for electronic surveillance and physical search of individuals engaged in espionage or international terrorism against the United States on behalf of a foreign power.[13] Requests are adjudicated by a special eleven-member court called the Foreign Intelligence Surveillance Court. Section 215, amended after 9/11, allows FBI agents to obtain a search warrant for "any tangible thing"[14]: books, records, discs, data tapes, and computers or hard drives. It does not require the agent to show "probable cause" or specific facts to support the belief that a crime may have been committed. The agent only need to *claim* that he or she believes that the records he or she wants may be related to an ongoing investigation relating to terrorism. Libraries that provide Internet access and e-mail service to patrons may become the target of a court order.

This has been objected to not only by libraries but by members of Congress and, indeed, by many in the public sector. An editorial cartoon strip published in the *New York Times* by featured artist Brian McFadden, titled "Urgent Government Recalls," included a block labeled "Recall Notice for the PATRIOT ACT." The "defect/hazard" noted is "a sweeping violation of privacy, hastily thrown together during a National crisis."[15]

On May 26, 2011, President Barack Obama signed the PATRIOT Sunsets Extension Act of 2011, a four-year extension of three key provisions: roving wiretaps, searches of business records (the "library records provision"), and conducting surveillance of "lone wolves"—individuals suspected of terrorist-related activities not linked to a terrorist group. Various sections of the PATRIOT Act were scheduled to "sunset" in 2005, 2011, and 2015. The PATRIOT Act was a large bill, as were the reauthorizations that followed in 2005 and 2006. Not all of it sunsets, but three provisions were set to expire on June 1, 2015: Section 215, the "lone wolf" provision, and the "roving wiretap" provision. Section 215, the "library records provision," also concerns the National Security Agency (NSA) secretly collecting the "to and from" information about nearly every American landline telephone call. (The public was made aware of this by former intelligence contractor Edward Snowden in 2013.[16])

Ultimately, these three key sections of the PATRIOT Act antiterrorism law that expired at midnight June 1, 2015, have been restored and extended through 2019.

"However, Section 215 of that law will be changed to stop the NSA from continuing its mass phone data collection program. Instead, phone companies will retain the data and the NSA can obtain information about targeted individuals with permission from a federal court."[17]

In chapter 4, we talked about integrated library systems (ILS) and how, in the interest of patron confidentiality, all of these ILS offer the option to *not* keep track of a reader's history—which most libraries choose, if it is not, in fact, the default setting. Once the item has been returned, the information relative to that transaction ceases to exist. While this can hinder a patron who would like to know if they have recently read a particular book, it is for their protection in case an inquiry is made by the authorities to learn that patron's reading habits. If the FBI wants to know if Mr. Jones checked out *The Anarchist Cookbook*, for example, there will be no record of anything that he has ever checked out. For Internet searches, many libraries use software that wipes out user history after a reboot of the computer. Products such as Fortres or Deep Freeze basically "freeze" the configuration of the computer system. In the case of any accidental or malicious changes made to the hard drive, the LSS simply reboots the computer to the original "frozen" state. Any changes made are not permanent. (Only when the software is deliberately "thawed" can any changes be made to the configuration.) This applies as well to any searches made on the computer. After a reboot, all search history is gone. Therefore, if the FBI asks to search a computer for evidence that someone has visited a suspicious site, the history doesn't exist.

Many libraries have patrons sign up to use a public computer in order to keep track of how much time is spent on them. Software such as Cybrarian or Time-Keeper can authenticate users through the ILS, manage the length of their online session, and manage printer use and costs. This saves the LSS a lot of time as managing patron Internet use can be time consuming and tedious. It is important to remember, however, that any software that tracks users can be subject to search unless the software provides a remedy to eliminate records or just uses numbers and not names. Record retention policies of individual states may require that manual time sheets, if used, be kept for a certain number of years and cannot be destroyed before that time. The LSS would do well to keep that in mind when considering patron computer-use sign-up sheets.

Libraries that are served with a search warrant issued under FISA rules may not disclose, under penalty of law, the existence of a warrant, and they cannot tell any patron that his or her records were given to the FBI. These rules override state confidentiality statutes. A case that received national attention occurred in Connecticut in 2005, when a national security letter was served to the Library Connection, a consortium of (at the time) twenty-six academic and public libraries, for records that would determine who had used a library computer between 4:00 p.m. and 4:45 p.m. on a specific day six months earlier. The chair and three board members opposed the FBI (under threat of imprisonment) and engaged the American Civil Liberties Union (ACLU) to fight the gag order preventing them from talking about the case. After a long year of litigation, the gag order was lifted and the demand for the records was dropped. The Connecticut Four, as they became known, were hailed as heroes and honored nationally for standing up to the government and for their support of the First Amendment.[18]

If the FBI comes to your library, be sure that there is *one person* designated to be in charge, usually the library director, who should then ask the agent for identification. In the absence of a court order, he can explain the library's privacy and confidentiality of records policy and say that the records are not available. If the agent does produce a warrant, be sure that it is examined thoroughly in order to understand exactly what it is and isn't asking for. The librarian has the right to ask for legal counsel before turning over any records or equipment and to have counsel present when the actual search is conducted. If the library does not have a lawyer, then it can contact the ALA Office of Intellectual Freedom and be provided a referral for advice. For more details, the U.S. Department of Justice provides readable summaries of the PATRIOT Act and FISA, the links to which can be found at the end of this chapter.

CHAPTER SUMMARY

The library profession takes seriously its responsibilities to uphold the First and Fourth Amendments to the U.S. Constitution and the Library Bill of Rights, the ALA Code of Ethics, the freedom of information, and the confidentiality of patron records and privacy issues. LSS also know and understand the principles of intellectual freedom and censorship. Any attempt to abridge these rights, including the PATRIOT Act, runs counter to our mission. We have the tools in place to fight censorship and book banning. Well-written material selection policies that include the Library Bill of Rights and the Freedom to Read Statement, as well as the Request for Reconsideration of Materials form, back this up. The knowledge that everyone has a right to information is critical, and we must understand that not everyone will like or approve of all of the materials in any given library. Patrons have the right to choose only those materials that meet their personal standards, but they do not have the right to prevent another from accessing those materials that do not. The LSS must be vigilant about keeping calm in the face of challenge and, in extreme cases, know how to handle challenges or visits from the FBI.

DISCUSSION QUESTIONS AND ACTIVITIES

1. Does your library (where you work or the one you patronize) do enough to protect the intellectual freedom of its patrons?
   a. Ask to see their policies, if available.
2. What is your understanding of the PATRIOT Act?
   a. Do you think it is still necessary?
   b. If not, what parts could be changed or removed?
3. Examine the mission of an organization (on the web) that is known by libraries for censorship, such as those mentioned in this chapter.
   a. Are they in compliance with ALA policies?
4. Choose two children's books from the list at http://www.ala.org/bbooks/top-100-bannedchallenged-books-2000-2009.
   a. Read them and write a brief review.
   b. Is it apparent why they were challenged?

NOTES

1. American Library Association, "What Is Censorship?," American Library Association, http://www.ala.org/advocacy/intfreedom/censorshipfirstamendmentissues/ifcensorshipqanda.

2. "Index: A Selective Timeline of Censorship 1235–2003," *Conscience*, Spring 2003, 54.

3. National Council of Teachers of English, "The Students' Right to Read," National Council of Teachers of English, http://www.ncte.org/positions/statements/righttoreadguideline.

4. American Library Association, "Frequently Challenged Books of the 21st Century," American Library Association, http://www.ala.org/bbooks/frequentlychallengedbooks/top10.

5. National Council of Teachers of English, "The Students' Right to Read."

6. Judy Blume, ed., *Places I Never Meant to Be: Original Stories by Censored Writers* (New York: Aladdin Paperbacks, 2001), 13.

7. Blume, *Places I Never Meant to Be*.

8. American Library Association, "Selection Policy," *Choice: Current Reviews for Academic Libraries*, http://www.ala.org/acrl/choice/selectionpolicy.

9. American Library Association, "Banned Books Week: Celebrating the Freedom to Read," American Library Association, http://www.ala.org/bbooks/bannedbooksweek.

10. Karen Jo Gounaud, "10 Ways to Create a Family Friendly Library," Family Friendly Libraries, http://www.ccv.org/issues/harmful-to-children/family-friendly-libraries/.

11. Gounaud, "10 Ways to Create."

12. American Library Association, "Analysis of the USA Patriot Act Related to Libraries," American Library Association, http://www.ala.org/offices/oif/ifissues/issuesrelatedlinks/usapatriotactanalysis.

13. Federation of American Scientists, "Foreign Intelligence Surveillance Act," Federation of American Scientists, last modified 1978, http://www.fas.org/irp/agency/doj/fisa/.

14. American Library Association, "Analysis of the USA Patriot Act."

15. Brian McFadden, "Urgent Government Recalls," *New York Times*, May 24, 2015, 2.

16. National Public Radio, "Senate Blocks Patriot Act Extension," National Public Radio, last modified May 23, 2015, https://www.eff.org/foia/section-215-usa-patriot-act.

17. Erin V. Kelly, "Senate Approves USA Freedom Act," *USA Today*, last modified June 2, 2015, http://www.usatoday.com/story/news/politics/2015/06/02/patriot-act-usa-freedom-act-senate-vote/28345747/.

18. Amy Goodman and David Goodman, "America's Most Dangerous Librarians," *Mother Jones*, September/October 2008, 42–43.

REFERENCES, SUGGESTED READINGS, AND WEBSITES

American Library Association. "Analysis of the USA Patriot Act Related to Libraries." American Library Association. http://www.ala.org/offices/oif/ifissues/issuesrelatedlinks/usapatriotactanalysis.

———. "Banned Books Week: Celebrating the Freedom to Read." American Library Association. http://www.ala.org/bbooks/bannedbooksweek.

———. "Frequently Challenged Books of the 21st Century." American Library Association. http://www.ala.org/bbooks/frequentlychallengedbooks/top10.

———. "100 Most Frequently Challenged Books by Decade." American Library Association. http://www.ala.org/bbooks/frequentlychallengedbooks/top100.

———. "Selection Policy." *Choice: Current Reviews for Academic Libraries*. http://www.ala.org/acrl/choice/selectionpolicy.

———. "What Is Censorship?" American Library Association. http://www.ala.org/advocacy/intfreedom/censorshipfirstamendmentissues/ifcensorshipqanda.

Blume, Judy, ed. *Places I Never Meant to Be: Original Stories by Censored Writers*. New York: Aladdin Paperbacks, 2001.

Federation of American Scientists. "Foreign Intelligence Surveillance Act." Federation of American Scientists. Last modified 1978. http://www.fas.org/irp/agency/doj/fisa/.

Five Years of Florida Book Challenges. http://www.flalib.org/fl_lib_journal/2014/Spring2014.pdf.

Goodman, Amy, and David Goodman. "America's Most Dangerous Librarians." *Mother Jones*, September/October 2008, 42–43.

Gounaud, Karen Jo. "10 Ways to Create a Family Friendly Library." Family Friendly Libraries. http://www.ccv.org/issues/harmful-to-children/family-friendly-libraries/.

GSLISatIllinois. "Perspectives on Intellectual Freedom, Part I." YouTube, September 24, 2013. https://www.youtube.com/watch?v=1ENoZiN6UQE.

———. "Perspectives on Intellectual Freedom, Part II." YouTube, September 26, 2013. https://www.youtube.com/watch?v=SvrFKMuYKZE.

———. "Perspectives on Intellectual Freedom, Part III." YouTube, September 27, 2013. https://www.youtube.com/watch?v=TolHzPPTOrE.

"Index: A Selective Timeline of Censorship 1235–2003." *Conscience*, Spring 2003, 54.

Kelly, Erin V. "Senate Approves USA Freedom Act." *USA Today*. Last modified June 2, 2015. http://www.usatoday.com/story/news/politics/2015/06/02/patriot-act-usa-freedom-act-senate-vote/28345747/.

Lessenberry, Jack. "Plymouth-Canton School District Banning Books." Michigan Radio, January 17, 2012. http://michiganradio.org/post/plymouth-canton-school-district-banning-books.

Lodge, Carey. "California School Bans All Christian Books." *Christian Today*, September 29, 2014. http://www.christiantoday.com/article/california.school.bans.all.christian.books/41072.htm.

McFadden, Brian. "Urgent Government Recalls." *New York Times*, May 24, 2015, 2.

National Council of Teachers of English. "The Students' Right to Read." National Council of Teachers of English. http://www.ncte.org/positions/statements/righttoreadguideline.

National Public Radio. "Senate Blocks Patriot Act Extension." National Public Radio. Last modified May 23, 2015. https://www.eff.org/foia/section-215-usa-patriot-act.

O'Brien, Luke. "Librarians Describe Life under an FBI Gag Order." *Wired*. Last modified June 24, 2007. http://www.wired.com/2007/06/librarians-desc/.

Public Concern Foundation. "Gagged National-Security-Letter Recipients Find Their Voice." *Washington Spectator*. http://washingtonspectator.org/gagged-national-security-letter-recipients-find-their-voice/.

TED Talk. "Glenn Greenwald: Why Privacy Matters." YouTube, October 10, 2014. https://www.youtube.com/watch?v=pcSlowAhvUk.

U.S. Department of Justice. The Foreign Intelligence Surveillance Act of 1978 (FISA). Justice Information Sharing. Last modified September 19, 2013. https://it.ojp.gov/default.aspx?area=privacy&page=1286.

U.S. Government. "The USA PATRIOT Act: Preserving Life and Liberty." United States Department of Justice. http://www.justice.gov/archive/ll/highlights.htm.

CHAPTER 15

Children and Intellectual Freedom

Library support staff (LSS) will know the ethics and values of the profession, including an understanding of the Library Bill of Rights, the ALA Code of Ethics, the freedom of information, confidentiality of patron records, and privacy issues. They will also know and understand the principles of intellectual freedom and censorship. (ALA-LSSC Competency #2)

Topics Covered in This Chapter:

- Children's Internet Protection Act (CIPA)
- Filtering
- Children and Libraries
- Social Media

Key Terms:

Bandwidth: Bandwidth is a measurement of the ability of an electronic communications device, such as a computer network, to send and receive information. This is particularly important in a school or library, as the greater the bandwidth, the faster the speed of the Internet connection.

Broadband: Broadband refers to high-speed Internet access, including using cable modem, fiber optic, wireless, satellite, and digital subscriber lines (DSL). Libraries use any and all of these technologies in providing fast Internet access to their patrons.

CIPA: The Children's Internet Protection Act (CIPA) was enacted by Congress in 2000 to address concerns about children's access to obscene or harmful content over the Internet. This is relevant to public and school libraries in terms of their Internet connections and availability of web content.

Filtering: To filter means to slow or obstruct the passage of something, like blinds filtering sunlight. In a library context, it means restricting or screening information on a computer so that it is not available to the viewer.

Social media: Social media is the interactive, web-based electronic communication through which users create online communities in order to share information, ideas, and personal messages. This is a popular use for library computers for patrons, and can be used by staff to share library news.

CHILDREN'S INTERNET PROTECTION ACT

By now it has become apparent that libraries rely on computer technology both to perform the functions of a library and to offer Internet access to the public—to the library's online catalogs, to its webpages, to its electronic resources, and to all of the content available on the Internet. This is a given in the twenty-first century. One of the problems with this, particularly in schools and libraries, is that there is a plethora of information available online, and not all of it is appropriate for children. In 2000, Congress enacted the Children's Internet Protection Act (**CIPA**) to address concerns about children's access to obscene or harmful content over the Internet.[1]

To make enforcement of CIPA affordable for schools and libraries, Congress mandated the Schools and Libraries Program in 1996. It was implemented in 1997 by the Federal Communications Commission (FCC) and is funded by the Universal Service Fund (USF); this is known as the E-Rate. The E-Rate connects schools and libraries to **broadband**. Those that are eligible can get discounts in two categories: (1) for telecommunications and Internet access and (2) for internal connections and broadband services. In short, they receive discounts for Internet-installation equipment and Internet access. The increase in Internet use by students, teachers, and the public created increasing demand for **bandwidth**, so in 2014, the FCC adopted the E-Rate Modernization Order to increase Wi-Fi networks while continuing to support broadband connectivity to schools and libraries.[2]

To receive E-Rate discounts, schools and libraries must first determine their eligibility: public and private K–12 schools and public and privately supported libraries are usually eligible. The school or library then has to file a lengthy application, which includes having a current technology plan, participating in competitive bidding to find a service provider, selecting the service provider, applying for discounts, reviewing the application, and starting the service. It is a competitive process, and eligible libraries will be funded depending on their level of poverty and the urban or rural status of the population served. Discounts range from 20 percent to 90 percent of eligible services.[3]

CIPA imposes certain requirements on schools or libraries that receive discounts for Internet access or internal connections through the federal E-Rate program. These include adopting an Internet safety policy and implementing the means to filter computer Internet access. The textbox on page 191 shows the elements that need to be addressed.[4] A more detailed sample policy can be accessed on the CIPA website or through E-Rate Central.

SAFETY POLICY ELEMENTS

1. Access by minors to inappropriate matter on the Internet;
2. The safety and security of minors when using electronic mail, chat rooms and other forms of direct electronic communications;
3. Unauthorized access, including so-called "hacking," and other unlawful activities by minors online;
4. Unauthorized disclosure, use, and dissemination of personal information regarding minors; and
5. Measures restricting minors' access to materials harmful to them.

Source: Federal Communications Commission

FILTERING

Filtering, as it applies to libraries and schools, denies access based on *content.* Blocking denies access based on a site's URL.[5] Libraries and schools that receive E-Rate funding are required to adopt an Internet safety policy and install filtering software on all computers. An Internet safety policy would contain wording that the school or library in question would then use to prevent user access to a computer network to transmit inappropriate material. This material is defined as content harmful to minors, such as visual depictions of obscene materials or pornography, including child pornography. It would further authorize supervision and monitoring by staff with regard to behavior while visiting social networking sites.[6] Supervision and monitoring, it must be noted, does not mean that Internet *use* can be tracked.

Schools and libraries receiving E-Rate funding are also required to install filtering or content control software on all computers. It is designed to restrict what websites can be accessed. Such software can both restrict some sites and identify others that can be visited. Internet sites can be blocked by content (by keyword scanning) or by image recognition. The ALA's position is that

> publicly supported libraries are governmental institutions subject to the First Amendment, which forbids them from restricting information based on viewpoint or content discrimination. Libraries are places of inclusion rather than exclusion. Current filtering software not only prevents access to what some may consider "objectionable" material, but also blocks information protected by the First Amendment.[7]

Remember, only libraries that accept E-Rate funding are subject to these regulations. Misunderstanding of CIPA can lead some institutions to worry about losing funding unless they block all potentially offensive sites.

The problem with filters is that most of them don't work or don't work well. The Internet is vastly different than it was in 2003, when the Supreme Court last upheld the constitutionality of CIPA. It doesn't account for social networking or collaborative websites. CIPA is seen as an outdated law that does a disservice to children today.[8] Such stringent control of content can block legitimate research. Filters such as

NetNanny, CyberPatrol, or Smartfilter can be used in schools and libraries to block inappropriate content, but such software often blocks access to needed materials for research while still allowing inappropriate content to come through. The classic example is that filters that block the word *breast* prevent someone from doing research on breast cancer. "According to the ALA, studies have found that filters can block out resources dealing with topics such as war and genocide, safer sex, and public health. One study found that a filter blocked a website required for an online nursing exam!"[9]

In Connecticut, all schools and libraries that are E-Rate eligible get their Internet service through the Connecticut Education Network (CEN). As such, content filtering is provided automatically to public schools as part of their CEN connectivity. This provides a baseline of filtering that is determined by the Commission for Educational Technology. Public schools can opt for another filtering system in addition to that which is provided by CEN, and public libraries, which do not automatically receive filtering, may choose to opt in. Even CEN provides a disclaimer that no filtering system is foolproof and that users are so warned.[10]

Libraries and schools can also create "whitelists" and "blacklists" of sites (by URL), but the creation of these lists can be subjective. As we noted in a previous chapter, librarians and LSS all have personal lives and opinions that may influence the inclusion or exclusion of various sites. In 2013, Deborah Caldwell-Stone, deputy director of ALA's Office for Intellectual Freedom, reported that

> according to legal complaints, some libraries are denying users access to websites that discuss Wicca and Native American spirituality; blacklisting websites that affirm the lesbian, gay, bisexual, and transgender (LGBT) communities while whitelisting sites that advocate against gay rights and promote "ex-gay" ministries; and refusing to unblock web pages that deal with youth tobacco use, art galleries, blogs, and firearms. School librarians, teachers, and even Department of Education officials are openly complaining that the overzealous blocking of online information in schools is impairing the educational process.[11]

Even while CIPA requires that filters be installed, there are legitimate times when those filters can be disabled, such as when adults are doing research and necessary sources are being blocked. Under the law, the library can disable a filter for adults on request, and the patron does not have to explain why. Tech-savvy kids have always found ways to work around Internet filtering by using their own personal devices in school or the library. While the Internet may filter their school or library computers, kids can use their smartphones or tablets that use digital cellular systems—bypassing the Internet altogether. Students have also been known to use their school computers as proxy servers (using certain websites to get around barriers that would otherwise be between you and the content that you want to see)[12] in order to access their home computers.

An important component to filtering is to teach good Internet searching skills and to recognize what databases are safe to use. Many schools and libraries subscribe to electronic databases, some of which are specific to children, such as Primary Search or Kids Search by Ebsco or Kids InfoBits by Gale Cengage. These databases offer searching on a variety of topics appropriate to the child from kindergarten through grade 12.[13]

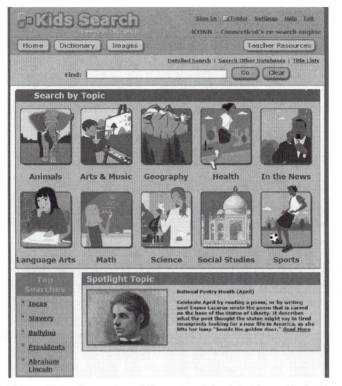

Figure 15.1. Screenshot of Elementary School Database. *Used with permission of EBSCO and the CT State Library*

Libraries that do not accept or qualify for E-Rate funding are not required to use any filtering software at all. This was the case at the public library at which I worked. For a variety of reasons, we did not qualify for E-Rate funding, so we had no requirement to filter. We did, however, find that a number of patrons were accessing pornography and other materials that were upsetting to library users. The decision was to try a filter called Photo No-No!, an image-based product that claimed to block thousands of known porn sites, as well as using image-scanning software to recognize inappropriate images. It only worked sporadically and also blocked completely neutral sites, such as weather maps. Another filter that we tried was iShield, which worked marginally better but also frequently blocked common sites, including Yahoo.com.

Having any filtering or blocking software is problematic for librarians as the Library Bill of Rights and the First Amendment encourage us to provide open and equal access to all. No one wants to expose children to harmful materials, but the best defense may be a good offense. Have a strong Internet use policy in place that clearly spells out what is and is not acceptable use—and post it in a visible place. Have the policy include user behavior rules as well. Laws that prohibit the production of child pornography and obscenity apply to the Internet and also provide protection for the library. Educate LSS, patrons, and board and community members about the websites and search engines on the library's computers that satisfy user needs and interests. Provide Internet information and training to patrons and families. Providing privacy screens and careful placement of computer stations can also minimize the viewing of materials not suitable for all eyes, should it occur.[14]

CHILDREN AND LIBRARIES

As we saw in chapter 8, children are an important component of library use and the reason that many families begin to use the library. The first proposition in the ALA Freedom to Read Statement asserts that libraries make available the widest diversity of views and expressions.[15] This tenet of intellectual freedom applies to children as well and may mean that there will be books in the children's collection that some parents find objectionable for a variety of reasons. It is critical, then, that the parent be part of their child's library visits. No one can fault a child who chooses a book that looks appealing to them but unknowingly violates his or her family's values. It is the job of the parents to supervise their children's books selections if they feel strongly about those choices. It is not the library's job to act in loco parentis, "in the place of the parent."

Challenging materials that a library owns is different from objecting to a book that a child brings home, but it is *not* the job of the LSS to "censor" what kids take out, however inappropriate it may be. There are several examples in the previously referenced book *Places I Never Meant to Be*, where authors recall being told by their librarians that they could not take a particular book out because it came from the adult section or because they thought that the content was "too mature." One thing I have found is that if a book is "too mature" for a child, they probably won't read it because it would be over their head or beyond their level of comprehension.

A good example of this was when Judy Blume, the popular (and often challenged) author of books for children and young adults wrote an adult novel; every underage Judy Blume fan in the library wanted to take it out. Besides being well written, her books sometimes touched on sexual issues. We knew that the adult novel was not an appropriate choice for children, but it was not our place to tell a child that she or he could not take it out. It was very unlike her other titles, so it often came back the next day, unread. Some of the savvier kids may have been looking for "the good parts," but by and large the book did not hold their interest. Surprisingly, no parents came in to complain about it either. It cannot be overstated that everyone has free and equal access to library materials, and it is not the job of library staff to object to anything patrons may choose, however inappropriate it may seem. I lived up the street from my childhood library and remember being scolded by the children's librarian for only reading mysteries. You can be sure I went back and repeatedly chose as many mysteries as I could find.

The following textbox that I have compiled from ALA's Office of Intellectual Freedom lists of frequently challenged children's books shows examples of ten titles that have been repeatedly challenged over a twelve-year period from 2001 to 2013[16]:

FREQUENTLY CHALLENGED BOOKS

Captain Underpants series, by Dav Pilkey
    Reasons: Offensive language, unsuited for age group, violence
The Absolutely True Diary of a Part-Time Indian, by Sherman Alexie
    Reasons: Drugs/alcohol/smoking, offensive language, racism, sexually explicit, unsuited to age group
The Hunger Games, by Suzanne Collins
    Reasons: Sexually explicit, unsuited to age group, and violence
The Chocolate War, by Robert Cormier
    Reasons: Nudity, offensive language, sexually explicit, unsuited to age group
The Adventures of Huckleberry Finn, by Mark Twain
    Reason: Racism
Scary Stories series, by Alvin Schwartz
    Reasons: Insensitivity, occult/Satanism, unsuited to age group, violence
It's Perfectly Normal, by Robie Harris
    Reason: Homosexuality, nudity, sexual content, sex education
Alice series, by Phyllis Reynolds Naylor
    Reasons: Sexually explicit, unsuited to age group
Forever, by Judy Blume
    Reasons: Offensive language, sexual content
And Tango Makes Three, by Peter Parnell and Justin Richardson
    Reasons: Homosexuality, unsuited for age group

Source: American Library Association

SOCIAL NETWORKS

The ubiquitous presence of computers gives children virtually unfettered access to the Internet. We know that schools and most public libraries filter content in order to keep children from accessing harmful or obscene materials, but there are other dangers. Children are prolific users of **social media**: blogs, Facebook, Twitter, Instagram, Flickr, Tumblr, MeetUp, and so on. As we discussed in chapter 8, children and teens tend to reveal a lot about themselves on social media, including personal information, photographs, and contact information. Anything that they post can be reposted, retweeted, tagged, and sent all over the world. "Take that instantaneous availability, and mix in the processing and maturity of the adolescent brain, and, in the blink of any eye, circumstances may be set in motion which can immediately change the course of your child's life."[17]

Most states have enacted laws that make it a crime to engage in anything that can endanger the health and safety of children. Sexting, if the child is under sixteen, violates statutes related to possessing or transmitting child pornography. State and federal statutes also ensure that bullying or cyberbullying does not impact the child's learning environment. Signs that your child may be cyberbullied include an avoidance of his or her computer or device, nervousness when using his or her device, not wanting to go to school, changes in appetite, and loss of interest, among others. Signs that your child may be doing the cyberbullying include quickly switching screens or closing the device, becoming insensitive or violent toward others, and other behavioral changes.[18] Obviously any changes in a child's behavior can be significant and not necessarily a sign of bullying and should be immediately addressed.

Social media can be a powerful tool for keeping in touch with young patrons— but should LSS "friend" them? If it is through the library's Facebook account, then it would be a good way to let young patrons know what programs are coming up or what new books have arrived or even to have informal conversations. Institutional accounts, administered by designated LSS, are safe and, if set up correctly, private. This is a great way to enforce your "brand" and creates a dynamic, online social networking presence for the library.[19] Social media is a big part of young patrons' lives, and it is the responsibility of the LSS to stay current with emergent technologies. Libraries have an obligation to do all that they can to facilitate this access in a safe, nonthreatening environment.

CHAPTER SUMMARY

LSS must understand the Library Bill of Rights, the ALA Code of Ethics, freedom of information, confidentiality of patron records, and privacy issues. They must also know and understand the principles of intellectual freedom and censorship. In this chapter, we addressed the intellectual freedom of children and how it is impacted by CIPA and filtering software in the school or public library. Children need to be kept safe from harmful or obscene materials, but the use of filters does not necessarily assure this. Content filters can block needed information while also allowing access to websites that are not appropriate for children. The technical expertise of children also allows some of them to "work around" the filters in order to access sites that are not permissible. Their familiarity with social media sites can also be problematic, as they may lack judgment in what they post and to whom. We are also concerned about the intellectual freedom that children have to choose books that interest them, and it is the job of the parent, not the LSS, to monitor children's reading or borrowing choices.

DISCUSSION QUESTIONS AND ACTIVITIES

1. Do you agree with the filtering requirements of CIPA in order to receive funds?
   a. Explain your answer.
2. Filtering is in violation of the First Amendment.
   a. Is it ever okay to block speech online?
3. Research the merits of several commercial filters and give your opinion of the benefits or effectiveness of each.
4. What are some of the potential problems with children using social media?

NOTES

1. Federal Communications Commission, "Children's Internet Protection Act," Federal Communications Commission, last modified December 31, 2014, http://www.fcc.gov/guides/childrens-internet-protection-act.

2. Federal Communications Commission, "The E-Rate Program," Federal Communications Commission, last modified January 13, 2015, http://www.fcc.gov/e-rate-update.

3. Universal Service Administrative Company, "Schools and Libraries E-Rate: Getting Started," Universal Service Administrative Company, http://www.usac.org/sl/about/getting-started/default.aspx.

4. Federal Communications Commission, "Children's Internet Protection Act."

5. Marcel H. Faulkner, "Filter Schmilter: Libraries and Internet Filtering Software," Web junction, last modified March 21, 2012, http://www.webjunction.org/documents/webjunction/Filter_Schmilter_Libraries_and_Internet_Filtering_Software.html.

6. E-Rate Central, "Sample CIPA-Compliant Internet Safety Policy," E-Rate Central, http://e-ratecentral.com/CIPA/cipa_policy_sample.pdf.

7. American Library Association, "Statement on Library Use of Filtering Software," American Library Association Office of Intellectual Freedom, http://www.ala.org/Template.cfm?Section=IF_Resolutions&Template=/ContentManagement/ContentDisplay.cfm&ContentID=13090.

8. Mies Ginny, "Internet Filtering: Don't Do It," *TechSoup for Libraries* (blog), last modified April 8, 2014, http://www.techsoupforlibraries.org/blog/internet-filtering-dont-do-it.

9. Ginny, "Internet Filtering."

10. State of Connecticut, "Connecticut Education Network Policy for Content Filtering," Connecticut Commission for Educational Technology, last modified May 28, 2008, http://www.ct.gov/ctedtech/cwp/view.asp?a=2597&Q=416360&ctedtechPNavCtr=%7C45373%7C.

11. Deborah Caldwell-Stone, "Filtering and the First Amendment," *American Libraries* 44, no. 3/4 (March/April 2013): 58–61.

12. Chris Pollett and Jonathan Strickland, eds., "How Proxy Servers Work," *How Stuff Works* (blog), last modified February 10, 2009, http://blogs.howstuffworks.com/transcript/how-proxy-servers-work.htm.

13. iCONN, "Resources for Elementary Schools," iCONN, http://www.iconn.org/classic elementary.

14. American Library Association, "Statement on Library Use of Filtering."

15. American Library Association, "The Freedom to Read Statement," American Library Association, http://www.ala.org/advocacy/intfreedom/statementspols/freedomreadstatement.

16. American Library Association, "Frequently Challenged Books of the 21st Century," American Library Association Office of Intellectual Freedom, http://www.ala.org/bbooks/frequentlychallengedbooks/top10.

17. Michael A. Blanchard, "Technology Can Be Worrisome for Parents," *Suisman Shapiro Blog*, last modified January 13, 2015, http://www.suismanshapiroblog.com/2015/01/13/technology-can-worrisome-parents/.

18. Sameer Hinduja and Justin W. Patchin, "Cyerbullying Warning Signs," Cyberbullying Research Center, last modified October 2014, http://www.cyberbullying.us/cyberbullying_warning_signs.pdf.

19. Nedda H. Ahmed, Adriana Edwards-Johnson, Karen Antell, and Molly Strothman, "Should Librarians Friend Their Patrons?," *Reference and User Services Quarterly* 53, no. 1 (Fall 2013): 9–12.

REFERENCES, SUGGESTED READINGS, AND WEBSITES

Ahmed, Nedda H., Adriana Edwards-Johnson, Karen Antell, and Molly Strothman. "Should Librarians Friend Their Patrons?" *Reference and User Services Quarterly* 53, no. 1 (Fall 2013): 9–12. https://search.ebscohost.com/login.aspx?direct-true&db-aph&AN-90455091&site-ehost-live&scope-site.

American Library Association. "The Freedom to Read Statement." American Library Association. http://www.ala.org/advocacy/intfreedom/statementspols/freedomreadstatement.

——. "Frequently Challenged Books of the 21st Century." American Library Association Office of Intellectual Freedom. http://www.ala.org/bbooks/frequentlychallengedbooks/top10.

——. "Statement on Library Use of Filtering Software." American Library Association Office of Intellectual Freedom. http://www.ala.org/Template.cfm?Section=IF_Resolutions&Template=/ContentManagement/ContentDisplay.cfm&ContentID=13090.

American Library Association Washington Office. "Introduction and Overview of CIPA 10 Years Later." YouTube, August 5, 2013. https://www.youtube.com/watch?v=gtxcxk3zJO0.

——. "Revisiting CIPA 10 Years Later Part 1." YouTube, streamed live July 30, 2013. https://www.youtube.com/watch?v=l2v-SDig3IM.

——. "Revisiting CIPA 10 Years Later Part II." YouTube, streamed live July 30, 2013. https://www.youtube.com/watch?v=G2Bae9wRl30.

Blanchard, Michael A. "Technology Can Be Worrisome for Parents." *Suisman Shapiro Blog.* Last modified January 13, 2015. http://www.suismanshapiroblog.com/2015/01/13/technology-can-worrisome-parents/.

Caldwell-Stone, Deborah. "Filtering and the First Amendment." *American Libraries* 44, no. 3/4 (March/April 2013): 58–61. https://search.ebscohost.com/login.aspx?direct=true&db=aph&AN=85906996&site=ehost-live&scope=site.

Cyberbullying Research Center. http://cyberbullying.us/resources/parents/.

E-Rate Central. "Sample CIPA-Compliant Internet Safety Policy." E-Rate Central. http://e-ratecentral.com/CIPA/cipa_policy_sample.pdf.

Faulkner, Marcel H. "Filter Schmilter: Libraries and Internet Filtering Software." Webjunction. Last modified March 21, 2012. http://www.webjunction.org/documents/webjunction/Filter_Schmilter_Libraries_and_Internet_Filtering_Software.html.

Federal Communications Commission. "Children's Internet Protection Act." Federal Communications Commission. Last modified December 31, 2014. http://www.fcc.gov/guides/childrens-internet-protection-act.

——. "The E-Rate Program." Federal Communications Commission. Last modified January 13, 2015. http://www.fcc.gov/e-rate-update.

Ginny, Mies. "Internet Filtering: Don't Do It." *TechSoup for Libraries* (blog). Last modified April 8, 2014. http://www.techsoupforlibraries.org/blog/internet-filtering-dont-do-it.

Hinduja, Sameer, and Justin W. Patchin. "Cyerbullying Warning Signs." Cyberbullying Research Center. Last modified October 2014. http://www.cyberbullying.us/cyberbullying_warning_signs.pdf.

iCONN. "Resources for Elementary Schools." iCONN. http://www.iconn.org/classicelementary.

Pollett, Chris, and Jonathan Strickland, eds. "How Proxy Servers Work." How Stuff Works (blog). Last modified February 10, 2009. http://blogs.howstuffworks.com/transcript/how-proxy-servers-work.htm.

Rainey, Reitman. "The Cost of Censorship in Libraries: 10 Years under the Children's Internet Protection Act." Electronic Frontier Foundation. Last modified September 4, 2013. https://www.eff.org/deeplinks/2013/09/cost-censorship-libraries-10-years-under-childrens-internet-protection-act.

Resnick, Paul, Caroline Richardson, and Derek Hansen. "See No Evil: How Internet Filters Affect the Search for Online Health Information." Kaiser Family Foundation. Last modified December 2002. https://kaiserfamilyfoundation.files.wordpress.com/2013/01/see-no-evil -how-internet-filters-affect-the-search-for-online-health-information-appendices.pdf.

State of Connecticut. "Connecticut Education Network Policy for Content Filtering." Connecticut Commission for Educational Technology. Last modified May 28, 2008. http:// www.ct.gov/ctedtech/cwp/view.asp?a=2597&Q=416360&ctedtechPNavCtr=%7C45373 %7C.

Universal Service Administrative Company. "Schools and Libraries E-Rate: Getting Started." Universal Service Administrative Company. http://www.usac.org/sl/about/getting-started/ default.aspx.

Glossary

Access: Access is a way of getting to something. In the context of libraries, it means facilitating the means of getting information to the user.

Acquisitions: The acquisition of materials in a library means ordering and receiving print and nonprint materials. It does not refer to the selection of these materials, nor does it refer to the ordering of office supplies or library equipment. The former is done by collection development or selection staff, the latter by the business or technical services department. Some materials are not ordered at all but come to the library as gifts or through library exchange.

Active older adults: Active older adults are those individuals (usually fifty-five and older) who have little or no physical or cognitive impairment and maintain a healthy and active lifestyle.

Adaptive technology: Adaptive technologies are methods of making visually or audibly delivered materials available to individuals with those impairments, such as magnified screens, closed-captioning, and enhanced telecommunications devices. It also relates to provisions for physical disabilities.

Archives: Archives are a collection of documents or records that are not available to the general public because they may be valuable or fragile. It also can refer to the place where these items are stored, such as a special room in the library. LSS can provide access to archives or archived materials for their patrons.

Art release: The art release is the creation of a design or a graphic that can be used for posters, flyers, and handouts. It is included in a newsletter or other sources to advertise a library event.

Attending skills: Attending skills are those that show that the LSS is giving full attention to the patron. They show active interest in what patrons say and do and show respect for their needs.

Baby boomers: "Baby boomers" is the name given to those born between 1946 and 1964. They are so named because of the increase in births in the years following World War II. As of 2012, they made up close to one quarter of the U.S. population.

Bandwidth: Bandwidth is a measurement of the ability of an electronic communications device, such as a computer network, to send and receive information. This is particularly important in a school or library, as the greater the bandwidth, the faster the speed of the Internet connection.

Banned books: A banned book is one that is subject to objection and/or is physically removed from the library shelf on the basis that it is in some way offensive to someone. In so doing, it is made unavailable to anyone.

Behaviors: Behaviors are the ways in which one acts toward another. This is important for LSS to understand when dealing with the public, as people have a variety of ways in which they respond to various situations.

Bibliographic verification: Bibliographic verification is the process whereby items to be ordered are carefully checked to make sure that they exist, are in print, and can be acquired. This is done by checking the item against the library's catalog, a consortium or state catalog, the Library of Congress, or OCLC/WorldCat. It also includes making sure that the library doesn't already own the item or have it on order, in process, or in repair.

Bi-Folkal kits: Bi-Folkal kits are themed multisensory kits designed to encourage older people to reminisce and create connections. This is just one of the ways that libraries can provide outreach to the older adult or the elderly.

Bill of Rights: The Bill of Rights is the first ten amendments to the Constitution that were written in response to calls from several states for greater constitutional protection for individual liberties. Ratified in 1791, they are the basis for the Library Bill of Rights.

Body language: Body language is a constant, nonverbal flow of communication, including eye contact, posture, hand gestures, touch, and the use of space. The LSS must be aware of this in his or her interactions with patrons.

Branding: Branding is the process involved in creating a unique name and image in the consumer's mind for a product (or library) through advertising campaigns with a consistent theme.

Broadband: Broadband refers to high-speed Internet access, including using cable modem, fiber optic, wireless, satellite, and digital subscriber lines (DSL). Libraries use any and all of these technologies in providing fast Internet access to their patrons.

Censorship: Censorship is the "suppression of ideas and information that certain persons—individuals, groups or government officials—find objectionable or dangerous."[1] Censorship of materials is a major issue in libraries.

Challenged materials: A challenge to materials is a formal, written complaint requesting the restriction or removal of a book based on the objections of a person or group. The majority of these people are parents, and the location is often the school library.

Child development: Child development is the physical, intellectual, language, and social stages that occur in children from birth to young adulthood. This is especially important when planning library services for that age group.

CIPA: The Children's Internet Protection Act (CIPA) was enacted by Congress in 2000 to address concerns about children's access to obscene or harmful content over the Internet. This is relevant to public and school libraries in terms of their Internet connections and availability of web content.

Circulation: Circulation is the process of checking materials out to a patron and back in to the library. The book is stamped or the borrower is provided with a receipt with the date that the material is due back. There are several other associated circulation tasks, including placing holds, tracking overdues, and interlibrary loan.

Classification systems: A classification system is the numerical or alphabetical system a library uses to organize materials by subject. The two most often used are the Dewey Decimal Classification System and the Library of Congress Classification System. These systems provide for the arrangement of materials on a shelf in a logical order, making it easy for patrons to find that for which they are searching.

Collection development: A library's objective is to serve the informational needs of its users. The purpose of collection development is to select materials that serve the needs of the primary service population. This service population will vary by library type and community and relies on the demographics of that community to determine what choices the library makes.

Common Core Standards: The Common Core is a set of high-quality academic standards in mathematics and English language arts/literacy (ELA). These learning goals outline what a student should know and be able to do at the end of each grade.[2] Libraries are aligning material selection to this concept.

Copyright: Copyright is a form of protection grounded in the U.S. Constitution and granted by law for original works of authorship fixed in a tangible medium of expression. Copyright covers both published and unpublished works[3] and protects them from unauthorized use.

Customer service: Customer service means assisting patrons (users, customers) with their needs in person, by phone, or electronically by providing high-quality service. The LSS does this in order to achieve a goal or complete a transaction while showing respect, courtesy, and interest in the patron.

Demographics: Demographics are the statistics of a given population by age, sex, race, and income. This is important for libraries so that they can know whom they are serving and so that they can provide the appropriate resources.

Disability: A disability is a physical or mental impairment that substantially limits one or more major life activities of such individuals, such as having difficulties with mobility, speech, or hearing.

Discrimination: Discrimination means limiting, segregating, or classifying someone in a way that adversely affects the opportunities or status of that person. LSS must learn to treat all individuals equally, regardless of ethnicity, physical ability, or economic status.

Disruptive patron: A disruptive patron is one whose behavior interferes with the use of the library by other patrons or interferes with a staff member's completion of his or her duties; one who interferes with the normal functioning of the library.

Diversity: Diversity is the state of people of more than one nationality, race, gender, color, sexual orientation, and socioeconomic status. It encourages acceptance of these differences and the uniqueness of each individual. Libraries are an example of a place where diversity is encountered on a regular basis, and libraries must strive to make their services acceptable and sensitive to the demographic.

Document delivery: Document delivery is the means to provide electronic or digital copies of materials to a patron, instead of a book or physical journal. This is most commonly done in academic and special libraries.

Filtering: To filter means to slow or obstruct the passage of something, like blinds filtering sunlight. In a library context, it means restricting or screening information on a computer so that it is not available to the viewer.

First Amendment: The First Amendment to the U.S. Constitution is that part of the Bill of Rights that prohibits the making of any law "respecting an establishment of religion or prohibiting the free exercise thereof; or abridging the freedom of speech, or of the press, or of the right of the people peaceably to assemble."[4] Thus, libraries can purchase whatever materials they deem relevant to their collections and can make their meeting and exhibit space available to the public without restriction.

Fourth Amendment: The Fourth Amendment to the U.S. Constitution is that part of the Bill of Rights that prohibits unreasonable searches and seizures. This protects the privacy of library patrons from having their reading or Internet searching history accessed without their permission.

Handicap: A handicap is a situation or barrier imposed by society or the environment, such as too-narrow doorways or curbs that are too high for a wheelchair, doors that are difficult to open, or signage that is too small to read.

Homebound: The homebound are those who, for reasons of infirmity or lack of mobility, cannot come to the library. Libraries then must consider strategies to reach this segment where they live, be it home, a retirement community, or a nursing facility.

Homelessness: The homeless are those who, through lack of employment, poverty, mental illness, substance abuse, or other factors, are without permanent housing. This includes those who live in transitional housing or shelters, either temporarily or chronically. The homeless are frequent library users because libraries provide shelter from the weather.

ILS: An integrated library system, or ILS, is the system that a library uses to perform the many functions of circulation, such as checking materials in and out. An ILS also tracks overdue materials, assesses fines, and provides for statistics and reports relevant to the library, as well as keeping a database of patrons and materials. Other modules provide for cataloging, acquisitions, and serials.

Intellectual freedom: Intellectual freedom is the right of everyone to seek and receive information from all points of view without restriction. It encourages free access to all ideas and is protected under the First Amendment. Libraries provide a variety of materials so that users can choose the information that suits their needs.

Interlibrary loan (ILL): Interlibrary loan is the process by which one library will provide books and other materials to another library. This is usually done by obtaining or delivering materials not owned by one library to another library or sharing multiple copies for a book discussion.

Internal customer service: Internal customer service means assisting coworkers, subordinates, or managers in the workplace by providing the same high-quality service in order to achieve a goal or complete a transaction, showing respect, courtesy, and interest, as the LSS would to a patron. Treating coworkers with this same level of customer service ensures excellent relations throughout the library.

Library Bill of Rights: The Library Bill of Rights is a document created by the American Library Association (ALA, the national professional library association) affirming basic policies that guide library service.[5] It is based on the principles of the U.S. Constitution and guides librarians in providing equal service to all patrons.

Library Code of Ethics: The Library Code of Ethics is a document created by the ALA that recognizes the ethical responsibilities of library personnel toward the public and guides how the public is served.[6]

Marketing: Marketing is based on thinking about the library in terms of customer needs and satisfaction. It relies on designing the library's offering in terms of those needs and on using effective communication to inform and motivate them.

Media: While *media* refers to any means of communication, including books, newspapers, magazines, CDs, DVDs, television, and radio, for example, in libraries, *media* is often the term used for formats other than print.

Microcosm: A microcosm is a smaller version of something else or having the characteristics of a larger version. The children's room is a microcosm of library service to adults as it provides all of the same services, such as reference and reader's advisory, to children as it does to adults.

Nonprint materials: Nonprint materials refers to those items not in the traditional form of a book, such as audiobooks on CD, DVDs, and electronic books. Some libraries also maintain maps, microforms, games, and toys. Virtually all libraries have most of these materials in their collections.

Older adults: Older adults are individuals generally considered to be of retirement age, usually sixty-five and older. They make up an important library demographic as they may have more time to spend using the library.

OPAC: The online public access catalog in a library is the online bibliography or database of a library's holdings. This is searchable from a computer in the library, and often from home, and contains a record of all print and nonprint materials held by that library.

Open-ended questions: An open-ended question is one that cannot be answered by "yes" or "no." This is useful when conducting a reference interview and encourages the patron to tell the LSS what, specifically, he or she is looking for.

Poverty: Poverty is the circumstance of having little or no money to purchase goods and services or lacking a means of financial support. This can impact a patron's liabilities if he or she gets a library card: paying fines or being responsible for lost materials.

Preservation: Preservation is a term in general use to define activities that will prolong the life of materials. It includes concerns about the environment, handling, and storage. Preservation can be done by LSS trained in a few basic concepts.

Press release: The press release uses the "5 Ws"—*who, what, when, where,* and *why,* plus *how*—to create a narrative that can be distributed to multiple media outlets in order to advertise a library event.

Privacy: Privacy is the right to be left alone and free from surveillance; the right to determine whether, when, how, and to whom one's personal information, including any history or records of library materials borrowed or Internet sites accessed, is to be revealed.

Programming: Programming is the offering of events, classes, and other programs to the variety of library patrons in any given community. It serves to bring people to the library, as well as to create community spirit.

Public services: Public services are those tasks performed by LSS that involve direct contact with the customer. They include the circulation and reference functions, as well as helping the patron find materials of interest for research or pleasure reading and helping patrons with library computers and equipment. Public services also include the functions of interlibrary loan and reserves.

Reference: Reference transactions are information consultations in which LSS recommend, interpret, evaluate, and/or use information resources to help others meet particular information needs.[7]

Resource sharing: Resource sharing is not limited to interlibrary loan and document delivery but also applies to cooperative purchasing of library materials and supplies. It can also refer to physical collections when libraries agree to collect materials in different subject areas.

Security risk management: Security risk management means being aware of your immediate physical environment and identifying potential problem areas in the library—including areas where one can hide and inadequate lighting in the parking lot, as well as knowing who has keys to the library.

Selection policies: A selection policy is necessary in order to provide guidance for the librarian or LSS who do collection development. This policy follows a set of guidelines to consider when choosing materials and includes such criteria as positive reviews, reputation of the author, local interest, demand, and budget limitations.

Serials: Serials is an all-inclusive term covering a variety of publications in various forms, content, and purpose, like magazines and newspapers. They are issued in successive parts, at regular intervals, and are intended to continue indefinitely.[8]

Service attitude: The service attitude is how LSS behave toward patrons: a positive attitude shows warmth, friendliness, and helpfulness; a negative attitude may show disinterest, disdain, or annoyance. Both can affect return visits to the library.

Shelving and stack maintenance: Shelving and stack maintenance refers to returning materials to the shelves and the maintenance of materials on those shelves in proper order so that they can be easily found in the library. Stack maintenance also includes shifting and weeding.

Social media: Social media is the interactive, web-based electronic communication through which users create online communities in order to share information, ideas, and personal messages. This is a popular use for library computers for patrons and can be used by staff to share library news.

Technical services: Technical services are those tasks performed by library staff associated with selecting and preparing new materials for circulation, such as adding barcodes, spine labels, and plastic covers, so that the materials can be protected and ownership can be identified. They also include cataloging and classification of materials, acquisitions, and the mending, repair, and preservation of materials.

USA PATRIOT Act: This is the acronym made by the Uniting and Strengthening America by Providing Appropriate Tools Required to Intercept and Obstruct Terrorism Act. Created by Congress in the wake of 9/11, it substantially expanded the authority of U.S. law enforcement for the stated purpose of fighting terrorism in the United States and abroad. It expanded the authority of the FBI to gain access to library records, including stored electronic data and communications.

Word-of-mouth marketing (WOMM): Word-of-mouth marketing is a powerful marketing tool that consists of people talking and listening to each other and spreading the word about library services and activities.

NOTES

1. American Library Association, "What Is Censorship?," American Library Association, http://www.ala.org/advocacy/intfreedom/censorshipfirstamendmentissues/ifcensorship qanda.

2. Common Core State Standards Initiative, "About the Standards," Common Core State Standards Initiative: Preparing America's Students for College and Career, http://www.core standards.org/about-the-standards/.

3. U.S. Copyright Office, "Copyright in General," U.S. Copyright Office, http://copyright .gov/help/faq/faq-general.html#what.

4. Constitution Facts, "Learn about the United States Bill of Rights," Constitution Facts, http://www.constitutionfacts.com/us-constitution-amendments/bill-of-rights/.

5. American Library Association, "Library Bill of Rights," American Library Association, http://www.ala.org/advocacy/intfreedom/librarybill.

6. American Library Association, "Library Code of Ethics," American Library Association, http://www.ala.org/advocacy/proethics/codeofethics/codeethics.

7. American Library Association, "Guidelines for Behavioral Performance of Reference and Information Service Providers," Reference and User Services Association, last modified May 28, 2013, http://www.ala.org/rusa/resources/guidelines/guidelinesbehavioral.

8. Library Corporation, "What Is a Serial?," Cataloger's Reference Shelf, http://www.its marc.com/crs/mergedProjects/conser/conser/module_2_1__ccm.htm.

Index

About the Author

Hali R. Keeler has been an adjunct professor since 1998 in the Library Technology Program at Three Rivers Community College in Norwich, Connecticut, where she formerly served as program coordinator. She teaches Library Public Services, Library Technical Services, and Management Strategies. Hali also served as a special faculty consultant for Charter Oak State College, performing portfolio reviews for their students in the area of library science. Hali earned her MLS from the University of Rhode Island and has an MA in French. Retired after thirty-five years in public library service as a children's librarian and a library director, she has been a longtime member of the American Library Association (ALA), Public Library Association, and the Connecticut Library Association (CLA). Offices she has held include chair of the Public Libraries Section of CLA, trustee of CLA, and president of the Southeastern Connecticut Library Association. She is the author of "Library Technology Program: Three Rivers Community College," *Library Mosaics: The Magazine for Support Staff* 16, no. 1 (January/February 2005): 12.